TAIWAN'S DEMOCRACY

Taiwan's rapid industrialization during the 1960s and 1970s, combined with the democratic revolution that began with the lifting of martial law in 1987, were of deep historic importance. Over the next decade Taiwan's "political miracle" matched its earlier "economic miracle," creating a vibrant liberal democracy complete with freedom of speech, association and assembly, rule of law, and competitive and fair multiparty elections. The continuation of these achievements and the new challenges that have surfaced are addressed in rich detail in the chapters of this volume by an international team of experts. One of the biggest challenges is Mainland China's economic success, which has added to the complexity of Taiwan's economic and political policy options. A number of the contributors to this volume consider Taiwan's response to China's economic rise and show how Taiwanese companies have strategically taken advantage of the changing economic environment by moving up the value chain of production within Taiwan while also taking the opportunity to invest overseas.

Chapters cover a wealth of topics, including:

- Constitutional reform
- National identity
- Party politics
- Taiwan's development model
- Industrial policy
- Trade and investment
- Globalization
- Sustainable development

Taiwan's Democracy will be of huge interest to students and scholars of Taiwan studies, Chinese politics and economics, international politics and economics, and development studies.

Robert Ash is Professor of Economics at the School of Oriental and African Studies, UK.

John W. Garver is Professor at the Georgia Institute of Technology, USA.

Penelope B. Prime is Professor of Economics at Mercer University, USA.

Routledge Research on Taiwan
Series Editor: Dafydd Fell
SOAS, UK

The *Routledge Research on Taiwan Series* seeks to publish quality research on all aspects of Taiwan studies. Taking an interdisciplinary approach, the books will cover topics such as politics, economic development, culture, society, anthropology and history.

This new book series will include the best possible scholarship from the social sciences and the humanities and welcomes submissions from established authors in the field as well as from younger authors. In addition to research monographs and edited volumes general works or textbooks with a broader appeal will be considered.

The Series is advised by an international Editorial Board and edited by Dafydd Fell of the Centre of Taiwan Studies at the School of Oriental and African Studies.

TAIWAN'S DEMOCRACY

Economic and political challenges

*Edited by Robert Ash, John W. Garver and
Penelope B. Prime*

Routledge
Taylor & Francis Group

LONDON AND NEW YORK

First published 2011
by Routledge
2 Park Square, Milton Park, Abingdon, Oxon OX14 4RN

Simultaneously published in the USA and Canada
by Routledge
710 Third Avenue, New York, NY 10017

Routledge is an imprint of the Taylor & Francis Group, an informa business

British Library Cataloguing in Publication Data
A catalogue record for this book is available from the British Library

Library of Congress Cataloging in Publication Data
Taiwan's democracy: economic and political changes / edited by Robert Ash,
John Garver, Penelope B. Prime.
    p. cm — (Routledge research on Taiwan ; 6)
    Include bibliographical references and index.
    1. Taiwan—Economic policy—1975- 2. Taiwan—Economic
conditions—1975- 3. Taiwan—Politics and government—2000- I. Ash,
Robert F. II. Garver, John W. III. Prime, Penelope B.
    HC430.5.T38245 2011
    320.95124'9—dc22   2011000558

ISBN 978-0-415-60457-4 (hbk)
ISBN 978-0-415-60458-1 (pbk)
ISBN 978-0-203-80904-4 (ebk)

Typeset in Bembo by
Pindar NZ, Auckland, New Zealand

Printed and bound in Great Britain by
CPI Antony Rowe, Chippenham, Wiltshire

Contents

Illustrations

Figures

Tables

1

INTRODUCTION

Taiwan's democratic consolidation

John W. Garver

Taiwan's economic and political "miracles"

When Taiwan reverted to China's control upon Japan's surrender in 1945, its economy was overwhelmingly agricultural. Under a half-century of colonial rule which sought to make the island an agricultural base serving Japan's strategic needs, Taiwan's agriculture had been commercialized and given a strong foreign trade orientation. Sugar and rice were exported to Japan, while Japanese manufactured goods were imported into Taiwan as part of Japan's effort to create an economically integrated East Asian empire.[1] Japan created a fairly strong physical and institutional infrastructure in support of trade. But there was only a modest expansion of modern manufacturing. Chinese control brought to Taiwan the devastating inflation that racked Mainland China in the late 1940s. There followed, within a few years, the arrival of over a million demoralized and angry soldiers, desperate refugees, and officials of the Chinese Nationalist Party (Kuomintang, or KMT) that had lost the civil war in China. Absorbing this flood was a heavy burden and created considerable disruption. Meanwhile, across the Taiwan Strait the powerful military forces commanded by the Chinese Communist Party (CCP) were preparing to invade and "liberate" Taiwan. Prospects for Taiwan's survival as anything other than another province of the People's Republic of China (PRC) under the rule of the CCP looked extremely remote.

In the event, the intervention of the Korean War and the dispatch of the US Seventh Fleet to the Taiwan Strait forestalled an invasion from the Mainland. There followed one of the most remarkable periods of economic transformation experienced by any developing country in the aftermath of World War II. During the 1950s a far-reaching debate within the KMT leadership paved the way for a dramatic reversal of the previous commandist thrust of the KMT's economic strategy in favor of large-scale privatization and the creation of a market economy.[2] By the 1960s, following a period of import substitution industrialization during the previous decade, Taiwan had irrevocably embraced a strategy of export-led industrialization. A package of government policies – some of them modeled on Japan's earlier experience – supported and encouraged Taiwanese businesses to export. Many of the newly emerging Taiwanese businesses cut their teeth supplying goods to US military forces in the Western Pacific, a focus of Cold War conflict.[3] Taiwan was a major supply and repair location for US forces during the Vietnam War, creating a strong source of demand in the 1960s. Familiarity with US commercial procedures and practises facilitated penetration of US civilian markets by Taiwanese companies. Taiwan's invention of export processing zones (EPZ) – the first was set up in Kaohsiung Harbor in 1966 – encouraged and facilitated the establishment of wholly export-oriented manufacturing enterprises by Taiwanese and foreign firms. By the 1970s Taiwan had emerged as a world leader in the manufacture of simple, labor-intensive goods: umbrellas, zippers, bicycles, shoes, camping equipment, clothing, and, a little later, simple electrical appliances such as fans, mixers, hair dryers, and tape players. By the early 1980s the people of Taiwan enjoyed a quite comfortable midrange of development and standard of living, with an average per capita income of over US$3,000. Meanwhile, a large, financially secure, and internationalized class of Taiwanese businessmen, alongside an even larger class of professionals (journalists, publishers, scholars, lawyers, scientists, engineers, teachers, etc.), had emerged. These new groups were to be important social bases for Taiwan's eventual transition to democracy – a process that got under way toward the end of the 1980s.

A major drive by Taiwan's "developmental state," as scholars term the particular pattern of state-business relations pioneered in East Asia, was to engineer a shift of export production from low-value goods to higher-value electronic goods. This drive began with the establishment in 1973 and 1980 of the Industrial Technology Research Institute (ITRI) and, as an associated venture, Hsinchu Science Park (HSP), both located about forty miles southwest of Taipei and close to two of Taiwan's major engineering universities. The benefits of Taiwan's large pool of highly educated engineering talent, boosted by the return to Taiwan of key ethnic Chinese with long experience in US industrial research and development, now made themselves felt. So too did generous government support for new high-tech start-up firms, and for research and development targeted toward innovation. By this time semi-conductors and integrated circuits were revolutionizing economic activity, and Taiwan was to emerge as a key supplier of core components: IC wafers and the devices using those chips – motherboards, hard disks, keyboards, monitors, printers, laser optical devices, liquid crystal displays, mouses, etc.

By 2009 Taiwan was an upper-middle income country with an average per capita income of US$16,000 – about the same as South Korea, although still significantly less than in the United Kingdom (US$35,000), Japan (US$39,000) and the United States (US$46,000). In fifty years the people of Taiwan had hauled themselves out of abject poverty to a level of considerable economic affluence. Moreover, they had done so whilst achieving a relatively equal distribution of income. Indeed, the attainment of high growth alongside relatively high levels of income equality led the World Bank to designate Taiwan along with the rest of the East Asian "Newly

Average growth of GNP per capita, 1965–90

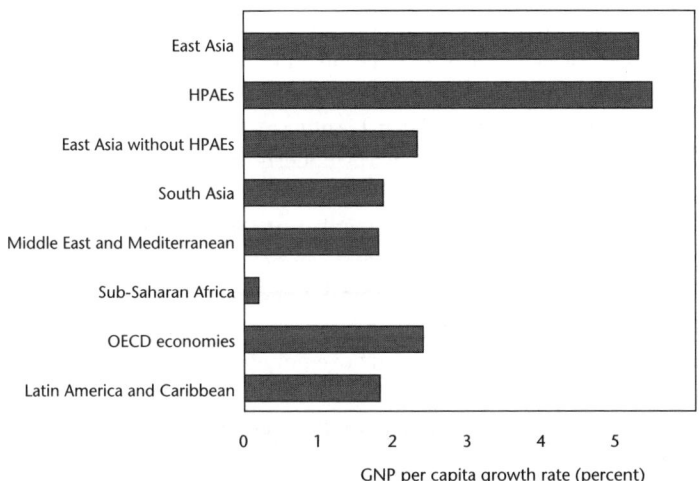

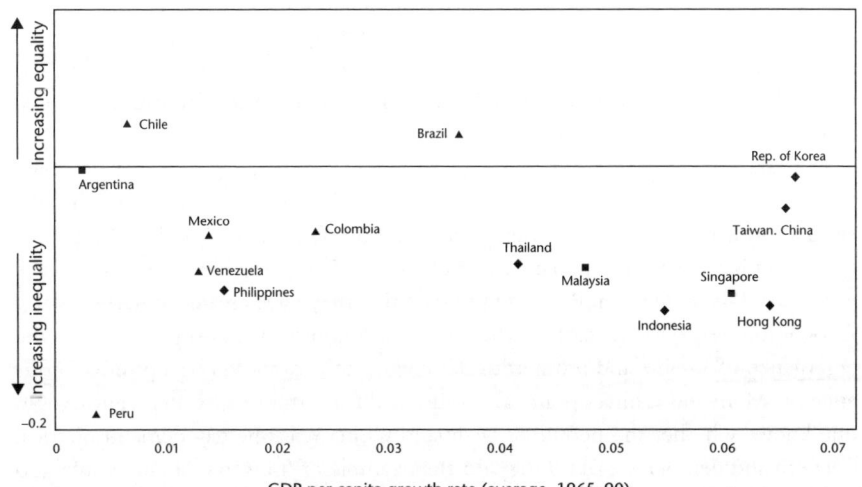

GDP per capita growth rate (average. 1965–90)

FIGURE 1.1 Taiwan's economic developmental success.

Source: World Bank, *The East Asian Miracle: Economic Growth and Public Policy*, New York: Oxford University Press, 1993. pp. 2–4.

Industrialized Countries" (NICs) as "High Performing Asian Economies" (HPAEs). Figure 1.1 uses several figures developed by the World Bank to illustrate Taiwan's outstanding success at economic development.

Taiwan's "political miracle" was its peaceful transition to liberal democracy – a process that began in late 1986. This was an event of even greater historic importance than Taiwan's economic accomplishments. Taiwan's political transition, alongside similar peaceful transitions to democracy in South Korea and the Philippines that took place at about the same time, was part of what Samuel Huntington called "the third wave" of global democratization.[4] These events considerably expanded the sphere of liberal democracy in East Asia, and thereby hammered the final nail in the coffin of the hoary belief that Confucian political culture of paternalistic authoritarianism was incompatible with modern democracy.[5] Between 1987 and 1996 the people of Taiwan created a vibrant political system, complete with freedom of speech, association and assembly, rule of law, and competitive and fair multiparty elections that enabled the island's citizens to choose and change their rulers. In short, the people of Taiwan had created a liberal democracy. In 1996, for the first time in the long history of the Chinese people, the highest leader of a Chinese political system was chosen by a free and competitive popular vote. Four years later, in 2000, a similarly historic transition of power from a long-time incumbent ruling party to an opposition party was accomplished. In the aftermath of election defeat, a group of people who had held power for many years, the KMT, freely and peacefully surrendered their authority. It is one thing to conduct a fair and competitive election; it is quite another thing for the losers to give up power. Yet another milestone came in 2008, when the people of Taiwan returned the KMT to power under the leadership of Ma Ying-jeou – a politician of Mainlander descent who had learnt to speak Taiwanese only as an adult. In an act of remarkable political maturity, 58 percent of the voters of Taiwan selected a member of a formerly much disliked minority, the Mainlanders, to lead them in search of their common destiny. There were similarities in this regard between Ma's election and that, eight months later in the United States, of an African-American as president.

It bears repeating that the free and democratic political system that has been created in Taiwan is the first stable democratic polity in the long Chinese political tradition. This is a momentous political accomplishment of which the people of Taiwan have been, and remain, intensely proud. This pride is one reason why the people of Taiwan feel that they, and the state that they have created, deserve greater recognition, respect and status in the world community. It is also possible that the emergence of a stable and prosperous democracy in Taiwan will be a positive influence on Mainland China's political evolution during the twenty-first century. No one knows whether the people of Mainland China will one day demand political freedom and democracy. But if they do, the example of Taiwan's vibrant, stable, and prosperous democracy may be one reason for Mainland China's embrace of the same kind of political system.

Many people in Taiwan, from across Taiwan's political spectrum as Dafydd Fell makes clear in his chapter, take pride in imagining that Taiwan may one day play such a historic, positive role. In a landmark speech at Beijing University in April 2005, the KMT leader Lian Chan talked of "the potential for Taiwan to be a beacon for political transformation on the other [PRC] side of the Strait, drawing encouragement from the modernizing sprit of the May Fourth Movement and the democracy movement that was crushed in 1989."[6] In his second presidential inauguration speech in 2004, Democratic Progressive Party (DPP) leader Chen Shui-bian appealed to the same sense of pride in more "Taiwanese" terms.

> A half century of toil and labor by the people of this land has culminated in what is now known as the "Taiwan experience," the fruits of which ... have become the proud assets not only of the peoples on both sides of the Taiwan Strait, but of all Chinese societies. ... Taiwan is a completely free and democratic society. ... If both sides are willing ... to create an environment engendered upon "peaceful development and freedom of choice," then in the future, the Republic of China and the People's Republic of China ... can seek to establish relations in any form whatsoever. We should not exclude any possibility, so long as there is the consent of the 23 million people of Taiwan.

One should not take Taiwan's democracy for granted. It is too easy for people raised and living in stable democracies to forget that history is littered with democracies that proved incapable of meeting the challenges confronting them.[7] From ancient Athens, which succumbed first to Sparta and then to Macedonia, to Germany in 1933, Japan's Taisho democracy *c.* 1926, to France's first three republics in 1793, 1848, and 1940, democratic systems have frequently failed. As Samuel Huntington pointed out – and contrary to the common American belief that democracy is somehow a natural form of government – democracy was rare in the world until the period after World War II. In many recently democratic countries, the initial spread of democracy was followed, according to Huntington, by waves of retreat from democratic forms. Many countries – Germany and Japan, for example – have achieved durable democratic systems only on "the second try." China's own first attempt to establish a liberal democracy, the Republic of China (ROC), established in 1912 following China's 1911 revolution (*xinhai geming*), was also a failure. The ROC was based on Western-style parliamentary institutions, which, however, failed completely to assert effective power. Instead, a powerless parliamentary government was soon completely overshadowed by regional warlords who exercised real power. The PRC's white paper on "Building of Political Democracy in China," issued in 2005, touts this post-1911 failure of "bourgeois democracy" copied from the West as proof of the unsuitability for China of that type of institutional arrangement and of the need for "socialist democracy" under the leadership of the Chinese Communist Party.[8] One could also consider the collapse of the ROC under its 1947 Constitution, and under the CCP's insurrection, as a second failure to institute democracy in China.

As Jean-Francois Revel demonstrated, the failure of democratic states has typically resulted from a conjuncture of powerful external enemies and deep domestic division.

Philosophers from Aristotle to James Madison have noted that internal strife has been an endemic and sometimes fatal bane of democracies. Where access to power is open to all citizens, there is a danger that state institutions will be unable to contain the antagonistic consequences of such strife, which may escalate into violent conflict. From an empirical study of several score Greek city states, Aristotle concluded that the natural evolution of political development was from democratic to tyrannical forms. This was so, he argued, because those contesting parties would discover tyrannical forms to be a more effective weapon in that struggle. There is also the possibility that contending groups will reach an impasse that makes it impossible to respond effectively to challenges. Such paralyzing and conflict-ridden polarization has been a central ingredient in the terminal crises of democracies throughout history.

In the case of Taiwan, the salient division of society has been between two groups that scholars refer to as "sub-ethnic groups." Both groups are ethnic Chinese, but they have very different views of themselves and the world. Taiwan's population is 98 percent ethnic Chinese (i.e. they speak a dialect of Chinese, are similar racially, and share life customs and rituals), but there are important differences in life experiences and perspectives that distinguish one group of ethnic Chinese from another. On the one hand, 85 percent of Taiwan's ethnic Chinese population are people whose ancestors migrated to Taiwan from Southern China prior to Japan's acquisition of Taiwan in 1895. Many of these ancestors had arrived in Taiwan in the seventeenth and eighteenth centuries. This group is known in the vernacular as "Taiwanese" and it includes speakers of both Southern Fujianese and Hakka dialects of Chinese. A further 13 percent of Taiwan's ethnic Chinese population comprise those who fled CCP rule and sought refuge in Taiwan in 1948–50. This group is loosely known as "Mainlanders." Taiwanese and Mainlanders have different dialects of Chinese as their mother tongue (Mainlanders speak Mandarin or a Mainland dialect other than Fujianese or Hakka). But more important than such linguistic traits are their different life experiences. Multiple foreign invasions, wars, defeats in war, revolutions, chaos, civil wars, and more savage invasions: these were the lot of people on Mainland China between 1895 and 1950. By contrast, the Chinese who had moved to Taiwan simply did not experience those multiple and heavy calamities. Instead, during these same years they experienced steady and orderly, if strictly disciplined, progress under Japanese colonialism's efforts to modernize Taiwan. The Taiwanese were also heavily influenced by Japanese culture, many of them building Japanese-style homes, learning to speak Japanese, adopting Japanese names and customs (e.g. removing shoes inside one's home, favoring Japanese music and movies, eating sushimi). These Japanese-like habits dismayed the Mainlanders when they arrived in 1948–50. Taiwanese, for their part, frequently compared Nationalist officials unfavorably with the Japanese officials who had ruled before 1945. Japanese police and judges might have been strict, but they were not corrupt or arbitrary. In short, there was a huge perceptual gap between "Mainlanders" and "Taiwanese" in the early 1950s. It has taken many years to narrow, if not quite eliminate this gap.

As Dafydd Fell notes in his essay in this volume, "Almost all political scientists working on Taiwan agree that national identity is the most salient issue in Taiwan's electoral politics." One great danger confronting Taiwan's new democratic polity is that its sub-ethnic divisions may become so antagonistic and polarized that they will pull the polity apart, paralyze it, or render it vulnerable to external enemies. The essay by Christopher Hughes reaches optimistic conclusions in this regard, finding that Taiwan has, in fact, moved toward a consensus on national identity. Hughes raises the possibilities of polarization over identity and that the Chinese Communist Party might exploit this polarization. But he finds that the main trend has been toward consensus and formulation of a concept of identity inclusive enough to encompass native Taiwanese, Mainlanders, and the 2 percent of Taiwan's population who are non-Chinese aboriginals.

Dafydd Fell and Shelley Rigger reach more somber conclusions. Fell finds severe polarization having occurred during the second half of the 2000s, corresponding to the second term of President Chen Shui-bian. Fell also traces Taiwan's paralysis over important issues from national defense to partisan antagonism. Rigger finds that the first decade of Taiwan's constitutional revision/amendment was "hasty and ill-considered" and based on short-term partisan gain rather than deliberation about what arrangements were most likely to produce a stable and effective yet democratic polity. The end result has been, Rigger suggests, institutionalization of an extremely high bar for further constitutional amendments (namely, a three-quarter majority of at least 75 percent of eligible legislators, *plus* 50 percent of all eligible voters). The core ideological objectives of one wing of the DPP were not previously achieved and are likely to prove impossible to achieve under the stringent amendment requirements now in place. The result may be to entice extremists toward the use of violent means.

An important part of the process of democratization in Taiwan has been forma-tion of a coherent vision of collective identity sufficient to persuade those who are to be citizens of – that is, who collectively constitute – the emerging democratic polity. Over the past several decades, scholars have come to realize that nationhood is ultimately best characterized not by some set of shared, objective characteristics (for example, those of race, religion, language, or even geographic propinquity), but rather by a *belief* in shared identity and destiny.[9] Nationalism – this belief in shared identity, of who a "people" are, where they come from, and what unites them in search of a common destiny – need not lead to democracy. It may, in fact, point in non-democratic directions, as has happened on the Chinese Mainland since 1989. But where stable democracies have developed, those polities have typically been underpinned by evolution of a concept and sense of nationhood. If democracy places sovereignty in "the people," the question of who "the people" are must be defined. Taiwan is now following this historically well-trodden path.

As for the external threat to Taiwan's young democracy, it is greater and perhaps clearer than for most new democracies. It comes from the powerful state, the People's Republic of China, a mere hundred miles across the Taiwan Strait. The multiple "challenges and opportunities" facing Taiwan's young democracy must be understood in the context of this very substantial external threat.

The external challenge to Taiwan's democracy

The People's Republic of China claims Taiwan as part of its sovereign territory. Taiwan, Beijing insists, belongs to China because the people who live there, at least, the overwhelming majority of them, are ethnic Chinese. Moreover, the same argument runs, Taiwan has been part of China's empires for many centuries. Taiwan was stolen by Japan in 1895, Beijing says, but was returned to China by the United States and Britain under the terms of the 1943 Cairo Declaration. The Republic of China was defeated and effectively destroyed in the Chinese Civil War, leaving the People's Republic of China as its successor. Under accepted principles of international law, a successor state succeeds to the territory of its predecessor state. Since Taiwan lay within the recognized boundaries of the ROC, it lies equally within the legitimate boundaries of the PRC. It follows from this that the putative governmental institutions of Taiwan are without any legitimacy whatsoever, and constitute a *de facto* rebellious organization opposed to China's legitimate government, the PRC.[10]

Beijing insists that Taiwan should be integrated into the state system of the PRC as a special autonomous region along the lines of the "one country, two systems" model used to manage Hong Kong's 1997 reversion to Chinese sovereignty. China is prepared, it says, to be very generous with the people of Taiwan. As in the case of Hong Kong, Beijing is willing to allow Taiwan to continue to enjoy, largely unchanged and for a quite long period of time, its own social and political system, even though this is very different from the Leninist system dominant on the China Mainland. This is the "two systems" aspect of Beijing's proposal. At the same time, Taiwan must come under the sovereign control of the PRC, which means that Taiwan's foreign affairs and its security against foreign powers will be handled by Beijing. This is the "one country" aspect. The Chinese government's view has been that details of such an arrangement should be worked out by negotiations between the two sides.

A major problem, however, is that the people of Taiwan, by overwhelming majority, have not found this proposal attractive. Public polls indicate that only a small proportion of Taiwan's people favor accepting Beijing's "one country, two systems" approach – in 2003 a mere 8.3 percent, compared with 74.9 percent who opposed it. In the same year only 2 percent favored moving toward "unification [with the PRC] as soon as possible," whereas 7.2 percent favored "independence as soon as possible." In other words, the pro-independence extreme of Taiwan's spectrum was over three times larger than the pro-unification extreme. The people of Taiwan have struggled long and hard to create a free and democratic polity for themselves, and are not inclined to risk this by giving Beijing, and the Chinese Communist Party, sovereign control of Taiwan. The huge middle of Taiwan's political spectrum favors maintaining the status quo: neither subordinating Taiwan to the CCP, nor provoking the CCP and risking war by "Taiwan independence." Figure 1.2 illustrates shifts in public opinion in Taiwan over the issue of "unification" versus "independence."

The continuing partition of Taiwan from the PRC rouses great passion and sometimes anger in China. In the Chinese view, following the reversion to Chinese

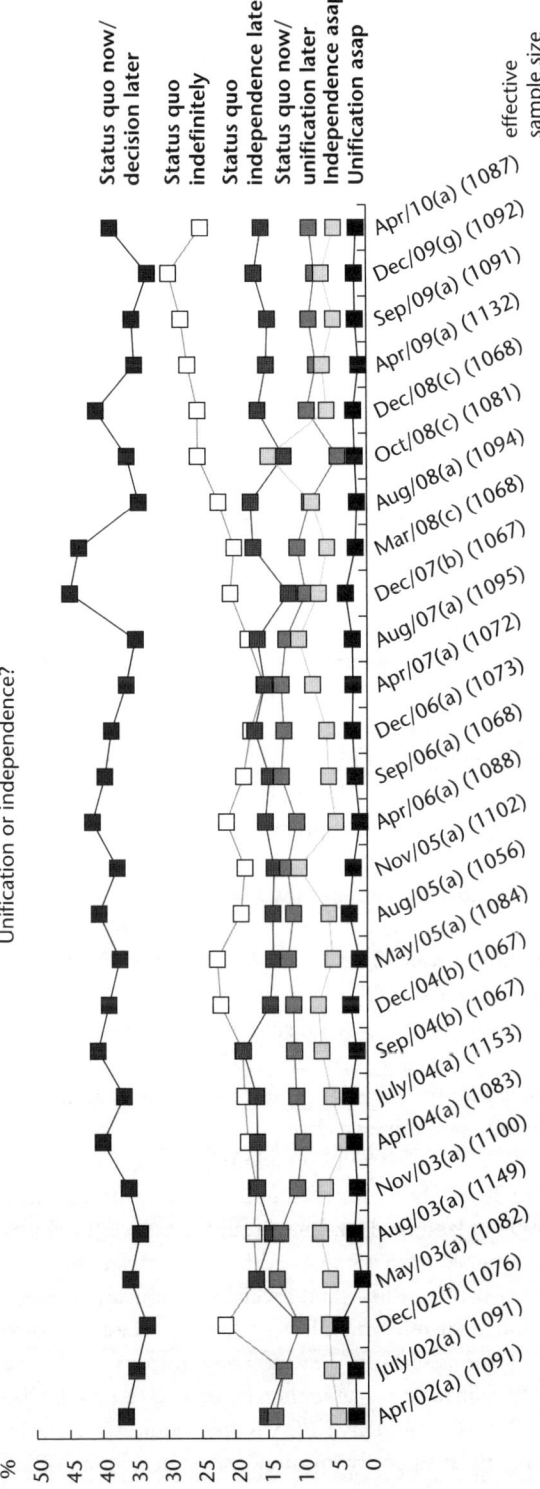

Unification or independence?

FIGURE 1.2 Public opinion toward cross-Strait relations.

Survey conducted by: (a)   Election Study Center, National Chengchi University, Taipei (886-2-29387134)
                           (b)   Burke Marketing Research, Ltd., Taipei (886-2-25181088)
                           (c)   China Credit Information Service, Ltd., Taipei (886-2-87683266)
                           (d)   Center for Public Opinion and Election Studies, National Sun Yat-Sen University, Kaohsiung (886-7-5252000)
                           (e)   Survey and Opinion Research Group, Dept. of Political Science, National Chung-cheng University, Chiayi (886-5-2720411)
                           (f)   e-Society Research Group, Taipei (886-2-27213658)
                           (g)   Center for Public Opinion and Public Policy, Taipei Municipal University of Education, Taipei (886-2-23113040)

Respondents: Taiwanese adults aged 20–69 accessible to telephone interviewers sovereignty of Hong Kong (1997) and Macao (1999), the separation of Taiwan from the PRC is the last remaining vestige of the "century of national humiliation" suffered by China at the hands of imperialist powers between 1839 and 1949. It also reflects interference by the United States in the internal affairs of China. The Taiwan issue is a wholly domestic issue, Beijing asserts, and the use or non-use of military force to settle that issue lies exclusively within the decision-making remit of China's sovereign government, the PRC. The United States has no standing to interfere in this matter and its attempts to do so trample on the core interests of the Chinese nation. As nationalism has replaced Marxism-Leninism as the philosophical legitimation of PRC authority, resentment of US "interference" in the Taiwan issue has become increasingly widespread and heated.

China's military power has grown rapidly since 1989–91. The 1989 uprising in China against CCP rule, and its brutal military suppression, began a trend toward larger defense budgets. The collapse of Communist regimes in East Europe and subsequently in the former USSR itself reinforced the trend. The availability of Russian weapons systems after 1992, and, during the same period, the flood of advanced technology into China in the form of foreign investment have facilitated the growth of PRC military capabilities. By 2010, US analysts were already debating when the PRC was likely to achieve military parity with the United States in the Western Pacific, and what the consequences of this would be for US security obligations in the region. Since 1979 Beijing has professed to seek unification with Taiwan by peaceful means. This was a core part of the delicate compromise of US and PRC interests toward Taiwan that emerged from difficult negotiations in 1971–2 and again in 1978. Beijing insists it retains the sovereign right to use force in domestic affairs, should it so decide, but adds that it would prefer to achieve unification by peaceful means.

Since about 1990, because of democratization in Taiwan and a new, far more suspicious view of US policy toward Taiwan, the PRC has paid considerable attention to improving its military capabilities toward Taiwan. By March 2008 the People's Liberation Army (PLA) had deployed along China's central coast opposite Taiwan 1,400 missiles – up from 350 or so in 2002. These missiles had the capacity to shut down Taiwan's airfields, telecommunications, and command and control facilities just prior to a PLA assault. Combined with the PLA's large and fairly potent submarine force, as well as its extremely potent naval mine warfare capabilities, they could slow and degrade a US response to a PLA attack.[11] The PLA's amphibious assault capabilities are also rapidly improving. In 2006 China launched its largest ever indigenously designed combat ship, an "amphibious landing dock" that greatly enhanced the ability to deliver combat vehicles and artillery onto a contested beach.[12] Meanwhile, the PLA is developing a wide array of tanks, artillery, and specialized vehicles designed for amphibious operations.[13] China's current amphibious capability is estimated to be capable of moving 30–40,000 troops across to Taiwan. These forces would seize several ports, and mobilized PRC civilian craft would then be used to ferry a further 150,000 troops to secure control of Taiwan. Large PLA forces would then dig in, leaving the United States to contemplate a costly invasion against determined PLA resistance – with US causalities perhaps similar to those suffered during the US invasion of Okinawa in 1945. Chinese threats of a nuclear response to US "interference in China's domestic affairs" (i.e. to a move to undo the PLA conquest of Taiwan) would fuel further anti-war opposition in the United States. Would the people of the United States be willing to sacrifice thousands of casualties and risk a nuclear war with China to reverse a PRC victory over Taiwan?

There is immense frustration in the PRC over repeated failed efforts to conquer Taiwan. Two such efforts in the 1950s to use military force to drive a wedge between the Americans and Nationalist China (as Taiwan was then called) failed. At the time of the 1971–2 US-PRC rapprochement, Beijing's calculation was that the United States would gradually distance itself from Taiwan, leaving it isolated before Beijing.[14] That did not happen. After 1978, Beijing began to court Taiwan via encouragement of tourism, visits to relatives on the Mainland, and investment. The hope was that by such means increased pride in "Chinese-ness" and in China would be stimulated. But again the CCP's hoped-for outcome was not forthcoming. The prime Taiwanese response to closer contact with the Mainland was one of disgust at the poverty and repression prevalent on the Mainland. The successful return of Hong Kong under the "one country, two systems" rubric was expected to encourage support for use of a similar model for Taiwan. It did not. Today, the CCP's hope is that increased economic integration will persuade Taiwanese people of the wisdom of political unification. What will be Beijing's response if this too fails? No one knows, but this uncertainty must be factored into any assessment of the resilience and sustainability of Taiwan's democracy. After all, an important finding of psychology is that frustration can reduce the rationality of one's behavior.

A final dimension of the PRC threat to Taiwan's democracy is the traditional skill of the CCP in implementing united front tactics. These entail systematic infiltration of enemy organizations: encouragement and/or utilization of conflicts within the enemy camp; use of carefully crafted political ploys and propaganda to find allies within the enemy camp; covert acquisition of intelligence about enemy plans and deployments; and careful coordination of internal subversion of the enemy with the use of military force. The CCP honed these tactics against the KMT in the 1920s–40s, and is probably using them today in its attempt to unify Taiwan with the PRC. In the event of a PLA assault on Taiwan, for example, it is virtually certain that a group of Taiwanese leaders, suborned by CCP united front efforts, will emerge to "request" and justify the invasion.

There is a fundamental asymmetry between the political systems of the PRC and Taiwan. The PRC is a Leninist system organized on the principles of democratic centralism. Policies can be imposed from the top. Opposition to those policies from within society can be repressed. Public opinion can be guided – or created. Powerful and large covert agencies of the PRC exist to fulfill these goals. Taiwan, on the other side of the Taiwan Strait, is a rambunctious and in many ways an immature democracy. It enjoys wide freedom of the press, assembly, demonstration, and opposition to the government. It is against the stark external challenges to Taiwan's democracy that any shortcomings of its democracy must be weighed.

The external opportunity for Taiwan's democracy

If the PRC is a challenge to Taiwan's democracy, it is also a major opportunity. Since abandoning policies of economic autarky in 1978, China has emerged as the core of extremely powerful East Asian transnational production networks which have become one of the drivers of the global economy. As the economics-oriented chapters in the second half of this volume explain, Taiwan's peculiar relationship with Mainland China confers on Taiwan's companies certain advantages over other East Asian economies (e.g. Japan, South Korea, Singapore) and over North American and European competitors in participating in these transnational production networks. But if Taiwan's government is unable to reach agreement with Beijing on core issues, Taiwanese firms may be disadvantaged vis-à-vis their competitors in their efforts to take advantage of China's extremely attractive low-cost production base. As more and more Asian nations are integrated into the China-centered East Asian dynamo, Taiwan's exclusion, or limitations on its involvement, would significantly diminish Taiwan's global business competitiveness. The consequence might be to slow economic growth and elicit an angry response from Taiwan's business class even to the extent of generating political conflict.

Let us now examine how these transnational production networks emerged. Over the past 150 years, East Asia has witnessed several waves of rapid industrialization. Japan led the way in the late nineteenth and early twentieth centuries, and gave a further boost to the process after losing its empire in 1945. Following the Communist victory in China, Hong Kong joined the process as a large part of China's capitalist class fled to the former British colony and began business operations there. So, in the 1960s, did South Korea and Taiwan. After 1978, China, with its mammoth economy, labor force, and land base, became the latest recruit. Development economists identify at least three waves of East Asian industrialization. Japan represents the first wave; Hong Kong, Taiwan, South Korea, and Singapore represent the second; the PRC, the third. A fourth wave may now be under way, as countries like Malaysia, Thailand, and even India become drawn into these same powerful transnational production networks.

At the heart of the East Asian model of industrialization is systematic, deep, and state-supported participation in the global economy. During much of the post–World War II period many developing countries – in Latin America, Africa, South and Southeast Asia – eschewed participation in the global capitalist system in the belief that such participation was "exploitative" and served merely to perpetuate underdevelopment and poverty. Ignoring this (as it then was) orthodoxy, the East Asian states embraced global markets. Export promotion, the production of goods for foreign markets (especially in the rich, industrialized countries of the West), was a core element. Systematic and large-scale transfer of technology from the West to the newly industrializing Asian countries was another. Inflows of capital from Western countries, either via direct investment or via government-supported bank loans, made possible large-scale acquisition of technology, machinery, and equipment, which in turn made possible expanded production of export goods. The net result of these forces was to generate a powerful virtuous cycle. Expanded exports produced more foreign currency, which generated expanded Western inputs for expanded export production.

The level of integration between earlier and later East Asian industrializing states has increased concomitantly with the advance of modern technology. In particular, the containerization and information revolutions made possible in the 1990s and 2000s a level of transnational division of labor in the production of certain goods that simply had not been economically feasible in, say, the 1960s. Today each East Asian country contributes its particular form of comparative advantage to the production of specific goods. Earlier industrializers such as Japan, South Korea, Taiwan, and Singapore contribute product research and development, innovation, recognized brands, marketing skills, managerial skills stressing quality control and efficiency, as well as knowledge-intensive and capital-intensive technology, components, materials, machinery, and equipment.[15] Later industrializing countries, especially the Chinese Mainland, contribute cheap but fairly well-educated and experienced labor, cheap land, cheap basic materials and components, and low external costs (the latter whether because of a willingness to accept environmental pollution or because of large state investment in infrastructure supporting industrial production). The result of this accelerating transnational division of labor has been the production of high-quality, low-cost, and frequently innovative goods for global markets. Those goods have enjoyed great market success. What is at stake in any deterioration of Taiwan's relations with the PRC is nothing less than the island's ability to continue to participate in this extremely powerful and successful engine of economic growth and prosperity. Figure 1.3 illustrates the general operation of these East Asian transnational production networks in a global context.

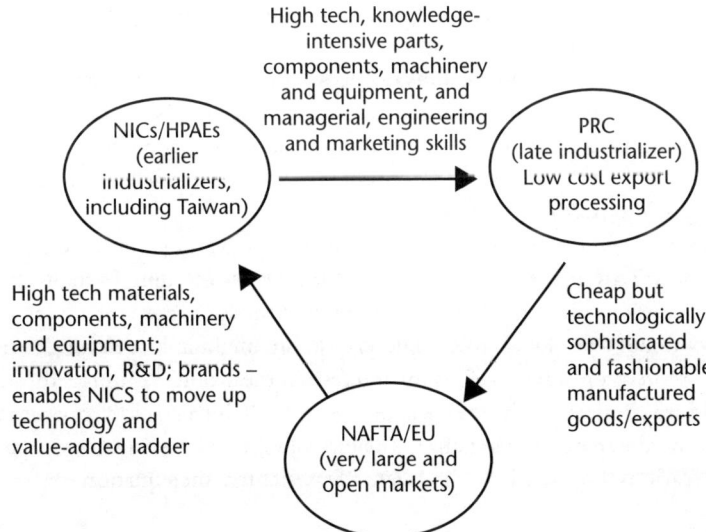

FIGURE 1.3   General model of East Asian production networks.

As already noted, Taiwan businesses enjoy certain advantages in terms of operating in China. There is the language: most Taiwanese businessmen speak Mandarin, thanks to the policies of forced sinicization of Taiwan's pre-democratic period. Cultural familiarity also increases the ease and comfort of interaction with PRC businesses. Geographical proximity is another advantage: Taiwan is quite close to South China's dynamic production bases in Guangdong, Zhejiang, and Fujian provinces, as well as to Shanghai and South Jiangsu. Political goodwill, emanating either from a sense of common Chinese-ness or from a calculated effort to win over Taiwan's business class, is another potential advantage. Political calculations may have led Beijing to court Taiwan's business community by conferring on them operational advantages over their "foreign" Korean, Japanese, or American competitors. It was with such advantages in mind that in the 2000s the Taiwanese government sought to make Taiwan an "Asia-Pacific Regional Operations Center" for major international firms. These hopes were not realized, in part because of the estrangement of Taipei and Beijing.

Yun-peng Chu and Gee San are at pains to highlight the potential advantages of close relations between Taiwan and the Mainland. By contrast, Barry Naughton and Peter Chow see dangers to Taiwan in its evolving relationship with the Mainland. One great danger confronting Taiwan, according to Naughton and Chow, is that it threatens to be disadvantaged vis-à-vis its East Asian competitors in its operations in China because of restrictions imposed by Taiwan's own government, or because of Beijing's refusal to allow wider Taiwan participation. China's vast and rapidly growing internal market offers major opportunities for countries able and willing to participate in it. From an objective economic perspective, a major challenge to Taiwan's continued strong economic growth has been uncertainty whether or not political obstacles (originating in Taipei or Beijing – or both) might impede its participation in China's markets. In this respect, the 2002 signature of a free trade agreement between China and the eleven countries of the Association of Southeast Asian Nations (ASEAN) threatened to put Taiwan at a competitive disadvantage vis-à-vis Southeast Asian suppliers.[16] A desire to maintain Taiwan's economic competitive edge by widening access to China was a major factor motivating Ma Ying-jeou's rapprochement with China starting in 2008. The most recent culmination of this process was the signing, in June 2010, of a landmark "Economic Cooperation Framework Agreement" (ECFA) (see also p. 28).

Meanwhile, quite apart from the obvious gain of averting war or other hostile action against Taiwan, there are clear *political* advantages accruing to the island from improved relations with the PRC. Assuming that the PRC's emergence as a global power continues, a favorable cross-Strait relationship might induce Beijing to use that power to protect and advance Taiwan's interests in the world. Countries throughout the world are pondering how they will be affected by China's rapidly growing power. Taiwan is no different, but its status in the face of China's growing power is perhaps more precarious. This is where the United States enters the equation.

The other half of Taiwan's international macro-climate: the United States

The United States's commitment to assist Taiwan in the event of an unprovoked PRC attack is the bedrock of Taiwan's security policy. That is the reason why most Taiwanese leaders are leery of alienating Washington via "provocative" actions. Some DPP leaders, however, believe that since the United States protects Taiwan out of self-interest, Washington will not abandon Taiwan, and therefore can be maneuvered into conflict with Beijing, thereby facilitating a greater degree of "Taiwan independence" for the island. Such an approach is extremely dangerous for Taiwan because, in the final analysis, it is the US government that will decide what is or is not "provocative," and because the United States places a higher premium on its relations with Beijing than on those with Taiwan.

This is not to deny that there are important US interests underlying the commitment to Taiwan's security. One is to prevent the destruction of the liberal democracy on Taiwan, to which several decades of American investment of money and diplomatic energy has significantly contributed. Throughout the authoritarian period of Taiwan's development, the United States worked to nudge it in more democratic and free directions.[17] The credibility of US alliances with other countries in Asia – Japan, South Korea, Australia, the Philippines, etc. – is also at stake. If the United States is unwilling to confront Beijing in support of America's "old friend," Taiwan, other Asian countries may well conclude that Washington is unlikely to come to their aid against Beijing in extremis, and that their interest lies in working out a new arrangement with the PRC – especially a PRC made even more powerful if Taiwan had fallen under PLA control – without the United States. Taiwan's incorporation into the PLA's military system would also greatly enhance China's relative military capabilities. Indeed, such considerations *may* be part of US calculations, although they are not articulated in public US policy statements. In such statements, the overriding US interest is said to be the peaceful resolution of the Taiwan question by the people on the two sides of the Taiwan Strait themselves.

Against these US interests in Taiwan is the simple but awesome fact that conflict over Taiwan between the US and PRC could escalate to all-out war, conceivably even involving a general nuclear exchange and lasting for many years.[18] Admittedly, this is a remote possibility, not least because it would destroy the transnational production networks described in the previous section, which have been the basis of China's remarkable developmental success since 1978. But both Washington and Beijing recognize war as a possibility, albeit a potentially catastrophic one which they both have a profound common interest in avoiding. This apart, there are many areas of common interest where it is in the US interest to cooperate. The influence of the PRC now extends from Asia, to the Middle East, to Africa, to outer space, and Beijing can use such influence to either oppose or help achieve US objectives. Throughout much of modern history, China and the United States actually have had a pretty good record of working together on international issues of common concern (Warren Cohen terms the twenty years of confrontation between 1950 and 1970 "the great aberration"[19]), and one of the overriding questions of the twenty-first century is whether they will be able to work cooperatively, or will move toward confrontation. China's stake in trying to build a cooperative Sino-American relationship is as great as Washington's. Under the shadow of these very weighty geopolitical considerations, Taiwan must move very carefully.

The US commitment to Taiwan's security is unilateral, undertaken by the United States through legislation defined by the 1979 Taiwan Relations Act (TRA). Part of the compromise between US and PRC interests regarding Taiwan worked out in 1971–2 and 1978 was that the United States would have no "official" relations with Taiwan and would abrogate the US-ROC mutual security treaty of 1954. Since US undertakings with Beijing precluded any sort of bilateral, government-to-government agreement with Taipei, Washington's enactment of the TRA was a unilateral one. Beijing did not like this, but it understood the compromise, and accepted it because it wanted normal diplomatic relations with the United States. Another aspect of the PRC-US compromise over Taiwan was Beijing's expression of its intent to resolve the Taiwan question via peaceful means – even while insisting that the issue was a purely domestic matter in which Beijing retained the sovereign right to use military force should it so decide.

Taiwan politics – its identity debate, partisan competition, its efforts for institutional reform, and its efforts to maintain and enhance its global economic competitiveness – takes place within these international parameters. To survive and continue to prosper, Taiwan's leaders and, since democratization, Taiwan's voters have had to find a balance that could accommodate both Washington and Beijing.

The politics of Taiwan's democratic consolidation

There are three key components of Taiwan's transition from an authoritarian, one-party dictatorship to liberal democracy, all of which are discussed in the first chapters of this book. These three dimensions are: identity debates, partisan competition, and institutional reforms. Identity debates have involved contending narratives of who the people of Taiwan are – are they "Chinese" or "Taiwanese"? – and the significance of those labels. Partisan competition involves the struggle for political power within the framework of law and strong, stable institutions. This struggle has frequently been intense and has aroused strong passions linked to conflicting identity narratives. Institutional reforms have involved the transformation of laws and governmental organizations inherited from Taiwan's pre-democratic period into forms appropriate to a liberal democratic system. Institutional reform efforts have also sometimes been linked to contending identity narratives. The chapters by Christopher Hughes, Dafydd Fell, and Shelley Rigger examine, respectively, Taiwan's identity debate, partisan competition and institutional reforms. Figure 1.4 seeks to integrate these domestic factors with the international factors discussed above.

Given the strong challenges it faces, the consolidation of Taiwan's democratic values and institutions is important. Taiwan must develop a collective identity that is inclusive, democratic, and persuasive enough to secure its citizens' commitment

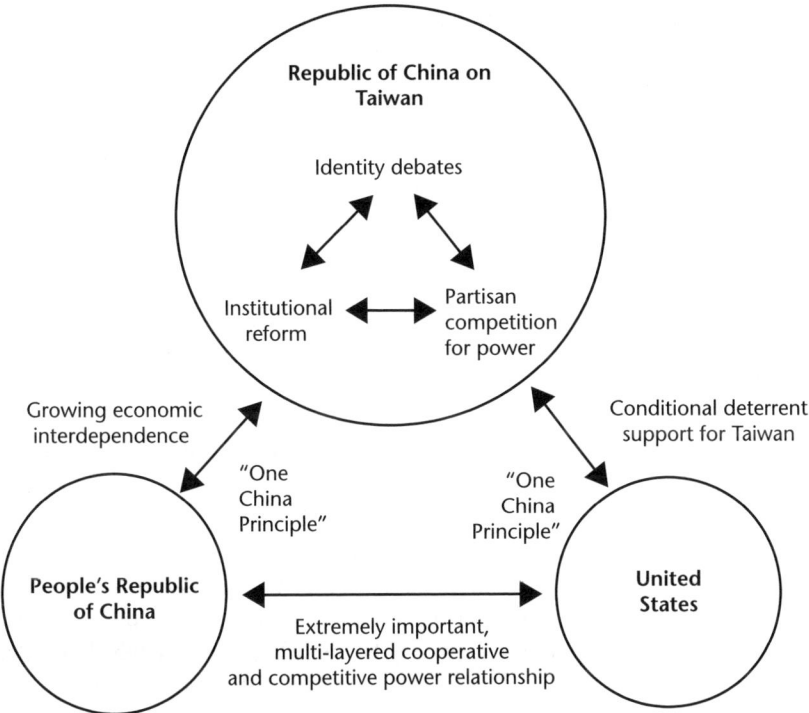

FIGURE 1.4 Key domestic and international variables in Taiwan's political process.

to it. It must develop a spirit of bi- or multiparty cooperation through which all parties commit themselves to the welfare of the polity. It must also put in place a political framework that is sufficiently strong to address whatever problems may arise, whilst also providing for national defense and the containment of domestic political conflict. As the first three chapters in this book show, Taiwan has already moved a considerable way toward such a democratic consolidation.

The thesis structuring Christopher Hughes's analysis is that both the Blue and the Green narratives were initially (that is, at the start of Taiwan's transition to democracy in around 1986) undemocratic in that they each delegitimized people in the other camp. The Blue narrative deemed native Taiwanese, who tended to be "Greens," as disloyal to "China." The Green narrative deemed people of "Mainlander" descent to be alien and foreign, and lacking in true loyalty to Taiwan. The consolidation of Taiwan democracy required and fortunately has achieved, according to Hughes, construction of a new non-ethnic (or sub-ethnic) narrative of identity able to include both the Blue and the Green viewpoints, as well as all views in between. Hughes traces the process through which this new identity – one defined not in ethnic but in territorial terms – has emerged. Democratization led most "Blues" to abandon their previous vision of military invasion and overthrow of the CCP, even if it did not remove their aspiration that Taiwan might one day – perhaps in the wake of the emergence of a democratic Mainland – become part of a reunited China. From the

Green perspective, however, this Blue narrative was a pretext for the continuation of alien rule over the people of Taiwan and the denial of their right to sovereign self-determination. Hughes argues that consolidation of Taiwan democracy demanded a new progressive Taiwanese identity that would embrace Blues, Greens, and everyone else in Taiwan. In his chapter, Hughes offers a masterful analysis of how this new "civil nationalism" was negotiated on Taiwan.

Fell explores movement among Taiwan's political parties through consideration of three issues: first, unification with China versus Taiwan independence; second, Taiwanese identity versus Chinese identity; and third, purchase of advanced weapons from the United States to defend Taiwan against possible PLA attack. He uses the first two issues to construct a useful Left–Right model of Taiwan's political spectrum, on the basis of which he traces shifts in Taiwan's political parties, whether toward each other and the center of the spectrum, or away from each other and toward the poles. Dr. Fell finds that Taiwan's political parties were deeply polarized at the beginning of the transition to democracy. Thereafter, through 2004 – that is, through President Chen Shui-bian's first term as president – they moved steadily toward one another, and the center of the political spectrum. Since 2004, however, a process of polarization has set in, as the political parties have shifted back toward their respective ideologically driven stances. Identity politics again takes a central role in Dafydd Fell's chapter, in which he offers a set of criteria for a model of Taiwan's political spectrum that can be used to analyze partisan competition in Taiwan. The model of the Taiwan political spectrum developed by Fell highlights the deep disagreements over the destiny of Taiwan associated with the extremities of political opinion on the island. Such disagreements did not, however, prevent five rounds of constitutional amendment from taking place between 1991 and 2005. Moreover, as Fell indicates, majority political opinion lies more toward the center, and competition for votes may therefore draw the parties back in that direction. Yet the danger remains. In October 2008 half a million "Green" supporters rallied in Taipei to protest the Ma Ying-jeou administration's putative "hollowing out of Taiwan's sovereignty" and "*de facto* unification" of Taiwan and the Mainland through a series of agreements with Beijing over the previous five months since Ma's inauguration.[20] Ma's bold moves to expand economic and cultural contacts with the PRC appear to bow to Beijing's objections to demonstrations of Taiwan's sovereignty and are certain to exacerbate Green fears and anger. Averting deepening polarization within Taiwan as cross-Strait relations expand will require political skill and acumen.

Taiwan's transition from one-party authoritarian dictatorship to multiparty democracy naturally required substantial change in political institutions. During the period of KMT dictatorship prior to 1987, Taiwan was governed in accordance with the Constitution that had been drafted on the Mainland of China in 1947. That Constitution, drawn up shortly after Japan's defeat, was intended to enfranchise citizens across the length and breadth of Mainland China. It created national Chinese organs of government, even specifying special measures to ensure representation from China's ethnic minority areas, such as Tibet and Mongolia. In 1948, however, "temporary provisions to deal with the period of communist rebellion" were adopted, as the struggle between the KMT and the CCP intensified during the Chinese Civil War (1946–9). These "temporary provisions" suspended many liberal aspects of the Constitution that would have restrained government power in favor of citizens' freedoms, and they were to remain in place until April 1991. After the defeated remnants of the KMT government and army fled to Taiwan in 1949, the 1947 Constitution, along with "temporary provisions," served as the legal basis for martial law, a military state, and one-party rule.

The 1947 Constitution dovetailed with the "Blue" Chinese nationalist narrative effectively to disenfranchise the Taiwanese. National representative institutions – both the legislature and a national assembly charged with electing the president and amending the Constitution, and putatively representing all China – remained in place. As representatives in those bodies grew old, vacancies that occurred because of death or retirement were filled by presidential appointment or through "special elections" by those who had originally lived in the relevant provinces but were now residing in Taiwan. Behind these institutions was the reality of a military state maintained by martial law. It is part of Taiwan's impressive political achievement, and a manifestation of Taiwan's commitment to the rule of law, that it was accomplished through a peaceful and legal process of constitutional amendment – a process analyzed by Professor Shelley Rigger in her chapter in this volume.

The exceptionally high bar to further constitutional amendment plus the "amendment exhaustion" that has apparently set in following two decades of amendment struggles, may have unfortunate results because of certain idiosyncrasies of Taiwan's constitutional arrangements. Most other democratic countries tend clearly toward either a presidential or a parliamentary system. By contrast, Taiwan has an unusual mixture of the two – what many analysts term a "semi-presidential system." This mixture of parliamentary and presidential elements is outlined in Figure 1.5. It is one of the factors that contributed to gridlock after the 2000 election, when Taiwan's executive and its legislative branches were controlled, respectively, by the DPP and the KMT. In this way, each party used the constitutional powers of the branch it controlled to combat its opponent.

In terms of attributes of a presidential system, under the ROC's Constitution the president of the Republic is not a figurehead, but holds a range of substantial powers explicitly and constitutionally enumerated (i.e. not derived from the legislature). These presidential powers include those of assuming the role of commander in chief of the armed forces, taking ultimate control of foreign relations (including negotiation of treaties and agreements), and appointing civil and military officials. The ROC president also has the power to veto legislation passed by the Legislative Yuan (the ROC legislative body), although this may be overridden by a simple majority vote of all legislators. In addition, the president is empowered to issue emergency decrees and declare martial law. He also has the authority to appoint and remove the head of the Executive Yuan (the cabinet of the ROC government, whose head is called a premier) without the consent of the legislature.[21] He may also dissolve the

Aspects of a presidential system	Aspects of a parliamentary system
President is granted a series of substantive powers directly by the constitution. He is not a figurehead.	Executive Yuan, not president, is highest administrative organ of state. Premier, not president, directs operation of cabinet and subordinate ministries and agencies. President technically not part of Executive Yuan.
President can appoint and remove the head of the Executive Yuan without approval of the legislature, and may dissolve the the legislature without the approval of the premier.	Simple majority vote of legislature may pass a no-confidence vote in the Executive Yuan resulting either in resignation of government or dissolution of legislature.
President can veto legislative actions, though that veto can be overridden by simple majority of all legislators.	Legislature approves Executive Yuan policy statements and reports, and may by 2/3 vote redirect policy of the Executive Yuan.
Head of the Executive Yuan and cabinet ministers are not members of legislature.	

FIGURE 1.5 Presidential and parliamentary elements of Taiwan's "semi-presidential" system.

Legislative Yuan without the approval of the premier in the aftermath of a legislative vote of no confidence in the government.

But there are also elements of the ROC constitutional arrangements that are typical of a parliamentary setup. For example, it is not the president, but the head of the Executive Yuan (the premier) who supervises the operation of governmental ministries and agencies – that is, oversees the routine conduct of the government. The Constitution also specifies that the Executive Yuan is the highest administrative organ of the state. This organ is presided over by the premier, not the president. Moreover, the government, that is the Executive Yuan, is responsible to the legislature and can be dissolved, by the president, through a simple majority of legislators. Finally, the legislature may, by a two-thirds vote in favor, redirect policy of the Executive Yuan.

Taiwan's democratic transition

The roots of Taiwan's democratization can be traced back to the 1950s, when elected village associations were set up as part of land reform. Elected county and city councils soon followed, and in 1959 an elected provincial assembly was established. Since Taiwan was considered to be merely a province of the ROC, a provincial assembly (representing a single province, Taiwan) could legitimately be elected by the electorate of Taiwan. In theory, however, "national" organs of government were meant to represent the rest of Mainland China, and their representatives were therefore appointed, not elected. Under these arrangements, all elected positions were parochial and rarely challenged KMT dominance. Nevertheless, such elections familiarized the populace of Taiwan with the workings of the electoral system. Elections remained tightly controlled under Chiang Kai-shek, but began to loosen under his son, Chiang Ching-kuo, who had handled security affairs for his father in the 1930s and was groomed as heir and successor throughout the post-1949 period. After Chiang Kai-shek's death in 1975, Taiwan under the leadership of Chiang Ching-kuo underwent a gradual transition from what analysts have called "hard" to "soft" authoritarianism." By the late 1970s opposition politicians had set up a de facto, if not yet legal, island-wide political organization, nominating candidates to stand for elections in opposition to KMT candidates. The two-week period of authorized debate preceding elections became known as "the holiday of democracy" and witnessed genuine, if still limited, free political debate. Police surveillance and intimidation continued to plague this opposition *dang wai* or "outside the [KMT] party" quasi-underground organization. But the government generally tolerated it and only rarely resorted to imprisoning those involved in it.

Perhaps Chiang's most important reform was his recruitment of Taiwanese professionals and businessmen into the KMT. By the mid-1980s the majority of KMT members were Taiwanese. One of the most important of these was Lee Teng-hui, an agronomist,[22] who was selected by Chiang as vice-president in 1984. After Chiang's death in January 1988, and despite unsuccessful efforts by hard-line Mainlander Chinese nationalists within the KMT to prevent succession by a native Taiwanese, Lee became the island's first native Taiwanese president and head of the KMT. It was Lee who presided over the most critical period of Taiwan's democratic revolution between 1988 and 2000.

As noted earlier, Taiwan embarked on its democratic revolution in 1986. Early in that year during a meeting of the KMT Central Committee, the ailing Chiang Ching-kuo called for major political reforms destined to precipitate full-scale democratization.[23] The quasi-legal underground opposition party, the *dang wai*, that had established itself during the previous decade seized the opportunity to emerge into open view and declared itself the Democratic Progressive Party (DPP). Chiang's government not only acquiesced in this, but initiated discussions with DPP leaders about the future of the country and the nature of its transition to democracy. This outcome emerged only after fierce debate within the KMT between reformers and hard-liners who favored repression rather than conciliation, compromise, and co-optation. Meanwhile, a similar debate took place within the DPP between advocates of a revolutionary approach to democratization, and those who favored compromise and incremental reform. Eventually the moderates in both parties won and negotiations between them made possible Taiwan's move toward democracy.[24] A watershed was reached in July 1987, when martial law was finally lifted. By now, Taiwan's transition to democracy was well under way.

In 1986 many of Taiwan's basic institutional arrangements were, not surprisingly, undemocratic. Non-elected "national" organs still dominated the political system. The legislature was still largely unelected. The president and vice-president were selected by a non-elected body, the National Assembly. Popularly elected bodies such as the provincial assembly, let alone the people themselves, had no role in the process of amending the Constitution. These non-democratic features were progressively transformed into genuinely democratic institutions through the several waves of constitutional amendment propelled by the interaction of national identity and partisan competition, which are analyzed by Shelley Rigger.

The point has already been made that, when Taiwan began its transition to democracy, it confronted a deep and often bitter divide between the two main sub-ethnic groups – Mainlanders and the Taiwanese. Although intermarriage and recruitment of Taiwanese into the KMT, and the rise of a dynamic and prosperous class of Taiwanese businessmen, had softened this cleavage, in the mid-1980s it was still much in evidence. The Mainlanders had formed the social basis for the KMT's dictatorship, assuming the most important positions in government, the military, and internal security, and in state-owned enterprises (which dominated Taiwan's economy into the 1960s).

Taiwanese resentment over their marginalization within their own land by "alien" Mainlanders was symbolized by the February 28 incident of 1947. During that episode a petty confrontation between a policeman and a cigarette merchant ended in police brutality. Protest demonstrations followed and quickly escalated into an island-wide protest against KMT rule, and then to brutal and bloody repression by KMT military forces. For the next forty years the mere use of the numerals "2 2 8" (for February 28) would attract the interest of Taiwan's internal security organs. There was an obvious and overt symbolism in the fact that when, under the presidency of Chen Shui-bian, the name displayed on Taiwan postage stamps was changed from "Republic of China" to "Taiwan," the date of issue of such stamps was chosen to be February 28, 2007. Moreover, the face of the stamp depicted a museum established in Taipei to commemorate the February 28, 1947, incident.[25]

During the pre-1987 dictatorship, Taiwanese were not permitted to debate their identity. Rather, the KMT dictatorship firmly repressed any discussion of who the people of Taiwan were. The orthodox narrative upheld by the repressive power of the KMT was that Taiwan was a province of the ROC, an entity that encompassed the length and breadth of continental China. Taiwan's destiny, according to this narrative, was to serve as a bastion of "freedom" and a base for eventual invasion of "the Mainland" by ROC military forces and the overthrow of the "bandit regime," the People's Republic of China, set up by the CCP. The whole of China would thereby be liberated from "communist slavery." Once the "red, communist bandits" on the Mainland had been overthrown and the legitimate authority of the ROC restored, the people of all of China, Taiwan included, might then proceed to dismantle the system of KMT "tutelage" and advance to liberal democracy.[26] Within this narrative, advocacy of Taiwan nationalism or of a Taiwanese identity distinct from that of China was nothing less than treason. During the pre-1987 period of authoritarian rule, many people in Taiwan were jailed or otherwise punished for challenging the KMT Chinese nationalist narrative. Journals that displayed too much "Taiwan sentiment" were closed down as subversive. The Chinese Nationalist orthodoxy was conveyed by the KMT controlled media and educational system. Brave writers periodically challenged this orthodoxy with greater or lesser degrees of directness. Almost always they suffered greatly for their efforts.

Starting in 1987, however, freedom of speech gave rise to a vigorous debate over Taiwan's identity. Long-repressed Taiwanese nationalist views were now powerfully and articulately expressed. This viewpoint came to be called "Green" because of the predominantly green flag of the pro-Taiwan independence opposition party, the DPP. The orthodox KMT point of view came to be referred to as "Blue" because of the blue field on the KMT and the ROC national flag. (The fact that these two were identical was a source of considerable grievance to Greens and used as one reason to justify changing the national flag: How could a Party's flag be the same as the national flag, they asked.) Because of splits in the KMT, two new, mainly Blue parties emerged: the New Party in 1993 and the People First Party in 2000. Together with the KMT, these have constituted what is often referred to as the "pan-Blue" camp. Meanwhile, Lee Teng-hui led a third group of people out of the KMT in 2001 and founded the Taiwan Solidarity Union (TSU). The DPP and the TSU together have informally become known as the "pan-Green" camp.

According to the Green viewpoint, the distinctive nature of Taiwan's historical experience had given the island's population a quite different character from that of the China Mainland. Nationality was not determined by language or ancestry. If it were, the United States, Canada, Australia, and New Zealand would still be part of Britain. Rather, according to the Taiwan nationalist interpretation, it was historical experience molded into a distinctive consciousness that determined nationality. The people of Taiwan were, and viewed themselves as, distinct from China. Taiwan was, and by rights ought to be recognized as, a nation and a state separate from China. Moreover, the people of Taiwan – the nation of Taiwan – deserved their own state, the Republic of Taiwan. From such perspectives, the name "Republic of China," or even "the Republic of China on Taiwan" (as Taiwan was increasingly styled by the KMT under Lee Teng-hui in the 1990s), was the residue of "alien" Chinese rule over the people of Taiwan.

Chen Shui-bian's presidency and the drive to assert Taiwan's sovereignty

The election in March 2000 and the subsequent (May) presidential inauguration of Chen Shui-bian marked the beginning of eight years of efforts, as Christopher Hughes phrases it, to "move decisively toward consolidation of a Taiwanese identity." Chen was an extremely bright lawyer, known for his forceful and often colorful rhetoric, who in 1980 defended pioneers of the *dang wai* movement who were on trial for their part in protests in Kaohsiung the previous year. In 1981 he became a *dang wai* member of the Taipei City Council, and in 1994 that city's DPP mayor. As noted earlier, Chen's 2000 election victory represented a significant advance for Taiwan's democracy. His election also marked the first time Taiwan's "Greens" had held Taiwan's highest executive power and been given responsibility for governing Taiwan. This was not an easy transition. Many analysts concluded that even after the 2000 election, the DPP still had the mentality of an opposition party, while the KMT continued to regard itself as the ruling party. By the time Chen left office in 2008, after completing a second term of office, the recklessness of his behavior had deeply alienated both Beijing and the United States, as well as many Taiwanese. Indeed, some had even begun to question whether Taiwan's democracy could survive its deep divisions over identity.

A manifesto, issued by the DPP a year before Chen's election in 2000, already demanded Taiwan independence. It stated: "Taiwan is a sovereign and independent country"; "Taiwan should renounce the 'One China' position [and] … incorporat[e] plebiscite into law in order to realize the people's rights."[27] Under intense pressure from the United States, Chen began his administration by backing away from these militant positions and giving assurances that, in spite of the previous year's manifesto, he would not act recklessly. In his inaugural address in May 2000, Chen pledged that, as long as the PRC "has no intention to use military force against Taiwan," he would not declare independence, change the name of the country, seek to include the "state-to-state" doctrine in the Constitution, promote a referendum on independence or unification, or abolish the National Unification Council or the National Unification Guidelines. In August 2002, however, he used a video conference to assert more provocatively that there was one country on each side of the Strait. Similar statements followed. In September 2003 Chen announced plans to hold a referendum on a number of sensitive issues, including the definition of the national territory and the name of the country. Such advocacy continued, and indeed several referenda took place at the time of the 2004 and 2008 presidential elections. In 2004, voters were asked whether advanced weapons should be purchased to counter China's steady buildup of missiles in Fujian province, opposite Taiwan. Four years later voters were asked what name – Taiwan or the Republic of China – should be used in the island's application for United Nations membership. In his 2004 New Year's speech, Chen defined the ROC in terms of the 36,000 square kilometers and the population of 23 million people that made up Taiwan. In early 2006 Chen announced that the National Unification Council – the body officially charged with responsibility for planning for eventual unification – would "cease to function." Meanwhile, in a "de-sinicization" campaign analyzed by Christopher Hughes, "China" was dropped from various state documents, as well as from the names of various Taiwan state-owned enterprises. These moves were highly symbolic assertions of what Chen and his fellow Greens believed was Taiwan's de facto sovereignty independence. This de facto independence was, in the Green view, no more than an assertion of "the existing status quo," and the various moves made by Chen sought merely to strengthen this status quo.

Washington had a different understanding of the "status quo." During negotiations in Beijing in 1971 and 1972, Washington had undertaken not to describe Taiwan as other than being a part of China. The exact nature of the US position regarding Taiwan's status was left unclear. To have done otherwise – to have recognized Beijing's position that Taiwan was a part of China – would have been to concede to China the legal principle that Beijing, China's sovereign government, had the right, under generally accepted principles of international law, to regulate Taiwan's relations with the United States and other countries. Thus in protracted, difficult, and delicate negotiations with Beijing, Washington agreed to "acknowledge" and "not to challenge" Beijing's view that Taiwan was part of China – while also insisting on a peaceful resolution of the cross-Strait dispute and on the US conduct of "unofficial" relations with Taiwan independent of Beijing's regulation. A similarly ambiguous but equally useful understanding was endorsed twenty years later by Beijing and Taipei during talks in Hong Kong. During this 1992 meeting, representatives from Beijing and Taipei had agreed on the "one China principle" that Taiwan was part of China, while each side retained its own interpretation of what "China" meant. For Beijing, "China" was the PRC of which Taiwan was an integral part. For Taipei, "China" was an ethnic community comprising – as in fact had been the case since 1949 – two different political entities, the PRC and the ROC, each ruling its own territory. The "Hong Kong consensus" on "one China" provided a way of easing cross-Strait tensions and expanding cross-Strait relations, while facilitating US-PRC cooperation. Chen Shui-bian, however, rejected the notion that a "consensus" on "one China" had been reached in Hong Kong in 1992. For him and his Green compatriots, acceptance of the proposition, however ambiguous its formulation, that Taiwan was part of China was a dangerous infringement of Taiwan's sovereignty. In the event, Chen's words and actions in the wake of his rejection of the "1992 compromise" alienated both Beijing and Washington.

By 2007–8, US-Taiwan relations were sour. Washington saw Chen's assertions of "Taiwan independence" as reckless, having been undertaken without consultation with the United States and even in contradiction of US advice and urging. From the perspective of Washington, Chen's actions endangered US-PRC cooperation, threatened peace, and put at risk the tranquility and prosperity of the people of Taiwan. US warnings became increasingly direct. In December 2003, for example, with PRC Premier Wen Jiabao standing by his side in the White House, President George W. Bush stated publicly that: "The comments and actions made by the leader of Taiwan indicate that he may be willing to make decisions unilaterally to change the status quo, [a course] which we oppose." Following the nullification of the National Unification Council several years later, the US State Department issued a written statement saying "We expect the Taiwan authorities [to] publicly ... affirm that [they] did not abolish the National Unification Council. ... We believe the maintenance of Taiwan's assurances is critical to preservation of the status quo. Our firm policy is that there should be no unilateral change in the status quo, as we have said many times."[28]

By the end of Chen's term in May 2008, his relations with the United States, and with Beijing, were extremely strained. In the US view, Chen had shown himself to be an ideologically driven partisan, prepared to promote his agenda regardless of the costs to his own people or his allies. In Beijing's view, he was a traitor devoid of sincerity who sought to "split" China's territory.

While US refusal to support Taiwan independence embittered many of Taiwan's Greens during the 2000s, it may have had the efficacious effect of teaching Taiwan's voters about the realities of politics among great powers. The United States has consistently viewed the existing status quo as entirely satisfactory. It has allowed the people of Taiwan to govern themselves with liberty and democracy. It has facilitated cooperation between the United States and the People's Republic of China, between Taiwan and the United States, and between Taiwan and the PRC. It has prevented the PLA from using Taiwan as a platform to project Chinese military power into the Western Pacific. And it has helped ensure that war has been avoided. The moral is that, except, perhaps, in the wake of a direct PRC attack on the island, Taiwan cannot expect to enjoy US support for independence (i.e. de jure status as a sovereign state in the community of states). This denial of full, legal status as a sovereign state, recognized as such by other members of the community of states, is a bitter injustice in the minds of many Taiwanese voters, especially but not only among Greens. Viewed abstractly, the twenty-three million people of Taiwan, with their powerful economy, vibrant society, and stable political system have a stronger entitlement to sovereign statehood than many current members of the United Nations General Assembly, many of which are impoverished micro-states with abysmal standards of governance. But the delicate compromise of PRC and US interests that is involved in denying de jure sovereignty to Taiwan serves the interests of both Beijing and Washington. Since that compromise has also facilitated economic prosperity – in part, a direct consequence of closer cross-Strait cooperation – democratic and free self-government, and peace for Taiwan, Washington and Taiwan's "Blues" would argue that that great-power compromise has served Taiwan's interests as well. By contrast, Taiwan's "Greens" decry the Beijing-Washington compromise as an immoral sacrifice of the Taiwan people's right to self-determination.

If Chen Shui-bian and DPP Greens have asserted Taiwan's independence, the Blue KMT camp has insisted on Taiwan's destiny as part of a future free and democratic China. The latter viewpoint was dramatically exemplified in the visit to China in April 2005 of a KMT delegation led by party chairman and recently defeated KMT presidential candidate, Lien Chan. At the time this was the highest-level public contact between the CCP and the KMT since before 1949. Lien and his delegation were welcomed warmly by the CCP. In a speech at Beijing University Lien Chan laid out the KMT vision of the "brotherhood" of Chinese on both sides of the Strait. He stressed the importance of freedom of thought and Taiwan's embrace of such freedom, while also expressing a conviction that the Mainland would eventually move in the same desirable direction. This was a metaphorical way of alluding to eventual unification. Meanwhile, Lien said, the status quo should be maintained and "neither side can or should challenge it or try to change it unilaterally."[29]

President Chen Shui-bian's involvement in a deepening corruption scandal during his last two years in office contributed to the collapse of Green political fortunes. In May 2006 Chen's son-in-law was arrested for insider trading involving a government development agency. The investigation expanded to include Chen's wife and, eventually, Chen himself, who was accused of misappropriating substantial monies from a secret account used to promote Taiwan's international standing. In November 2008, six months after the inauguration of a new president, Ma Ying-jeou, the former president was arrested. The following September, he was convicted of wide-ranging graft offenses and sentenced to life imprisonment.

Ma Ying-jeou and the return to cross-Strait amity

With Ma Ying-jeou's election in March 2008, the KMT recaptured Taiwan's presidency. The KMT victory ended eight years in which Taiwan's executive and legislative branches had been controlled by different parties. It also shifted identity politics back toward the pro-status quo center, and put cross-Strait relations on a new track in search of closer cooperation.

Ma's background was different from that of either of Taiwan's previous popularly elected presidents (i.e. Lee Teng-hui and Chen Shui-bian). Born in Hong Kong of Mainlander parents, Ma went to university and then law school in the United States – becoming fluent in English in the process – but also taught himself Taiwanese, once he had embarked on a political career. He served as minister of justice in 1993–6 before being forced to resign for pursuing corruption investigations against high-ranking KMT officials.[30] Subsequently, in 1998–2006 he served as elected mayor of Taipei.

Once inaugurated as president, Ma moved quickly to repair Taiwan's ties with Beijing and Washington. There was a powerful economic logic to Ma's effort to improve cross-Strait relations (see p. 29). But political objectives – ending Taiwan's alienation from Washington and lessening the intense hostility emanating from Beijing – were also high on Ma's agenda. As he said in his May 21, 2008 inaugural address, "Support for Taiwan from abroad had suffered an all-time low" in recent years. Taiwan's democracy had "been treading down a rocky road" but now was set to "enter a smoother path." Accordingly, "the Republic of China must restore its reputation in the international community as a peacemaker."[31] Renewed embrace of the "1992 consensus" of "one China, respective interpretations," which Ma signaled in his inaugural address, was an initial move toward reconciliation with Beijing. Ma called for resumption of cross-Strait talks to achieve the "normalization of economic and cultural relations" as a first step toward even closer cooperation, and even raised the possibility of a cross-Strait peace accord. He also proposed a "three nos" strategy – no unification, no independence, and no use of force – in order to maintain the status quo in the Strait. His reference to the "common Chinese heritage" of people on the two sides of the Taiwan Strait and his hope that the Mainland would "continue to move toward freedom, democracy, and prosperity ... [in order] to pave the way for the long-term peaceful development of cross-Strait relations" hinted at the prospect of eventual unification. Shortly after Ma's inauguration, Taipei indicated willingness to accept Beijing's offer of two pandas for the Taipei Zoo, an offer rejected several years earlier by Chen Shui-bian's administration. Taipei also abandoned its previous efforts to enter the United Nations under the name of "Taiwan." Instead, the new government sought merely to achieve "meaningful participation" (and no longer full membership) in UN agencies – a formulation that pointed toward the old nomenclature of "Chinese, Taipei," which had been agreed by both sides in pre-DPP times.

Only three weeks after Ma's inauguration, talks began between the "unofficial" organs established by the two sides in 1991 to handle contacts: namely, Taiwan's Straits

Exchange Foundation (SEF) and the PRC's Association for Relations Across the Taiwan Straits (ARATS). A series of agreements were quickly reached. Instead of having to pass through Hong Kong or some other intermediate point, direct flights were inaugurated across the Taiwan Strait. The quota of Mainland tourists allowed to visit Taiwan was substantially increased, and agreement was reached to establish permanent SEF and ARATS liaison offices in Beijing and Taipei. A second round of talks in November led to even broader agreements regarding expanded air connections, postal services, maritime communications, and food safety. The November 2008 talks also saw the first visit to Taiwan by the head of ARATS – an event which, as noted earlier, led to huge protests. Over a half million people demonstrated against the ARATS chief's visit and the accelerating pace of Ma's embrace of the PRC.

The shift in policy between Chen Shui-bian and Ma Ying-jeou was dramatic, as Taiwan's political pendulum swung sharply from Green to Blue. Many people, and not only deep "Greens," felt that Ma was moving too fast, deepening Taiwan's dependency on the Mainland and endangering Taiwan's ability to resist Beijing's pressure.[32]

In spite of opposition, Ma pressed forward. In December 2008 SEF and ARATS began negotiation of an Economic Cooperation Framework Agreement (ECFA) that would create a virtual free trade zone between the PRC and Taiwan economies.[33] The DPP was revitalized (following the disgrace of Chen Shui-bian) by widespread popular concern about the proposed ECFA. The DPP opposed ECFA on both political and economic grounds. Politically, it charged that Ma's management of the process of economic integration with the Mainland lacked transparency and democratic responsibility. Taiwan's legislature had, it said, been denied oversight of the negotiating process, even though it involved a number of issues likely to touch on Taiwan's sovereignty. Many Greens regarded ECFA as unification by stealth and believed that the people of Taiwan would see this and reject it, if given a chance. Submission of any ECFA to popular referendum became a central Green demand. In the words of one Green newspaper:

> The most important thing is that Ma should promise to let the people decide through a referendum whether an ECFA should be signed. Since Ma took office, Taiwan has already signed twelve agreements with China without putting any of them to a referendum. At the most, they were submitted to … the legislature. … In other words, these agreements have been signed … without being monitored by the legislature or the public. … In short, the government pushed the agreements through unilaterally. Now, as it prepares to sign an ECFA, the government is playing the same tricks again. The government is only willing to submit the agreement to the legislature because … the KMT holds an absolute majority. … The president's words are not to be believed, nor are his actions to be trusted. The only way forward for Taiwan's people is to decide things for themselves through a referendum.[34]

In the event, the ECFA was signed in June 2010 – and on terms which one source described as being "remarkably sweet" for Taiwan.[35] By the time the agreement was made public, polls showed much greater popular support for it, although the two main political parties – KMT and DPP – remained (as they still are) divided on its advisability. It has yet to be seen to what extent ECFA succeeds in delivering the hoped-for economic and trade benefits – and perhaps encourages other countries to sign their own free trade agreements with Taiwan – without increasing the island's political vulnerability vis-à-vis the Mainland.

Taiwan's next economic miracle?

Taiwan faces strong competitive economic challenges. Other East Asian states, including the rest of the first-echelon NICs (South Korea, Hong Kong, and Singapore), pose strong competition. Thanks to its low costs, generous state sponsorship of key sectors and activities, large investments in education, and large pool of engineering talent (not to mention its increasing success in enticing high-level ethnic Chinese talent with years of experience in Western countries "back" to the Mainland), China itself poses very strong competition. Meanwhile, over everything looms widespread apprehension of many Taiwanese that too deep an economic integration with the PRC will lead to political vulnerability, which Beijing will exploit to coerce Taiwan to accept a new status as part of the People's Republic of China. Be that as it may, the political pendulum in Taiwan has swung sharply in a less skeptical, more optimistic direction under Ma Ying-jeou. The economic logic of Ma's drive for expanded economic integration with the Mainland is laid out in the chapters that comprise the second half of this volume.

Anne Booth's chapter argues that Taiwan's development from the 1950s, characterized by its successful transition from an agricultural export economy to one that exported higher-value and increasingly sophisticated industrial goods, was grounded in education and employment policies. Unlike other export-oriented East Asian economies, Taiwan relied only to a limited extent on foreign investment. Rather, its approach focused on local companies that built strategic alliances with foreign firms in order to increase exports and gain access to technology. Government-business relations were close, but no attempt was made to target specific firms to become internationally competitive at the expense of others. While this experience, including the establishment of appropriate institutions and infrastructure, promises to serve Taiwan well as it embarks on the next phase of growth, Booth highlights a series of new challenges that have arisen.

For some years now, Taiwan has experienced slower growth than comparable Asian economies, averaging 6 percent or less per year since 1998. Manufacturing as a share of GDP has declined and internal demand has shifted toward services. Nearly 74 percent of Taiwan's GDP now derives from the tertiary sector. Since services tend not to be traded, growth is becoming increasingly determined by domestic demand, as a result of which the premium on maximizing productivity has tended to be lost. Moreover, the development of financial services activities, which the government would like to promote in order to make Taiwan an Asian financial center, has to date lagged behind that of other centers in the region. At the same time, inequalities (especially wage inequalities) have in recent years begun to widen. Against the background of an aging work force, migrant workers have also increasingly been hired to fill labor gaps and/or to keep costs down.

In short, Taiwan's relatively equal, high growth economy seems to be in retreat. Combine this with Taiwan's evolving democracy and what economic role is left for the Taiwan government? Professor Booth argues that former Asian "developmental states" have weakened considerably. In Taiwan the rise of electoral politics, including the increasing influence of organized labor, has weakened the government's ability to directly influence the economy. The legacy of early government leadership in education has been the emergence of a highly educated labor force suitable for a knowledge-based economy. The challenge now facing Taiwan is to employ this work force effectively.

Yun-peng Chu and Gee San's analysis suggests that despite appreciation of the Taiwan currency and rising labor costs, manufacturing in Taiwan has been able to adapt and remain competitive through the 1980s and 1990s. However, they too see clear challenges for Taiwan as it faces the next stage of its development trajectory. Like Booth, they examine the slowing of economic growth that began with the dot-com troubles in 2000, but to which a fundamental change in the role of Taiwan government-led industrial policy also contributed. One of their findings is that government policies, including measures to enhance education and attract overseas Taiwanese to return home, had in the past helped underpin Taiwan's economic success. The central challenge now is for the government to establish, maintain, and enhance a strong business environment. Chu and San argue that getting Taiwan's China policies right is an essential condition for fulfilling this goal and thereby guaranteeing Taiwan's future.

The authors demonstrate the substantial scale of investment which Taiwan has undertaken in China. They also show how Taiwan's investment activities in China have increased the capital and technology intensity of China's exports. This has, in turn, facilitated China's emergence as a rival, competing with Taiwan's own exports. Against this background, it is not surprising that the former DPP government should have sought to impose restrictions on Taiwan firms investing in China. Be that as it may, the authors argue that such action was bound to damage Taiwan's economic interests in the long run.

Through a careful and detailed comparison of Taiwan with the Netherlands, Finland, and Ireland, Chu and San argue that the quality of Taiwan's labor force compares favorably with that of those three European countries, but that Taiwan's R&D is insufficient, and its scientific and technological base inadequate, to enable it to compete in the next knowledge-intensive phase of development. Taiwan has so far failed to meet the core challenge of converting its strong educational capabilities into high value-added products. Another important finding is that exploitation of locational advantages vis-à-vis the European Union contributed significantly to the three European countries' economic success. Taiwan too has the potential to reap similar benefits from its propinquity to the huge Chinese market. However, Taiwan government regulations current at the time of writing had prevented such benefits from being realized. Indeed, the irony of the then situation was that companies' efforts to circumvent official restrictions meant that far fewer benefits accrued to Taiwan and its people. Some might detect a further irony in Chu and San's suggestion that efforts to limit Taiwan's economic integration with the Mainland threatened to discourage foreign investment in Taiwan itself, and to create a second brain drain, as Taiwanese entrepreneurs moved elsewhere to set up their new companies. The challenges of moving up the value chain are formidable enough. The moral of Chu and San's analysis is that the effect of adding new barriers to existing challenges was likely merely to further impede Taiwan's economic progress.

In the penultimate chapter of this volume, Barry Naughton also identifies Taiwan's propinquity to China's large market as a potential advantage for Taiwan. His analysis, which complements that of Chu and San, focuses on the challenges of technological upgrading at the sub-sector level. The key to Taiwan's success, Naughton argues, lies in the way in which its own companies integrated themselves into global production networks. Having built relationships with the key companies responsible for creating networks (for example, IBM), Taiwan's highly educated labor force was the catalyst for the promotion of, first, original equipment manufacturing (OEM), and, subsequently, original design manufacturing (ODM). Thereafter, Taiwanese companies incorporated Mainland China-based production into their business strategies, thereby maintaining low costs. The success of this model lay in such firms' ability to continue to profit from their alliances with global companies, rather than independently seeking to create their own brands. The independence of specifications and tasks – otherwise known as "modularity" – within the personal computer and IT industry facilitated the efficient functioning of decentralized and mobile production units. The same factors also enabled Taiwanese firms to make incremental improvements to the modules which they themselves managed, although more fundamental innovation fell within the remit of the global firms with which they were allied.

In the most recent past, changes in the global economy – above all, the changing role of China – have begun to challenge this successful business model. Professor Naughton carefully shows that Taiwan's proximity to the Mainland Chinese market offers a unique opportunity for Taiwan companies to upgrade their innovation capabilities in terms of new and improved products. With its low costs and skilled expertise, China is also one of the main locations for new R&D efforts. Taiwanese firms are well placed to exploit these expanding global innovation networks (GIN). Meanwhile, the modularity of production may finally have reached its limits. Finding new ways to combine production with market demands will therefore be required, and Naughton argues this is much more likely to occur in China than in the US or EU markets.

The final chapter on Taiwan's economy by Peter Chow analyzes how the island's embrace of globalization has altered its comparative advantage, and considers the implications of such changes for its future efforts to achieve sustained development.

Professor Chow argues that as a small country and a latecomer dependent on trade, Taiwan's development will hinge critically on finding an appropriate niche for itself. Chow shares the views of other authors in this volume in finding that Taiwan's past developmental efforts have been hugely successful. But if, like Booth, he applauds the strengths of its educational system, he also highlights major weaknesses in its financial sector development. At the core of his analysis is his use of indices on revealed comparative advantage for technology, and an export sophistication index, to demonstrate how, as comparative advantage has changed over time, significant progress in technology levels has taken place.

However, there are two issues of concern. First, while free trade areas (FTA) have proliferated in the region, Taiwan's "awkward" status vis-à-vis China has been a political impediment that has prevented it from joining any of them. A critical question is how much this isolation will hurt Taiwan.[36] To the extent that multilateral trade liberalization can be accomplished, Taiwan can also benefit. Chow's chapter was of course written before the recent thaw in relations with the Mainland. However, he makes the interesting observation that despite having been penalized by policy-driven considerations, market-driven forces had already made Taiwan a de facto economic partner. He notes too that discriminatory treatment was likely to impact on Taiwan's trade, not its FDI.

The second issue of concern for Taiwan's future economic development highlighted by Chow (as it is by other authors in this volume) is whether Taiwan companies can build their own innovative capability. Chow argues that if it is to succeed in promoting innovation, Taiwan must utilize its core industries, add a complementary service component, and find appropriate niche markets. He identifies eight innovative sectors that may serve as possible core industries. Of the four economics-orientated authors, Chow is the strongest advocate of government intervention in this regard. Government's role, as he sees it, is to nurture core industries and help industrial restructuring.

A clear message is conveyed by all four economics-orientated chapters: the slowing of Taiwan's growth since 2000 indicates that the underlying conditions for Taiwan's continued economic development have fundamentally changed. From an internal perspective, the role of Taiwan's government as an agent of economic growth and change has been in steep decline as it has assumed the tasks of running a modern democracy. Externally, global production chains are in flux, not least because of the rise to economic pre-eminence on Mainland China. Taking advantage of the new opportunities that have presented themselves will demand creativity and entrepreneurship. The benefits that accrued to Taiwan in the past as a result of its integration into global markets were huge. However, merely trying to replicate this past will not propel Taiwan to the next stage of its economic development. Herein lies the challenge facing Taiwan at the end of the first decade of the twenty-first century.

Notes

1 Ramon H. Myers and Mark Peattie, *The Japanese Colonial Empire, 1895–1945*, Princeton, NJ: Princeton University Press, 1984.

2 See Tai-chun Kuo and Ramon H. Myers, *Leadership, Property Rights and Institutional Change: Taiwan's Economic Transformation, 1949–1965*, London: Routledge. Forthcoming.

3 For an analysis of the "East Asian miracle" stressing the role of war and preparation for war, see Richard Stubbs, *Rethinking Asia's Economic Miracle: The Political Economy of War, Prosperity and Crisis*, London: Palgrave, 2005.

4 Samuel P. Huntington, *The Third Wave: Democratization in the Late Twentieth Century*, Norman and London: University of Oklahoma Press, 1991.

5 South Korea and Taiwan, like Japan and Vietnam, are heirs to Confucian political culture. The Philippines is not. During the twentieth century many people argued that Confucianism was intrinsically incompatible with liberal democracy, seeing this as an explanation for China's embrace of Communism, the fact that South Korea and Taiwan were ruled by dictatorships, that viable democracy came to Japan only via American occupation, and/or why the Communist side won in Vietnam. This "cultural explanation" seemed to explain a lot and was very attractive for many years. The East Asian democratic revolution significantly contributed to the rejection by most scholars of the earlier cultural approach.

6 *Swords Must be Turned into Plowshares: How to End History of Conflict*, April 29, 2005. KMT Cultural Commission.

7 One of the few works to examine this phenomenon is Jean-Francois Revel, *How Democracies Perish*, Garden City, New York: Doubleday, 1983.

8 Available online at http://www.china.org.cn/english/2005/oct/145718.htm#1.

9 The classic statement of this view is Benedict Anderson, *Imagined Communities, Reflections on the Origin and Spread of Nationalism*, London: Verso, 1983 and 1991.

10 The PRC claim to Taiwan is laid out in a white paper "The Taiwan Question and Reunification of China," August 1993. Issued jointly by the Taiwan Affairs Office and the Information Office of the State Council. An ROC rebuttal is *How Taipei Views Beijing's White Paper*, April 2000, Mainland Affairs Council, Executive Yuan, ROC. Available online at http://www.mac.gov.tw/. A neutral view of the "One China" issue is Shirley A. Kan, *China/Taiwan: Evolution of 'One China' Policy – Key Statements from Washington, Beijing, and Taipei*, October 18, 1999. CRS Report for Congress, FL30341, Library of Congress.

11 Regarding PLA mine capabilities see Andrew Erickson, Lyle Goldstein, and William Murray, *Chinese Mine Warfare*, China Maritime Studies Number 3, June 2009. Naval War College. Available online at http://www.usnwc.edu/cnws/cmsi/default.aspx.

12 Richard Fisher, "China's New Large Amphibious Assault Ship," International Assessment and Strategy Center, 8 January 2007. Available online at http://www.strategycenter.net/research/.

13 Richard Fisher, "China Builds Up Amphibious Forces," *Aviation Week*, 21 May 2010. Available online at http://www.aviationweek.com/.

14 "Reference Materials Concerning Education on Situation," in *Chinese Communist Internal Politics and Foreign Policy*, Taipei: Institute of International Relations, 1974, pp. 132–9.

15 Western economies of course contribute these things too, but for the sake of brevity discussion of these countries is omitted here.

16 The 2002 agreement finally came into full effect in January 2010.

17 See John W. Garver, *The Sino-American Alliance: Nationalist China and American Cold War Strategy in Asia*, Armonk: M. E. Sharpe, 1997, pp. 230–45.

18 Richard Bush and Michael E. O'Hanlon, *A War Like No Other: The Truth about China's Challenge to America*, New Jersey: John Wiley Sons, 2007.

19 Warren Cohen, *America's Response to China: A History of Sino-American Relations*, New York: Columbia University press, 1990.

20 "Six hundred thousand protest in Taipei," *Taiwan Communiqué*, Formosan Association for Public Affairs, November/December 2008, pp. 3–5.

21 Contrary to the usual arrangement in a parliamentary system, the head of the Executive Yuan (the premier) and cabinet ministers are not members of the legislature.

22 Lee trained at Kyoto Imperial University in Japan, and Iowa State and Cornell Universities in the United States.

23 These included full election of the legislature by the electorate of Taiwan, lifting a ban on formation of new political parties, and ending martial law. A good review of Taiwan's evolution is John F. Copper, *Taiwan: Nation-State or Province*, Boulder: Westview Press, 2003.
24 On the role of these factional divisions within the KMT see Tse-kang Leng, *The Taiwan-China Connection, Democracy and Development Across the Taiwan Straits*, Boulder, CO: Westview Press, 1991, Chapter 2, "Democratic Transition in Taiwan," pp. 16–36.
25 The name used on stamps was changed back after Ma Ying-jeou's election. Under Ma the "2 – 28" museum in Taipei was also reorganized in order to downplay rather than highlight harsh aspects of KMT rule.
26 The notion of one-party "tutelage" may be traced to Sun Yat-sen (the founding father of the KMT and the Republic of China), who argued that a transitional period of tutelage would be necessary to prepare the Chinese people for democracy.
27 Resolution Regarding Taiwan's Future, DPP National Party Congress, 8 May 1999.
28 Press Statement, US Department of State, 2 March 2006. Available online at http://www.state.gov/.
29 *Swords Must Be Turned into Plowshares: How to End History of Conflict*, 29 April 2005. KMT Cultural Committee.
30 Part of Chen Shui-bian's defense against the corruption charges was that he had only done what previous KMT officials had also done.
31 *China Post*, 21 May 2008. Available online at http://www.chinapost.com.tw/.
32 Hugo Restall, "Ma Ying-jeou is Taiwan's Trojan Horse," *Far Eastern Economic Review*, vol. 171, no. 3 (2008), pp. 21–3.
33 "China, Taiwan Set Stage for Landmark Pact on Trade," *Wall Street Journal*, 18 December 2009, p. A19.
34 "The Liberty Times Editorial," *Taipei Times*, 2 May 2010. Available online at http://www.taipeitimes.com/.
35 *The Economist*, 21 June 2010.
36 Since Chow's chapter was written, a new question is to what extent the recent ECFA agreement with Mainland China will facilitate the signing of FTAs with other countries.

PART I

Constitutional debate amidst political challenges

2

THE POLITICS OF CONSTITUTIONAL REFORM IN TAIWAN

Shelley Rigger

The constitution of the Republic of China took effect on December 25, 1947; the first substantive amendments were not added until 1991. In the intervening decades the ROC constitution's spirit was honored mostly in the breach, for its democratic elements were suspended in the wake of the Chinese Civil War. Since 1990, the constitution has encountered a new set of challenges, undergoing seven significant reforms: 1991, 1992, 1994, 1997, 1999, 2000 and 2005. How was it, then, that in 2007 – before the 2005 reforms had even taken effect – Taiwanese politicians were once again consumed by a rancorous debate over yet another round of constitutional change, potentially the most far-reaching to date?

Constitutional reform in Taiwan involves a wide range of political actors and forces. It includes both pragmatic and political calculations; constitutional reformers seek to address real issues of representation, deliberation, efficiency and accountability, but they are not above using constitutional debates to mobilize support for partisan political goals. The complexity of the issue has produced a great deal of debate and analysis, but little consensus.

Scholars generally divide Taiwan's constitutional reform process into stages, although there is disagreement about precisely how those stages should be defined (e.g. Linn 2002; Yeh 2002). This chapter considers the constitutional changes since 1990, as well as the current debate over constitutional reform. It follows the model developed by Lin Jih-wen, which regards the reforms of 1991, 1992, 1994 and 1997 – the "Lee Teng-hui Era" reforms – as manifestations of a single political dynamic. During this period, Taiwan updated and rejuvenated the ROC constitution to suit the needs and demands of a democratizing polity.

This first round of constitutional reforms had two objectives: facilitating democratization and balancing power among democratically elected governing bodies. In 1991, constitutional revisions restored the popularly elected nature of the ROC's legislative organs (including both the parliament, or Legislative Yuan (commonly referred to as "the LY"), and the National Assembly, whose purpose was to elect the president and amend the constitution). The following year's reforms gave voters the right to choose the provincial governor (the highest-ranking executive official below the central government). The 1994 reforms implemented direct popular election of the president and adjusted the relative power of the president and premier (the head of Cabinet, appointed by the president but accountable to the Legislative Yuan through a vote of confidence). The 1997 revisions reversed the 1994 reforms by eliminating the post of provincial governor; they also increased the power of the president relative to the premier and legislature.

The second round of reforms encompassed amendments passed in 1999 and 2000. In 1999, the National Assembly tried to preserve its institutional influence by changing the mechanism by which Assembly members were chosen while simultaneously extending the term of office of sitting members. Facing a fierce backlash from the public for its self-serving behavior, the Assembly reversed itself the following year. Its power to elect the president already had been handed to the people; now it transferred nearly all the rest of its powers to the Legislative Yuan. The reform reduced the National Assembly to an *ad hoc* body that would convene infrequently, only to ratify constitutional amendments already approved by the LY, or to vote on a bill of impeachment against the president. In considering the 1999/2000 reforms as a separate reform round, I part company with Lin, who considers all the Lee Teng-hui Era reforms together. Looking at those two years' peculiar events as a separate round helps clarify their logic, and helps bridge the gap between those reforms and the subsequent rounds.

The third round of constitutional reform was concluded in 2005, when the National Assembly ratified amendments that cut the size of Taiwan's legislature in half and changed its electoral system from single, non-transferable voting (SNTV) in multi-member districts to a combination of proportional representation and single-member simple plurality voting. The 2005 round also substituted popular referendum for a National Assembly vote as the mechanism for ratifying future constitutional changes and transferred its impeachment powers to the legislative and judicial branches. With nothing left to do, the National Assembly ceased to function.

The "fourth round" of constitutional reform is still in its infancy: while a wide variety of constitutional changes are proposed – including proposals for entirely new constitutions that would establish a "Second Republic" or a "Republic of Taiwan" – these are very far from ratification.

Explaining constitutional reform

Most writing on Taiwan's constitutional reform takes a normative or prescriptive approach; coming up with ways to improve the constitution is something of a cottage industry in law schools and political science departments (Yeh 2004; DeLisle 2004; Laliberté 2004). Analytical studies of the constitutional reform process tend to emphasize the importance of democratization (and democracy-minded leaders) as driving forces behind the reform process (Yeh 2002; Chao and Myers 1998). For example, Yeh argues that "the [pre-reform] regime's need to respond to crises has driven consecutive constitutional revisions. These crises came both from the regime's legitimacy in democracy (inward) and the regime's legitimacy in the international community (outward)" (Yeh 2002: 55). Other studies emphasize a related variable, partisan calculation (Copper 1998; Rigger 2001). Yet another popular academic approach is to contemplate the implications of constitutional reform for cross-Strait relations (Wachman 2004).

In 2002, Lin Jih-wen published a paper that placed Taiwan's constitutional reform process in a rational choice framework. He noted the popular view of the reform process which emphasizes "the struggle for power mingled with the debate of ideas, while calculated moves interwove capricious impromptus," but he insisted that it was possible to analyze the process more systematically (Lin 2002: 144). He argued that existing accounts of Taiwan's reforms tended to take one of three approaches: institutional engineering, historical-structural (path-dependent), or bargaining. His article synthesizes insights from each of these approaches, but most strongly endorses the institutional bargaining approach developed by William Riker (1964).

According to Lin, Taiwan's 1990s constitutional reforms occurred in a two-dimensional issue space that defined the preferences of the four actors in the process (the Lee Teng-hui/mainstream faction of the KMT, the DPP, the KMT's non-mainstream faction and the New Party). Although the constitutional reforms involved seventeen distinct issues, Lin shows that the positions taken by the four political actors on these issues were associated with two underlying dimensions. By carefully examining their positions on the various issues relative to the pre-reform status quo, Lin locates each of the four players in the two-dimensional space.

The first dimension, which Lin labels the "ideological dimension," captures the degree to which a party acknowledged the legitimacy of the ROC constitution. In the 1990s, the DPP regarded the ROC constitution as illegitimate and called for a new constitution; thus, Lin places the DPP at the extreme left end of the ideological dimension. The mainstream (Lee Teng-hui) faction of KMT, for its part, sought to "make Taiwan a de facto sovereign state, while keeping the fundamentals of the ROC Constitution intact." Lin locates the KMT mainstream between the DPP and the status quo on the ideological dimension (Lin 2002: 145). The New Party and the KMT's non-mainstream (conservative) faction preferred to affirm and invigorate the ROC constitution, placing them to the right of the status quo on the ideological dimension.

The second dimension, which Lin calls the "power dimension," captures each actor's position on the fundamental question of how to balance the power of the president and legislature. As Lin points out, parties that expected to win presidential elections (mainly Lee Teng-hui's KMT) supported constitutional reforms that increased presidential power, while the New Party, which had little hope of winning the top post, supported a more authoritative role for the legislature. As for the DPP, Lin says its interests prompted it to take a moderate position: "The DPP, although sharing the NP's criticism on the KMT's power expansion scheme, hesitates about restricting the president's power, because the possibility of their winning the presidential election is no longer remote. ... [Nonetheless,] the DPP, although supporting a capable president, does not abandon the Legislative Yuan as an effective political arena" (Lin 2002: 142–143).

Having placed the parties within the two-dimensional issue space on the basis of their preferences, Lin explains the first round of constitutional reforms as a bargaining process. A key constraint on the parties' actions was the requirement that constitutional amendments must receive a three-fourths majority in the National Assembly. The KMT mainstream held the required supermajority through the 1991, 1992 and 1994 reforms, so its proposals passed easily.[1] The 1996 National Assembly elections reduced the KMT's share of seats to 55 percent, while the DPP increased its share to 29 percent. As a result, additional reform required cooperation between the KMT mainstream and the DPP.

Because both the mainstream KMT and the DPP sought to change the status quo (while the non-mainstream KMT and the New Party sought to preserve it), a coalition of the Lee Teng-hui faction and the DPP was possible. To put it in the lingo of Putnam's two-level games, the two actors' "winsets" overlapped: there were alternatives to the status quo that both actors preferred over the status quo (Putnam 1988). And because there were two issue dimensions, the DPP and KMT mainstream were able to trade votes on one dimension for votes on the other. The result was the 1997 constitutional reform. Most importantly, the Lee Teng-hui faction achieved its goal of blocking a requirement that the premier undergo legislative confirmation (a measure that would have transferred much of the president's executive power to the legislature), and the DPP was able to achieve its goal of radically diminishing the status of the provincial government, which was a long-standing ideological goal (Lin 2002: 149). Meanwhile, "No progress was made on the empowerment of the Legislative Yuan, about which the two parties held divergent opinions" (Lin 2002: 150). The result was a new equilibrium which placed the status quo between the preferences of the mainstream KMT and the DPP.

Lin makes two very important observations about this equilibrium: first, it "made further constitutional reforms unlikely" (Lin 2002: 155) and second, it was closer to the KMT mainstream's preferences than to the DPP's ideal (Lin 2002: 149). Additional reform was unlikely because since the KMT mainstream had achieved its goals, there was no room for further compromise. For its part, though, the DPP remained dissatisfied because the first round of reform did not move the status quo far enough toward its preferred position on the ideological dimension.[2] Because the DPP was weaker than the KMT (having barely half as many seats in the Assembly, and much less political support overall), only a partial victory was possible. But the DPP's dissatisfaction meant that the equilibrium, too, was only partial – and, as it turned out, temporary.

Lin's article does an excellent job of explaining the first round of constitutional reform. Its account of the second-round reforms of 1999 and 2000 is somewhat less convincing. In considering the second round, Lin correctly points out that abolishing the National Assembly was an ideological imperative for the DPP. Eliminating the National Assembly would fundamentally reshape the ROC constitution in a more democratic and Taiwan-centric direction. To gain control over the body (a first step toward killing it), Lin says, the DPP offered KMT Assembly members a "poison pill" – an extension of their term of office that was sure to provoke a strong negative response from the public, and from other elected officials. The KMT delegates took the pill, but they did not deliver the Assembly; to put it bluntly, the DPP strategy failed. Lin concludes that "the DPP seemed to have committed political suicide. But … so long as the DPP's leaders believed they had made progress on the ideological dimension, the price they paid became justifiable" (Lin 2002: 152). And in fact, just a year later, the DPP won the prize it had sought all along: the Assembly voted itself out of existence.

Lin's analysis is plausible, but I will offer a slightly different explanation, one that also helps to explain why – contrary to Lin's prediction – the constitutional reform debate continued into the third and fourth rounds. My explanation uses the concept of heresthetics. In an article on the US Constitutional Convention of 1787, William Riker opens his discussion of constitution-making with a summary of the rational choice paradigm: "The fundamental assumption of this paradigm is that people maximize expected utility, namely that, given their goals, they choose those alternatives likely to result in the largest net achievement of goals" (Riker 1984: 2). He goes on to observe that the paradigm is useful for identifying constraints on political actions and decisions, and for identifying the partial equilibria that emerge from the utility-maximizing actions of different political actors. However, Riker identifies an important limitation in the rational choice framework: "Unfortunately, not very much effort has been devoted to … the study of creative adjustment, or what I have … described as heresthetics, the art of political strategy" (Riker 1984: 2).

Riker develops a detailed account of the Constitutional Convention's debate over the rules for electing US presidents to show how a small group of delegates used political strategy to redefine popular choices in ways that undermined support for those options. By shifting the terms of the debate, these actors were able to push through the proposal they preferred – one that had enjoyed little support in the initial stages of the debate. In his conclusion, Riker points out that in the dynamic, multistage negotiations in the Constitutional Convention, "creativity … emanated from the will to win in the face of prospective loss" (Riker 1984: 15). Through creativity and persistence, one group of actors was able to redefine the terms of the debate to attract partners for a coalition sufficient to pass their preferred policy change.

Adding the idea of heresthetics to our analysis of Taiwan's constitutional reform helps explain how the reform process restarted after reaching a partial equilibrium in 1997. The 1997 settlement resolved the disagreement between the DPP and the mainstream KMT – the only possible winning coalition – on Lin's power dimension. There was no potential for further reform deriving from that dimension. But the DPP was still unhappy, because it wanted the reform process to continue. For the Democratic Progressives, radically changing – or (ideally) replacing – the ROC constitution was a core ideological goal. But once the KMT mainstream got what it wanted on the power dimension, it lost interest in constitutional reform. To make matters worse, the DPP's ideology was not very popular in the mid- to late-1990s:

appealing to the public on ideological grounds was not going to bring the DPP the victory it sought (Fell 2005: 114). Getting the constitutional reform process moving again would require an act of political creativity – and the "will to win in the face of prospective loss."

Once the power and ideological dimensions both had lost their utility for the DPP, the only way forward was to create a new basis for reform. For the DPP, the best option was to advance a new issue dimension that would replace the power dimension and reinvigorate the reform process. The result was a new emphasis on rationality and efficiency in government.

The DPP was not the first to complain that Taiwan's constitutional reform had not been carried out rationally or methodically. Critics in the academic world had long accused the political parties of making hasty and ill-considered reforms. As early as 1992, a group of intellectuals pointed out that the early reforms lacked a "comprehensive framework" and showed no understanding of "the significance of political, constitutional principles" and were driven solely by self-interested partisanship (Chao & Myers 1998: 264). But it was only when the reform process stalled after the 1997 reforms that the DPP put these complaints at the center of its own discourse. The National Assembly, in particular, became a target of vehement criticism from the DPP.

The DPP had long complained that the National Assembly should be abolished because it was authoritarian, redundant, inefficient and expensive. But getting rid of it seemed impossible, since amending the constitution to eliminate the National Assembly was a task only the Assembly itself could perform. In the summer of 1999, DPP Assembly members reached a tentative agreement with their KMT colleagues under which their term of office would be extended by two years in exchange for reducing the Assembly's size and converting it into an indirectly elected body.[3] Most DPP leaders opposed the compromise, which they believed would implicate the DPP in corrupt and self-serving "reforms" aimed at giving sitting members of the body two more years' salary and benefits. Others, however, were more strategic. They understood that the "self-fattening" maneuver would undermine support for the Assembly, even among political moderates, ultimately benefiting the DPP's cause. As one DPP politician put it, "A lot of media and journalists' reports only focus on the term extension, but this is wrong. Everyone agrees on the reform of the assembly, but how to practically weaken its power and slowly dissolve it is a strategic consideration."[4]

In the end, the Assembly members voted to extend their term of office, but they also significantly reduced the body's authority and independence. This did not spare them the outrage of society, however. The mass media, party leaders, legislators, scholars and ordinary Taiwanese all excoriated the Assembly for putting the selfish interests of its members ahead of its role as a disinterested arbiter of the national interest on questions of fundamental importance. A year later, the Council of Grand Justices struck down the 1999 term extension and demanded that the Assembly hold elections for new members immediately. These elections were especially advantageous for the People First Party (PFP), led by KMT maverick James Soong. Soong had broken away from the KMT to pursue the presidency in 2000. After his narrow loss to the DPP's Chen Shui-bian (Soong beat the KMT nominee, Lien Chan, by 14 percentage points), he formed the People's First Party (PFP). Rather than help Soong's party gain momentum by participating in early elections, the KMT joined with the DPP to push through the constitutional reforms that transferred nearly all the Assembly's powers to the legislature, leaving it as an *ad hoc* body with extremely limited functions.

The environment in which this odd round of reform unfolded was different from that which had prevailed during the first round. The emphasis had shifted from a debate over the relative power of different governmental bodies to a discussion of how to rationalize the political system to eliminate corruption and inefficiency. In addition, the DPP had formally set aside the strong ideological stance that had undercut its credibility in the early 1990s. In May 1999 the DPP Party Congress passed the "Resolution on Taiwan's Future." The resolution stated:

> Taiwan is a sovereign and independent country. In accordance with interna-
> tional laws, Taiwan's jurisdiction covers Taiwan, Penghu, Kinmen, Matsu, its
> affiliated islands and territorial waters. Taiwan, although named the Republic
> of China under its current constitution, is not subject to the jurisdiction of
> the People's Republic of China. Any change in the independent status quo
> must be decided by all residents of Taiwan by means of plebiscite.

In explaining the resolution to the media, DPP officials characterized it as a moderate gesture. The DPP, they said, was no longer promoting the active pursuit of inde-pendence through a declaration or name change. On the contrary, the party's new strategy was to defend a status quo in which Taiwan – under the name Republic of China – already was independent.

The Resolution on Taiwan's Future marked the DPP's retreat from an ideologically driven strategy on constitutional reform; the sneak attack on the National Assembly represented a new strategy of undermining public confidence in the rationality and effectiveness of government institutions the DPP wanted to change.[5] This strategy got a huge boost in 2000, when Chen Shui-bian was elected president, even as the KMT held onto its majority in the Legislative Yuan. The introduction of divided government exposed the weaknesses built into the constitutional arrangements intro-duced during the Lee Teng-hui Era – mainly the lack of effective checks and balances between the president and the Legislative Yuan. A Western scholar summarized these flaws in an article published just a year after Chen took office:

> Taiwan's current troubles are to a large extent rooted in its constitution, a
> document that does not have the same gravitas as in mature Western democra-
> cies with a centuries-old tradition of the rule of law. Politicians have amended
> Taiwan's constitution randomly six times during the 1990s, and it has become a
> tool for their short-term goals, rather than the foundation for a durable politi-
> cal system … so much bad blood exists between the "sore loser" KMT and

the dilettante DPP, that it will probably take years before the two – and other parties – have developed a mature, pluralistic political culture in which comity prevails between the ruling party and a loyal opposition. A new overhaul of the constitution is a must but a lot of dust needs to settle first.

(van Kemenade 2001: 62)

Van Kemenade's observations are accurate, but they echo the DPP's rationale. As one Chen Administration official put it, "Incremental constitutional revision … exacerbated constitutional vagueness and institutional inconsistency, which created even more political deadlock and instabilities" (Yeh 2004: 4). This was the DPP's new strategic discourse: a line of argument aimed at manufacturing a popular demand for additional constitutional reforms.

Throughout Chen's first term in office, the DPP blamed an obstructionist Legislative Yuan for the gridlock paralyzing the government, and it blamed the constitution for enabling that obstructionism. In the run-up to legislative elections held in December 2001 the DPP proposed constitutional amendments to halve the size of the legislature and reform the electoral system. Although the reforms won wide popular support, they stalled in the legislature. The DPP ratcheted up the pressure; in 2003, DPP legislator Luo Wen-chia excoriated the legislature's performance. Said Luo, "Such an inefficient parliament failed to meet the general public's expectation. … President Chen Shui-bian hopes that the Legislature can throw its weight behind the government to help contribute to the island's democratic development and economic transformation."[6]

For his part, President Chen went even further than others in his party, calling for a new constitution. Chen's first inaugural address, delivered in May 2000, made only two mentions of the constitution; the first acknowledged his constitutional role as president of the Republic of China, the second was a pledge not to change the constitution in certain ways. Over the course of his first term, however, Chen's criticism of the constitution grew increasingly heated; in 2003, he issued the first call for a new constitution. In his 2004 inaugural address, constitutional reform (or, as the official English text put it, constitutional re-engineering) was a central focus:

The promotion of constitutional re-engineering and the re-establishment of the constitutional order are tasks that correspond with the expectations of the people. … The constitutional re-engineering project aims to enhance good governance and increase administrative efficiency, to ensure a solid foundation for democratic rule of law, and to foster long-term stability and prosperity of the nation. … To avoid repeating the same mistakes by past administrations – six rounds of constitutional amendments in ten years time – the proposed constitutional reform project must not be … undertaken merely for the short-term … we will invite members of the ruling party and the opposition parties, as well as legal experts, academic scholars and representatives from all fields and spanning all social classes, to collaborate in forming a "Constitutional Reform

Committee." By the time I complete my presidency in 2008, I hope to hand to the people of Taiwan and to our country a new version of our Constitution – one that is timely, relevant and viable – this is my historic responsibility and my commitment to the people.

In September 2005 Chen made his point even more sharply: "not only the design of the current constitution is laden with contradictions and incompatibilities, its actual implementation is also morbidly inefficient."[7]

Between 1999 and 2005, the DPP successfully introduced a new issue dimension into the debate over constitutional reform. Rational, efficient governance became a key demand, one that resonated deeply among Taiwanese citizens, who saw all too clearly the effects of gridlock. Respect for the Legislative Yuan plummeted, and even many Taiwanese who opposed the idea of a new constitution were persuaded that more reform was needed to rein in an over-reaching, obstructionist parliament.[8] This was the environment in which the DPP put forward the third round of constitutional reforms. Its proposal called for halving the size of the Legislative Yuan, enacting a two-vote system in legislative elections,[9] eliminating the National Assembly,[10] and instituting popular referendum as the mechanism for ratifying constitutional amendments initiated by the legislature.

The KMT had suffered electoral setbacks in 2001 and 2004 and was facing another tough legislative race in December 2004; it was reluctant to challenge the DPP on such a popular issue. As the KMT whip Huang Teh-fu told the *Taipei Times* on August 6:

> This time, the constitutional amendment bill halving legislative seats, taking on the electoral "single-member district, two-vote system," letting the public decide on the new constitution via referendum and abolishing the National Assembly, has received a high level of support in recent polls, so we insist that legislative reform responds to mainstream opinion.

The PFP tried to turn the DPP's past criticism of incremental reform against the new proposal – said a PFP leader "… we cannot agree to rush through the constitutional amendment bill" – but public support for the measure made it unstoppable.[11] The proposal passed on August 23 with support from 201 of Taiwan's 225 legislators; in June, the National Assembly convened for the last time, ratifying the third round of constitutional amendments, and putting itself out of business.[12]

The DPP's heresthetic maneuver had succeeded: it had persuaded the public that previous rounds of incremental reform had left Taiwan's political system chaotic and ineffective – in need of still more reform. But once the third-round reforms were in place, DPP unity on the constitutional issue began to unravel. The heresthetic maneuver had worked *too* well. For President Chen and the party's ideological wing, implementing the third round of reforms did not obviate the need for a new constitution. The National Assembly ratified the reforms on June 7; three days later, the DPP set up a fifteen-person commission to develop a plan for yet another round of constitutional revision. As one DPP official put it, "The improvement of government effectiveness and efficiency requires major structural reform."[13] It was as if the hard-fought third round of reform had never happened.

The "fourth round" of constitutional reform

Ironically, the third round of reforms turned out to be much like the earlier rounds: hasty and ill-considered. Even before the revisions were passed, constitutional scholars and some politicians were questioning the decision to cut the legislature to only 113 members. The reform drastically reduced per capita representation for Taiwanese citizens. But for the DPP, there was an even greater irony: passing the third round of reform once again produced an equilibrium that benefited the KMT more than the DPP, and made additional reform more difficult.

First, the reforms shifted the status quo closer to the KMT's ideal position than the DPP's, because, while they addressed the issue of efficiency (which the KMT did not oppose), they did very little to advance the DPP's ideological agenda. In fact, most scholars believe the changes in the electoral system will benefit the KMT more than any other political party.

Second, the third round of reforms gave the opponents of further constitutional revision a ready-made reason for postponing additional changes: Why should Taiwan revise its constitution yet again before the previous round of reforms had even taken effect? The shift enabled KMT leaders like Ma Ying-jeou to use the DPP's own arguments against it. In May 2006, Ma said, "There is no urgency for amending the constitution. What's truly important is to observe and implement the constitution."[14] Ma promised that if he were elected president in 2008 he would abide by the spirit of the constitution, rather than seeking to amend it. In particular, Ma said he would honor the parliamentary nature of the existing constitution and allow the party in control of the Legislative Yuan to select the premier and form the government. In effect, Ma shifted the blame for gridlock from the constitution to the president.

Third, the 2005 reforms set an extremely high threshold for further constitutional reform. Constitutional amendments must first pass through the Legislative Yuan with a three-fourths majority, with at least three-fourths of the legislators voting. Then they must win the support of 50 percent of all *eligible* voters. The consequence of this change is that no constitutional revision can proceed unless there is very broad support across parties, among political elites and the public. The barriers to successful constitutional revision are so high, in fact, that the most enthusiastic supporters of further reform have suggested they might use extra-legal methods to push through a new constitution.

Fourth, the reforms split the DPP, making it impossible for the party to produce a draft constitution. Some DPP members continue to support ideologically based reform, while others are concerned mainly about government efficiency. Some are willing to work outside the legal process, while others insist that any constitutional reform must be carried out through the established process. The result is a wide range of constitutional drafts and proposals that take vastly different approaches to institutional design and the definition of the nation. In other words, the new debate has moved the DPP away from the popular and unifying efficiency agenda, and back into the much more controversial realm of ideology.

Chen Shui-bian's own statements have contributed to the weakening of the DPP's position. On some occasions, including his second inaugural address, Chen has sought to allay fears that constitutional reform could provoke conflict with the PRC by promising to exclude the most controversial issues from discussion. On other occasions, however, he has said that no issue can be excluded from the debate.[15] In March of 2007 he said Taiwan "wants" independence and a change in the national name. He has from time to time endorsed the idea of a "Second Republic" – using a new constitution to redefine Taiwan's territory and political system, while "freezing" the original ROC constitution. Chen has asserted that such a maneuver would maintain enough of a tie to the ROC to satisfy Beijing – and Washington. In short, Chen himself never settled on a clear idea of how constitutional reform should proceed, and as the time for enacting constitutional changes grew short, he seemed to lose interest altogether.

While Chen focused on the ideological goal of enacting a new constitution, other DPP leaders carried on the mission to promote government efficiency. According to a leading DPP politician, Su Tseng-chang, the constitution needs to be overhauled to improve its functioning, a goal that can only be accomplished with support from across the political spectrum.[16] The DPP laid out an ambitious plan for a bottom-up process in which the whole society would debate constitutional reform proposals. A consensus proposal would emerge and be ratified in a popular referendum accompanying the March 2008 presidential election.

In mid-2007, numerous constitutional reform proposals and draft constitutions were vying for DPP legislators' support. President Chen seemed partial to the "Second Republic" draft sponsored by the pro-independence Taiwan Think Tank. Seventy-five legislators (including some from the Taiwan Solidarity Union) endorsed a proposal from the 21st Century Constitutional Reform Alliance that took an even stronger pro-independence stance. Other proposals ranged from a "Taiwan Constitution" supported by pro-independence legal scholar Lee Hung-hsi to proposals for constitutional amendments that would revamp Taiwan's institutional arrangements while leaving the part of the constitution that defines the "Republic of China" untouched. The wide variation in proposals, most of which came from the DPP and its allies, illustrates the lack of unity within the pro-reform camp.

The wave of enthusiasm for constitutional reform receded suddenly in mid-2007. After months of escalating rhetoric and intense politicking, a new debate drove constitutional reform off the front pages: Should Taiwan hold a referendum instructing the government to apply for membership in the United Nations under the name "Taiwan"? Within the space of a few weeks, the momentum for constitutional reform all but disappeared, and the political world appeared completely transfixed by the new controversy – and the national elections looming in early 2008.[17]

The most cynical explanation for the DPP's sudden abandonment of its constitutional reform project asserts that the party never really cared about it; it was never more than a device to help a DPP candidate win the March 2008 presidential election. Once it became clear that there would not be time to put a constitutional reform referendum before the voters on that date, the issue lost its political utility, so the DPP dropped it. A less cynical explanation relies on similar logic: the DPP cared about constitutional reform, but the goal simply was too ambitious. Faced with evidence that constitutional reform could not be accomplished in the time frame the party had hoped for, the ideologues found a more feasible vehicle for advancing their agenda: the UN referendum. DPP moderates found themselves facing an even more daunting problem: avoiding annihilation in the 2008 legislative and presidential elections. Neither side saw much advantage in continuing to pursue constitutional reform, at least in the near term. We should bear in mind, however, that the new issue dimension that the DPP put into play – government efficiency – still has not been addressed. Constitutional reform remains an unresolved issue, one that could reappear.

Conclusion

In the 1990s, the DPP declared itself in favor of a new constitution that would establish Taiwan as an independent state, but it made little progress toward its goal. It was only when the Democratic Progressives introduced a new argument for constitutional reform – improving government efficiency – that the idea attracted widespread approval. But after pushing through efficiency-oriented reforms in 2000 and 2005, the party revived its ideological agenda. After three rounds of constitu-tional amendments and years of browbeating from Beijing and Washington (both of which oppose ideologically motivated reform proposals), popular support for radical change is limited. Even many DPP supporters and politicians are more interested in the "new" reform agenda – government efficiency – than the "old" one. Without a sense of common purpose, and facing high hurdles for successful reform, the DPP set aside its plans for a fourth round of constitutional reform.

The election of a KMT president and legislative majority in early 2008 makes the kind of reform the DPP had in mind even more unlikely. However, the fact that the KMT controls almost enough legislative seats to pass a reform proposal means overcoming the technical barriers to constitutional reform is easier than before. Were the KMT to make solving the institutional problems identified in the earlier rounds of reform a legislative priority, constitutional reform debate would resurface.

Notes

1 The DPP's preference was for more far-reaching reforms in these years, but it was not opposed to the substance of the reforms that were passed. DPP politicians agreed with the KMT that the reforms would improve the democratic functioning of Taiwan's political system.
2 Demoting the provincial government *did* represent progress on the ideological dimension, from the DPP's point of view. The DPP viewed the provincial government as a redundant administrative layer that existed only to reinforce the idea that Taiwan was but one prov-ince of a much larger ROC. Thus, the provincial government was a symbolic reminder

that the ultimate goal of the ROC state was unification, and that Taiwan's interests should be subjugated to that goal. Getting rid of the provincial government was a significant breakthrough for the DPP.

3 While indirect election might seem to deviate from Taiwan's democratizing trajectory, the DPP believed that taking away the body's electoral mandate would further erode its legitimacy.

4 "DPP lawmakers tout extension as part of a larger plan," *China News*, September 2, 1999.

5 The DPP had been undermining public confidence in the National Assembly for years by deliberately disrupting its meetings with protests both inside and outside the chamber.

6 Lin Fang-yan, "DPP lawmakers discuss school, house reform," *Taiwan Journal*, June 20, 2003.

7 Chen Shui-bian, Address at the Opening Ceremony of the International Conference on Constitutional Reengineering in New Democracies, October 28, 2005. Available online at http://www.cpbae.nccu.edu.tw/tra/CRND/attach/president_address_941028_eng.pdf.

8 According to a *Taipei Times* editorial, public support for changes to the Legislative Yuan reached 70 to 80 percent by mid-2004. August 17, 2004.

9 The first vote would go to elect seventy-five district representatives according to single-member simple plurality rules; the second would be a party vote, used to determine the allocation of thirty-four proportional representation seats.

10 The Assembly's last remaining power, impeachment, was to be transferred to the Court of Grand Justices.

11 Debby Wu, "Pan-blues differ on approaches to constitution bill," *Taipei Times*, August 7, 2004.

12 The National Assembly convened in 2005 was elected on a party list vote. The two parties that most strongly supported the reform won more than 80 percent of the vote (DPP 43 percent; KMT 39 percent). Clearly, the public was eager to see the reforms ratified.

13 Dennis Engbarth, "DPP establishes group to draft policies on second-phase constitutional reforms," *Taipei Times*, June 10, 2005.

14 "Constitutional Change No Cure-All: Ma," *China Post*, May 1, 2006.

15 "Post Interview with Taiwan's Leader," *Washington Post*, March 13, 2006.

16 "Constitutional Reform Needed, Despite China, Su Proclaims," *CNA*, January 7, 2007.

17 This trend is evident in President Chen's own statements. For example, his New Year Address on January 1, 2007 contained several mentions of constitutional reform, while his 2008 address did not include even one. News coverage also illustrates the trend. In the first half of 2007, the Green-leaning *Taipei Times* published 194 stories containing the word "constitution." In the second half of the year, it published only 138.

Works cited

Chao, Linda and Ramon H. Myers. 1998. *The First Chinese Democracy: Political Life in the Republic of China on Taiwan* (Baltimore: Johns Hopkins University Press).

Copper, John. 1998. *Taiwan's Mid-1990s Elections* (Westport, CT: Praeger).

DeLisle, Jacques. 2004. "Reforming/Replacing the ROC Constitution: Implications for Taiwan's State (-Like) Status and U. S. Policy." *Asia Program Special Report No. 125* (Woodrow Wilson International Center for Scholars), November.

Fell, Dafydd. 2005. "Measuring and Explaining Party Change in Taiwan: 1991–2004," *Journal of East Asian Studies* 5 (Jan/April), pp. 105–33.

Laliberté, André. 2004/2005. "Constitutional Reform in Taiwan," *Pacific Affairs* 77: 4 (Winter), pp. 701–6.

Lin Jih-wen. 2002. "Transition through Transaction: Taiwan's Constitutional Reforms in the Lee Teng-hui Era," *American Asian Review* 20: 2 (Summer), pp. 123–55.

Putnam, Robert. 1988. "Diplomacy and Domestic Politics: The Logic of Two-Level Games," *International Organization* 42: 3 (Summer), pp. 427–61.

Rigger, Shelley. 2001. *From Opposition to Power: Taiwan's Democratic Progressive Party* (Boulder: Lynne Riener).

Riker, William H. 1984. "The Heresthetics of Constitution-Making: The Presidency in 1878, with Comments on Determinism and Rational Choice," *The American Political Science Review* 78: 1 (March), pp. 1–16.

Riker, William H. 1964. *Federalism: Origin, Operation, Significance* (Boston: Little, Brown).

Van Kemenade, Willem. 2001. "Taiwan: Domestic Gridlock, Cross-Strait Deadlock," *The Washington Quarterly* 24: 4, pp. 55–70.

Wachman, Alan. 2004. "Constitutional Diplomacy: Taipei's Pen, Beijing's Sword," *Asia Program Special Report No. 125* (Woodrow Wilson International Center for Scholars), November.

Yeh Jiunn-Rong. 2002. "Constitutional Reform and Democratization in Taiwan, 1945–2000," in Peter C.Y. Chow, Ed., *Taiwan's Modernization in Global Perspective* (Westport, CT: Praeger), pp. 47–75.

Yeh Jiunn-Rong. 2004. "Hope or Nope: The Second Call for a New Constitution in Taiwan," *Asia Program Special Report No. 125* (Woodrow Wilson International Center for Scholars), November.

3

NEGOTIATING NATIONAL IDENTITY IN TAIWAN

Between nativization and de-sinicization

Christopher R. Hughes

After the Chen Shui-bian administration came to power in May 2000, the charge that the state was consolidating Taiwan's separation from China by systematically purging the island of Chinese influences through a process of 'de-sinicization' (*qu zhongguo hua*) was increasingly made on both sides of the Taiwan Strait. It will be argued below that such accusations amount to an oversimplification of the unavoidable challenge of replacing the KMT's version of Chinese nationalism with a more participatory vision of politics. At the centre of this is a discussion of the nature of 'nativization' (*bentu hua*) that has been integral to Taiwan's democratization that goes back much further than the Chen administration.

It is quite appropriate to take the critical view of identity politics in Taiwan. History is replete with examples of nativist movements being appropriated to legitimize militarist, ultra-nationalist and fascist regimes. One need look no further than the Chinese and Japanese forms of nationalism that were imposed on Taiwan in the past to find such cases. Focusing on the concept of 'civic culture' is also certainly useful for explaining why excluding segments of the population from political life due to ethnic loyalties or characteristics is essentially undemocratic. Almond and Verba thus provide one of the most convincing explanations for how even a state that practises universal suffrage and has institutions such as political parties and an effective legislature can be totalitarian if its values are not drawn from a participatory civic culture.[1]

Yet if the civic culture model is applied to Taiwan, it can just as easily be argued that democratic erosion has not occurred, precisely because the need to increase political participation has been a dominant theme in the discussion of the relationship between identity and the state that has taken place during the process of democratization. This is because democratization has entailed unravelling the way in which the politics of Chinese nationalism reduces citizens to the passive status of what Almond and Verba would call 'participant subjects'. In Taiwan this took the particular form of excluding the majority of citizens from political life by suspending democracy until the Chinese nation was united and nationwide elections could be held. In terms drawn from nationalist theory, the process of recognizing that sovereignty is practised by the residents of Taiwan could thus be described as an attempt to replace Chinese 'ethnic' nationalism with a form of 'civic' nationalism. Whereas the former emphasizes that the nation is a community of birth with a native culture, the latter is a territorial and legalistic concept that stresses the existence of an historic territory, legal-political community, legal-political equality of members, and common civic culture and ideology.[2]

This chapter develops such an argument by looking first at the way in which accusations of state-led de-sinicization have been made against the cultural and educational policies of the Chen administration. The significance of such accusations is then explored by tracing their origins back to charges made against the Lee Teng-hui administration in the late 1990s, which reflected a consensus between the two main parties on the need to strengthen a nativized Taiwanese identity based on political loyalty as an alternative to the older ethnic-Chinese nationalism of the KMT. This is followed by an account of how the consensus was shaped by accommodation not only of the demands of domestic democratization but also the conflicting needs of maintaining Taiwan's sovereignty and place in the international economic system while benefiting from its special historical and ethnic relationship with China. Finally, it explains how accusations of de-sinicization increased in intensity under the Chen administration, as the DPP had to move the consensus further towards strengthening loyalty to Taiwan in response to the danger of being outflanked on this issue by the emergence of new domestic political forces on the one hand, and Beijing's attempts to isolate the government and win over the loyalty of sections of the population to China on the other. It concludes that, despite accusations that attempts to strengthen the loyalty of the population to Taiwan amount to a form of de-sinicization, the cross-party consensus on an inclusive form of civic nationalism in Taiwan remains as the KMT under Ma Ying-jeou has had to appropriate and articulate the discourse on nativization in order to become the credible force in Taiwanese politics that was able to capture the presidency for the KMT again.

The argument over de-sinicization

The accusation that a process of de-sinicization is occurring in Taiwan has arisen in the context of the general reorientation of identity that was supported and shaped by state policies under the Chen Shui-bian administration. This involves initiatives to rectify Taiwan's name, changes to institutions designed to promote unification with Mainland China and attempts to change the ROC Constitution.

Sometimes this has been highly visible, as with the removal of the placards in front of the Presidential Palace that advocated the unification of China under the Three Principles of the People and the departure of slogans urging a renaissance of Chinese culture and opposition to Taiwanese independence from military bases. The Government Information Office (GIO) has taken an active part in changing public symbols, such as the addition of 'Taiwan' and a map of the island to the front cover of the English version of the 2001 *ROC Yearbook* and the relocation of the map of China to the back. These modest steps have now developed into a more positive presentation of Taiwan itself. The 2006–7 edition of the yearbook features the five winning symbols of an online poll called 'Show Taiwan to the World', which asked netizens to select which images they think best symbolize their 'country'. These are the Taipei 101 skyscraper (at that time the world's tallest building), Jade Mountain (the highest peak in Asia east of the Himalayas), the folk art of glove puppetry, Taiwanese cuisine and the endangered Formosan landlocked salmon.[3]

The 'movement to rectify Taiwan's name' (*Taiwan zheng ming yundong*) has involved dropping references to 'China' and the ROC when referring to the state and its various organizations. Examples include the renaming of Chiang Kai-shek airport as Taiwan International Airport in 2006 and renewed efforts as of early 2007 to make state-owned enterprises such as China Petroleum Co., China Post Ltd and China Ship Building change their names. Name rectification is particularly sensitive, however, when it directly impacts on foreign relations, such as when Chen Shui-bian announced to a meeting of the Formosan Association for Public Affairs (FAPA) early in 2002 that a new ROC passport was to be produced with the name 'Taiwan' added and listed as the place of issue.[4] The Ministry of Foreign Affairs has extended this attempt to reorientate identity to foreign policy by pressing for 'Taiwan' to be used in the names of its overseas missions. The launching of a campaign for membership of the United Nations under the name 'Taiwan' in 2007 and attempts to make this the topic for a referendum in tandem with the March 2008 presidential election brought the issue of name rectification to a new head.

Among the transformation of institutions, the abolition of the National Unification Council (NUC) has drawn most attention due to its direct impact on cross-Strait relations. Concerns have also grown over the way in which the reorientation of identity is taking place in more subtle ways, especially through changes of personnel in key cultural institutions such as the National History Institute (*guo shi guan*) and the National Palace Museum. Professor Zhang Yanxian, a native of Chiayi County with a PhD from Tokyo University, was appointed to head the former. He is an expert on the relationship between the Han and aboriginal groups in Taiwan, social movements during the Japanese occupation and after, the February 28 Incident and political cases from the 1950s.[5] Under his leadership, the Institute has produced books coverings issues such as the lifting of martial law and the biographies of prominent Dang Wai and DPP figures.

The appointment of Professor Tu Cheng-sheng (Du Zhengsheng), an LSE (London School of Economics) alumnus, as head of the National Palace Museum in May 2000 has been even more controversial. Tu had in fact been singled out as one of the chief architects of 'de-sinification' well before the Chen administration came to power because he had been influential in steering a reorientation of the school curriculum and teaching materials to learning more about Taiwan and less about China in the late 1990s.[6] Having stewardship over the museum that was once used by the KMT as a kind of cultural umbilical chord linking Taiwan to China's grand tradition, Tu incurred the wrath of many critics when he proceeded to label the Chinese artefacts as 'Chinese' and established a gallery devoted to Taiwanese culture.

The reorientation of education that Tu had begun under Lee Teng-hui also continued under the Chen administration. Already in March 2001 the Ministry of Education had produced a policy on 'Nativization of Education' (*bentu hua jiaoyu*), according to which junior and middle school pupils have to select to learn a 'native language' (*xiangtu yuyan*) from Hokkien, Hakka and an aboriginal language. The controversial *Know Taiwan* (*renshi Taiwan*) textbooks became teaching material for history, geography and social studies from the academic year beginning in August. A Native Education Committee (*bentu jiaoyu weiyuanhui*) began to revise the *Know Taiwan* curriculum in 2002 and the following year published a draft outline for a new high school history curriculum in which Chinese history since the mid-Ming Dynasty became part of 'World History'. An increasing emphasis on native culture can also be seen in the way that the Ministry of Education has actively promoted and funded the establishment of departments of Taiwan Literature in national universities since 2000. When Tu Cheng-sheng was appointed minister of education at the start of Chen's second term in May 2004, accusations of de-sinification reached a new height of intensity.

This reorientation of education has not been confined to schools and universities, moreover. The military has also moved away from its old practice of inculcating its staff and recruits with anti-independence indoctrination. Civil service examinations have been changed too, with the 'Chinese History' paper now combined with 'Theories of Historical Methodology', while 'History of the Chinese System' has been replaced by 'Modern Taiwanese History'. There has even been the addition of a paper on 'Japanese Modern History'. The Examination Yuan decided that examinations for promotion on 'National Literature' (*guo wen*) and the ROC Constitution should be abolished. National examinations on 'National General Knowledge' (*guojia chang shi*) were also scrapped.

Even foreigners have not been spared from identity politics, as can be seen in the argument over what system of Romanization should be used for Chinese characters. In July 1999 a decision had been made to adopt the Pinyin system used in Mainland China and recognized by the United Nations. In September 2000 this was overturned by the Ministry of Education's Committee for Promoting the National Language (*jiaoyu bu guoyu tuixing weiyuanhui*), which revived the idea of adopting a new form of Romanization called 'Tongyong Pinyin' that would more accurately reflect the way that Chinese is pronounced in Taiwan.[7] Unfortunately, as some foreign critics of this policy were the first to point out, very few people know how to use this special Taiwanese system.

These steps affecting Taiwan's identity are bound to be at the centre of political controversy because they are supported by those who wish to see Taiwan consolidate its political independence from China on the one side, while they are treated with a mixture of anger and disdain by those who believe that the island is a part of China on the other. They have been made more controversial, however, because they were taken at the same time that Chen Shui-bian was taking measures affecting cross-Strait relations. Most notable among these was the launching of Chen's doctrine of the formula of 'one country on each side' (*yi bian yi guo*) of the Strait in August 2002 and the passing of a referendum law in time to hold the island's first ever referendum in conjunction with the 2004 presidential election.

Such initiatives have been condemned by observers in Taiwan, Mainland China and even the United States as symptomatic of a movement towards achieving Taiwanese independence and upsetting the 'status quo' across the Taiwan Strait. As a result, there has been a tendency to conflate charges of de-sinicization and nativization in a general barrage of criticism against Chen Shui-bian's 'secessionist policies'.[8] This, however, obscures the way in which the argument over de-sinicization is one manifestation of the complex attempt to negotiate Taiwan's identity within the constraints of domestic politics and international relations that has been part of Taiwan's democratization for many decades. To unravel this it is necessary to look at how de-sinicization is related to the longer-term discourse on nativization.

The consensus on nativization

The attempt to develop a participatory civic culture based on nativization in Taiwan has a long history, going back at least as far as the rejection of KMT authoritarianism by dissidents who formed the opposition 'Dang Wai' movement under martial law.[9] Fearing that the KMT's Chinese nationalism would destabilize a fragmented society like Taiwan's, leading figures in the Dang Wai movement rejected that version of nationalism and replaced it with a form of Taiwanese nationalism. If the state was to be based on a homogeneous ethnic identity, these Dang Wai leaders would ask, what would become of the many individuals who did not fit in, such as the unfortunate Manchurian who was labelled a 'Han traitor' in Mainland China because he had worked for the Japanese, fled to Japan where he was called by a derogatory epithet for 'Chinese', moved to Shanghai where he was called a 'Manchurian', then eventually settled in Taiwan where he was called a 'Mainlander'?[10]

The way in which this concern to develop an inclusive political culture led to the articulation of a kind of civic nationalism can be seen quite clearly in the work of the leading theorist of the independence movement in exile, Professor Peng Ming-min. Peng was most influenced by Ernest Renan's view that 'neither race, language, nor culture form a nation but rather a deeply felt sense of community and shared destiny' (*mingyun gongtongti*). His determination to break the link between ethnicity and the state is clear to see when he argues that the Chinese should learn:

> to distinguish clearly between ethnic origin, culture and language on the one hand, and politics and law on the other, and to abandon the idea that those who are ethnically, culturally, and linguistically Chinese must be politically and legally Chinese as well.[11]

Advocating this view of state and society as based on a social contract was a much more effective way of undermining the ethnic nationalism of the KMT than advocating an exclusive ethnic Taiwanese nationalism. It enabled Peng to refer positively to examples from history, such as the Anglo-Saxon nations, where people of a similar background and heritage had established separate political entities and, conversely, cases where people of different origin and background constituted a single state.[12]

This vision of national identity was eventually appropriated by the KMT as it sought to find a more democratic foundation for its own legitimacy. The primary reason was the erosion of the party's Chinese nationalist ideology by the crises that rocked Taiwan in the 1970s. These include the failure of the KMT to assert Chinese sovereignty when the Diaoyu/Senakaku Islands in the East China Sea were transferred to Japan by the United States, the departure of the ROC from the United Nations, the death of Chiang Kai-shek and the growing international isolation that culminated with the breaking of diplomatic relations with Washington on 1 January 1979. The acceleration and deepening of nativization that took place in the decades that followed, however, was shaped primarily by the domestic dynamics of political liberalization.

When Lee Teng-hui became the first Taiwan-born president and chairman of the KMT in 1988 he presided over a party and a state that were already undergoing a process of nativization in terms of the ethnic composition of its personnel, thanks to reforms introduced by his predecessor, Chiang Ching-kuo. By the mid-1980s more than 70 per cent of the KMT's members were 'native' Taiwanese, in the sense of having been born in Taiwan before the armed forces of the ROC took the Japanese surrender in 1945 or being the descendants of such people.[13] As this nativization met increasing resistance under Lee from a ruling elite that was dominated by those who had come from Mainland China after 1945, he consolidated his power base by looking for support outside the party. In doing this he could appropriate the idea that Taiwan was a 'community of shared destiny' that had already become part of common political discourse thanks to the activities of the Dang Wai and the recently established DPP. He could also develop a more inclusive vision of politics as a way to address concerns among academics that a Taiwanese ultra-nationalism might emerge if people were not clear about the difference between ethnic and civic nationalism.

Above all, Lee was also aware that identification with Taiwan was unavoidable if the KMT was to survive as a popular party in a democratic system. As he put it himself in 1994:

> Anybody facing the enthusiastic competition of party politics in Taiwan, if they cannot sincerely identify with Taiwan as the paramount objective, definitely cannot survive. Moreover, there are priorities [literally, things have roots and ends, prior and latter], the reasoning is plain to see. If you go beyond identifying with Taiwan, and just strive to identify with something at an even higher level, the result must definitely be the loss of both.[14]

By moving in the direction of nativization, Lee was responding not only to politics at the elite level but also the burgeoning demands of a stronger civil society. A good example of this is the way that the increasingly controversial education reforms that emerged during his administration grew out of a movement that originated in calls by students for campus democracy and autonomy that appeared at National Taiwan University as early as 1982. Other groups began to push for a more pluralistic school education, to be achieved through autonomous teacher and parent associations and the private production of textbooks. As political liberalization proceeded, links were created between educational pressure groups and broader elements of civil society, such as welfare groups and human rights organizations, in the context of a deteriorating social situation characterized by a rise in youth crime, suicides and drug abuse.[15]

Additional space and support for this kind of movement was provided as the DPP took control of local governments. In September 1989, for example, Ilan County decided to stop schools from holding daily flag-raising ceremonies and hanging portraits other than those of the National Father in classrooms. On 8 January the following year, a number of DPP local authorities announced their intention to practise bilingual teaching.[16] Pressure groups began to gain more access to the central-government policy-making process too after elections were held for the National Assembly in 1991 and the Legislative Yuan in 1992. The alliance of welfare and human rights organizations reached a peak in 1994 with a wave of protests involving some 210 pressure groups. Demands made by this movement for pluralism, teaching about Taiwan itself, taking ideology out of education and even instilling a sense of Taiwan consciousness in the young[17] received parliamentary support from both the DPP and elements of an increasingly 'nativized' KMT.

As the reform movement expanded, it became increasingly difficult to divorce problems of academic autonomy and the mental and physical health of children from the ideological use of education, especially in courses such as the Three Principles of the People and the Thought of Sun Yatsen, and in the standardization of textbooks. Other groups were more outspoken on the issue of nationalism, accusing the KMT of using education to 'brainwash' the residents of Taiwan in the ideology of Chinese unification, dissipating their identification with Taiwan and making them not dare to recognize that Taiwan is an independent sovereign state. Some teachers' groups even began educational work to promote an independent Taiwan and a strong sense of Taiwanese history and culture.[18]

Balancing domestic and external constraints

In responding to such pressures for nativization, however, Lee Teng-hui always had to keep one eye on the management of cross-Strait relations. Beijing's unchanging interpretation of China was reiterated in its 1993 white paper on *The Taiwan Question and Reunification of China*,[19] which merely stated that 'There is only one China in the world, Taiwan is an inalienable part of China and the seat of China's central government is in Beijing'. Taiwan's Mainland Affairs Council tried to find a way to satisfy the growing domestic demands for change while not provoking Beijing by asserting that while Taiwan and the Mainland could both be described as 'Chinese' territory, 'It is an undeniable fact that the two have been divided and ruled separately since 1949'.[20] Its description of China as an entity with 'multifaceted geographical, political, historical, and cultural meanings',[21] was an obvious attempt to break the relationship between ethnic identity and the state.

While this was not appreciated by Beijing, it is easy to overlook the way in which Lee Teng-hui tried to use Taiwan's 'special' relationship with a depoliticized vision of Chinese identity in a positive way. When, in December 1991, he stated that, 'We cannot break our relations with the rest of the Chinese people, nor can we cut our links with Chinese culture',[22] he was reminding the people of Taiwan that it would not be in their interests to develop an exclusive sense of their own identity that might alienate the island from the benefits that could be accrued from tapping into the Chinese political and cultural world. In this respect, one could be both Taiwanese and Chinese, as Lee explained:

> Identify with Taiwan, cherish Taiwan, struggle hard for Taiwan, that is Taiwanese; do not give up the hard work and hope of unifying the country and reviving the nation [minzu], that is Chinese ... This view of identity, is the understanding that 'with survival is hope, only with survival is there development'. Only by advocating this view of identity can the nationalism of the Three Principles of the People serve the new significance of the age.[23]

Lee was also aware of the immense economic and political capital that could be tapped into by maintaining good relations with the Chinese overseas. While his constitutional reforms disenfranchised these communities in Taiwan, they still maintained the appearance of representation in the ROC's parliamentary chambers through the allocation of a small number of seats filled according to the proportion of votes won by parties in elections held in Taiwan. As with relations with the people of the Chinese Mainland, political disenfranchisement was not meant to preclude the cultivation of special economic, social and cultural links.

Finally, Lee also had to develop a mode of nativization that was compatible with a vision of the post-Cold War international order that posed a challenge to Beijing's hard version of state sovereignty. It is within this context that we find the idea of Taiwan's identity being articulated in ways that make it compatible with the vision of a 'global village' established on respecting democracy and human rights, replacing the use of military force with negotiation, promoting a mixed market economy and strengthening collective security.[24] Of course, this international vision offers more room for Taiwan to carve out a new identity and status for itself because recognition is based not on the congruence of nation and state, but on the moral criteria of democratic and economic achievements. Rather than resist what Sun Yat-sen and Mao Zedong would have considered to be the imperialist forces of the global economy, Taiwan had everything to gain by diving in head first, joining NAFTA, working with multinationals and entering the GATT/WTO, becoming a hub for international air transportation and establishing itself as a major Asian financial centre.[25]

It is within these domestic and external constraints that developing an inclusive, civic form of nationalist identity was useful for Lee. It would have been far too controversial for him to use the exiled Peng Ming-min's vocabulary of the 'community of shared destiny'. As early as August 1991, however, he could tell a group of university professors that there was a need for 'grafting the concept of *Gemeinschaft* (*shengming gongtong tî*) onto the traditional family ethic and morality'.[26] While he traced this concept to Goethe and Kant, it shares the fundamental proposition with Peng that political community arises out of the subjective identification of the individual through the practice of politics. Lee thus explains the relationship between this concept and his emerging doctrine of locating 'sovereignty in the people' (*zhuquan zai min*) as follows:

> The establishment of the ideal of sovereignty in the people is to stir up every citizen to use his consciousness of being master of his own country [*guojia*], contributing his wisdom and strength, realizing the respect that should be given to a complete individual. And the cohesion of a *Gemeinschaft*, is to mutually integrate the free will of the individual with the whole wealth and good of society, to establish a civilized society with individual freedom, social harmony and prosperity.[27]

That Lee's vision of *Gemeinschaft* is again quite distinct from any notion of purging Taiwan of Chinese influences can be seen in the way that he emphasizes the need for the state to encourage a pluralistic identity as follows:

> Among the 21 million people in Taiwan, there are aboriginals, and there are the compatriots who have come from the mainland over several hundred years. Between us, there should be no argument about ethnic division. We are all Chinese. Only identify with Taiwan, give your heart to preserving and developing Taiwan, no matter what ethnic group, no matter whether you came to Taiwan early or late, then all are Taiwanese.[28]

The implications of this vision of identity for policy-making in areas related to culture can be seen when the raft of proposals for changes to the school curriculum and teaching materials drawn up under the guidance of Tu Cheng-sheng appeared in 1997. While the overall effect of this package was to include learning about Taiwan's own geography, history and culture rather than focusing mainly on China, Tu stressed how the reforms were not aimed at cleansing Taiwan of Chinese influences but at teaching identity in multiple layers that move out from the local community of Taiwan, through the national community (*guojia*) of China and into the pluralistic 'world village'. He explained that this had become possible due to political changes since the 'Chinese people in Taiwan' had acknowledged the existence of the Mainland regime and were no longer concerned with the kind of politics that is based on Chinese nationalist claims to legitimacy. He explicitly denied that this amounted to following fashionable trends of developing a 'Taiwan consciousness', pointing out that China still had a special place in the new curriculum as the second circle of learning, both because it was the key to understanding Taiwan's culture and history and because it posed the biggest threat to Taiwan's security. Moreover, he argued, it would be a shame to waste the academic achievements in Chinese studies that Taiwan had built up over the decades.[29]

Under Lee Teng-hui, therefore, it would be a gross oversimplification to describe the movement for nativization as an attempt to purge Taiwan of Chinese influences. The preservation of ethnic and cultural links with China was clearly seen as good for both domestic stability and maximizing Taiwan's economic and political advantages. Rather than the depoliticization of 'China' being an attempt to exclude a section of the population from politics and society, it was supposed to ameliorate the concerns of disaffected 'Mainlanders' by moving away from the politics of ethnicity. It was also supposed to minimize friction with the PRC and present a positive image to the liberal-democratic states upon which Taiwan depends for its security.

Within the overall scheme articulated by Lee Teng-hui, the residents of Taiwan were encouraged to identify themselves politically with Taiwan's destiny, but were left free to build beneficial relationships with other communities if they so wished. This merely reflected a popular trend of identifying with Taiwan that had grown dramatically since democratization began in earnest in the early 1990s (Figure 3.1). As unification with China was maintained as the long-term aim of the KMT under the Guidelines for National Unification and with the existence of the NUC, the breaking of the link between statehood and ethnicity left the choice of developing future political relations between Taiwan and China open to the democratic process. Overall, the emphasis was on a full democratic participation of all citizens of the island, based on a social contract between individual, society and the state.

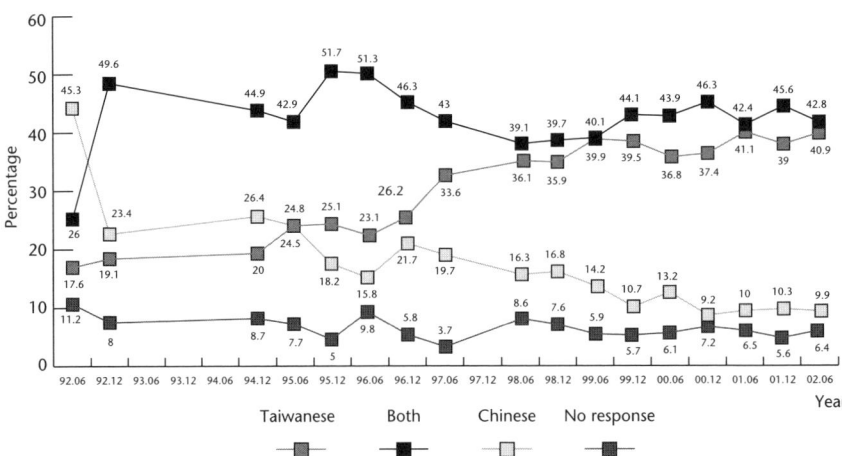

FIGURE 3.1 Taiwanese/Chinese identification trend distribution in Taiwan (June 1992–June 2002).

Source: Election Study Centre National Chengchi University. http://esc.nccu.edu.tw/modules/tinyd/content/TaiwanChineseID.htm

Building a cross-party consensus on identity

Contributing to this emerging consensus on identity politics was not a big problem for the DPP in opposition, given that its principles were drawn largely from the party's own intellectual heritage. Moderation was also increasingly attractive for a party leadership that was aware that the DPP had tended to succeed in elections when it appealed to the growing swell of disenchantment over the KMT's bad governance, rather than stressing identity politics. On the relationship with China, there was even a growing sense of impatience in society over Lee Teng-hui's cautious 'no haste, be patient' policy. This was fuelled by Beijing's appeal to interest groups in Taiwan, the most significant being the business community, many of whom were openly calling for more flexibility in opening up the Three Links.

Beijing's diplomatic efforts in Central America and Africa were also chipping away at the small number of states that formally recognized the ROC. Most important of all was the way in which attempts to mend the relationship between Beijing and Washington after the 1995–6 Taiwan Strait crisis were beginning to affect domestic politics in Taiwan. When a stream of recently retired high-level American officials had visited top leaders in Beijing and Taipei, they also visited DPP leaders, including Chen Shui-bian, who was then mayor of Taipei. The tone of these meetings that was conveyed by the media in Taiwan was one of increasingly firm pressure for a restarting of cross-Strait dialogue, an optimistic assessment of Beijing's sincerity, and the importance of maintaining the one-China principle.[30]

The DPP responded to these pressures under the chairmanships of the two veteran Dang Wai members, Shih Ming-teh (Shi Mingde) and Hsu Hsin-liang (Xu Xinliang). The first step in this process was to join with the KMT in a National Development Conference in December 1996, from which emerged the principle that Taiwan does not need to declare independence because it is already an independent state. This is the principle that was formalized as DPP policy before Chen Shui-bian came to power with the passing of the Resolution Regarding Taiwan's Future in May 1999, which has remained at the core of DPP policy-making since.[31]

The next step in preparing the DPP for power was Hsu Hsin-liang's initiative to build credibility with the public by convening a DPP conference in full view of the media in February 1998. This brought together 36 high-ranking members of the party,[32] and its findings were submitted to the Central Standing Committee as a reference for drafting the DPP's election strategy. The resulting compromise was encapsulated in the slogan 'strong base, westward advance' (*qiang ben, xi jin*) that combined the New Tide faction's concern with strengthening Taiwan's identity and economy with the Formosa faction's advocacy of the urgent need for greater economic integration with China.

The 'westward advance' position presented by the Formosa faction centred on the argument that growing interdependence across the Taiwan Strait would minimize the risks of talking to Beijing and opening up the Three Links, while also helping Taiwan to upgrade its own economy by moving out sunset industries. This made good sense as a way to counter the image of Taiwan as a regional trouble maker in a post-Cold War international order of growing interdependence and the development of a 'strategic partnership' between Washington and Beijing. Rather than Taiwan being absorbed into a Greater China, increased transactions in the context of globalization would link Taiwan not only with China, but also with the leading industrialized states. In this context, Taiwan's Chinese identity would be a positive advantage, because its historical, linguistic and cultural links would make it a good base for managing international enterprises in China, and would even help China to develop and become integrated into the global economy.[33]

The 'strong base' view advocated by the New Tide faction opposed such a view as being dangerously naïve in an international system characterized by a neo–realist balance of power within which Taiwan would be pressured to hold talks with China. National security would thus best be balanced by better diplomacy and efforts to strengthen Taiwan's economy by improving the island's investment environment.[34] Of most relevance for identity politics, increasing economic integration with China was said to pose a serious threat so long as there was little sense of solidarity and much indecisiveness over what the national interest was in Taiwan. When outside powers had to be dealt with, especially China, civic consciousness might just melt away and the status of the nation would become blurred. One of the main tasks for the DPP, therefore, was to strengthen Taiwan's civic consciousness.

Although both the Formosa and New Tide factions were to fall from grace after Chen Shui-bian rose to power in the DPP, the 'strong base, westward advance' strategy that emerged in 1999 represented a consensus within the party that offered continuity with the policies and principles that the KMT had developed under Lee Teng-hui. When Chen Shui-bian was elected president in 2000, continuity was further strengthened by the way in which many of the architects of the previous policy continued to be politically active. Lee Teng-hui, for example, remained highly influential out of power, transformed by his most dedicated followers into the spiritual leader of the independence movement. Tu Cheng-sheng became head of the National Palace Museum and was later appointed minister of education.

The continuation of Lee Teng-hui's balancing act can be seen quite clearly in Chen's 2000 and 2004 inauguration speeches.[35] Both of these reiterate Lee's strategy of building constructive relations with China and the US on the one hand, while strengthening Taiwan's nativization on the other. Chen's statement in the 2000 speech that he did not intend to abolish the National Unificiation Guidelines or the National Unification Council emphasized this continuity. His promise not to include in the ROC Constitution Lee's 1999 position that the two sides of the Taiwan Strait are two separate states enjoying a special relationship, known as his 'two states doctrine' (*liangguo lun*), could even be seen as backtracking from his predecessor's increasingly bold position on cross-Strait relations.[36]

Concerning the relationship between Taiwanese and Chinese identity, however, Chen moved the balance decisively towards consolidation of the former. He thus described Taiwanese culture as the result of the activities of grassroots organizations working to explore and preserve local history, culture, geography and ecology. This clearly remained in the context of advocating a pluralistic model of society, however, as he warned that cultural development had to be 'accumulated bit by bit' through a process of tolerance and respect, 'so that our diverse ethnic groups and different regional cultures communicate with each other, and so that Taiwan's local cultures connect with the cultures of Chinese-speaking communities and other world cultures, and create a new milieu of 'a cultural Taiwan in a modern century'.[37]

The implication was clearly that the Chinese cultural presence was welcome, albeit as something distinguishable from Taiwan's native culture and reduced to being on a par with 'world cultures'. Chen's explanation for the differences in political systems and lifestyles on the two sides of the Strait was based on their separate historical narratives over the past hundred years, rather than a cultural antipathy. While he accepted that 'The people across the Taiwan Strait share the same ancestral, cultural, and historical background', instead of seeing this as meaning that there is 'one China', he saw it as being a condition, along with the principles of democracy and parity, that would allow the leaders on both sides to 'possess enough wisdom and creativity to jointly deal with the question of a future "one China"'.

The DPP in power: between nativization and de-sinicization

Given the range of options open to Chen between the 'strong base' and 'westward advance' balance that he inherited, several factors can be proposed to explain why accusations that he presided over a process of de-sinicization grew after he came to power, despite attempts to maintain the inclusive vision of identity inherited from Lee Teng-hui and his own party's traditions.

First of all, attempts to shift state support away from privileging the grand tradition of Chinese culture in favour of allowing space for Taiwan's own history, traditions and innovations had already provoked criticisms of de-sinicization from sections of the political elite, media and academia during the Lee Teng-hui era. The event that triggered this was the release of plans for the reform of the school curriculum and teaching materials that had been drawn up under the guidance of Tu Cheng-sheng, the most concrete manifestation of which was the *Know Taiwan* series of textbooks produced by the National Institute of Compilation and Translation (NICT, *guoli bianyi guan*).[38] These initiatives were attacked by critics inside Taiwan and Mainland China for de-sinicization, promoting a Taiwanese national identity, lacking academic rigour, adopting a Japanese perspective on history that revealed a 'colonial mentality' on the part of the authors, eroding Taiwan's links with the Chinese Mainland and using education to separate the people of Taiwan from Chinese consciousness.[39] Critics also disliked the way in which the new historical narrative was confined to the 400 years that began with the Portuguese naming the island 'Formosa' and ran through a 'tragic history' (*bei qing de lishi*) during which the people of Taiwan had not been 'masters of their home'.[40]

It is not hard to see how the complaints about the education reforms largely stemmed from an attempt to defend ethnic Chinese nationalism. This is clear, for example, in anger over the way in which the whole population was no longer referred to as 'Chinese' in the political sense (*zhongguo ren*) or ethnic sense (*hua zu*). Instead, the textbooks merely stated that some of the population are 'people of Chinese culture' (*zhonghua <u>ren</u>*).[41] An attempt to defend the historical narrative of Chinese nationalism on political grounds can also be seen in the condemnation of the description of Japan's surrender of Taiwan to ROC forces in 1945 as merely 'the end of the war' instead of the 'glorious retrocession' (*guang fu*). This is even more clear in the way that critics were angry that Taiwan was openly referred to as the 'ROC on Taiwan', something they claimed was inconsistent with the official policy that the ROC is the sovereign government of the whole of China, which is only temporarily limited to Taiwan.[42] In all these respects, those who were angry over the education reforms were lagging well behind political and social changes that were taking place under democratization.

The charge that de-sinicization was being used to privilege the position of a new political elite and legitimize the concentration of power in the hands of Lee Teng-hui was not so easy to refute, however. This can be seen, for example, in the way that the new historical narrative of democratization culminated with the popular election of Lee Teng-hui as president in 1996.[43] Lee's influence could also be seen when the purpose of the reforms was said to be the consolidation and promotion of a Taiwan *Gemeinschaft*.[44] Elements in the textbooks such as the proclamation in the final chapter of the *Society* volume of the blueprint for 'creating a "new Taiwan"'[45] were also seen as part of a political programme rather than elements of education appropriate for the classroom. All of this added fuel to the charge that *Know Taiwan* was more of a political manifesto than a course devised for true education.[46]

The Chen administration also inherited a political climate within which issues of ethnicity had been given a new salience in politics by the overspill of events that surrounded the KMT's traumatic fall from power. The main reason for the party's failure had been the split between the 'native' Lee Teng-hui and Lien Chan on the one side and the 'Mainlander' James Soong on the other. Out of this emerged a more intense struggle over the nativization of the KMT and of Taiwan in general. The polarization of identity politics was further institutionalized when Soong established the People's First Party (PFP), drawing his support largely from disaffected 'Mainlanders' and advocating a pro-unification policy. Inside the KMT, the politics of ethnicity continued to simmer.

At the other end of the political spectrum, the Taiwan Solidarity Union (TSU) was established by those who took on themselves the responsibility for taking forward Lee Teng-hui's policies, claiming Lee as their 'spiritual leader' and proclaiming the new party's mission to be scrutinizing whether the DPP was truly 'taking the line of Taiwan's nativization'.[47] It must be said that the TSU was still careful to define 'nativization' in the inclusive, subjective terms of 'identifying with Taiwan, contribution to Taiwan, and being willing to work for Taiwan's future'. It even maintained the position that the two sides of the Taiwan Strait are separated by politics, but share the same language and culture.[48]

At the same time, however, the TSU could perform acts that are highly controversial and provocative within Chinese political culture, such as the visit to Tokyo's

Yasukuni Shrine made by the TSU chairman Su Jinqiang on 5 April 2005. This kind of activity not only radicalizes identity politics inside Taiwan, it also raises the profile of the island as a symbol in the much broader struggle between Chinese and Japanese nationalism that was given a new degree of animosity after Junichiro Koizumi became prime minister of Japan in 2001. Precisely because this is anathema to Chinese sentiments, it can also appeal to a core DPP constituency that has never accepted that anybody who is associated with China can have a legitimate role to play in Taiwanese politics, and who have refused to speak Mandarin or even associate with dissidents who had their origins in the Mainland since the earliest days of the party.[49] This tendency has occasionally emerged in wider social circles too under democratization, as in the spate of violent attacks against Mainlanders and their property that occurred at the time of the provincial and city mayor elections at the end of 1994.[50]

The emergence of the TSU thus presented a new challenge for a president who had been elected with only 39 per cent of the popular vote. Not only did the Chen administration have to compete with the TSU to maintain its core base of electoral support, it also had to rely on the new party to gain a majority in the Legislative Yuan after it won 13 seats there in the 2001 election and 12 seats in 2004. In short, Chen was in danger of being outflanked on the issue of consolidating Taiwan's identity.

Some weight also has to be given to the way in which the actions of the PRC have shaped the de-sinicization debate. Much attention has been given by observers of recent developments to the soft hand of Beijing's strategy of using the United Front to achieve 'peaceful unification' under 'one country, two systems', namely winning over the hearts and minds of key groups in Taiwan through economic and cultural transactions. Yet the United Front is also dedicated to isolating and neutralizing those whom the CCP deems to be advocates of Taiwanese independence. The increasing penetration of this policy inside Taiwan has only tended to politicize the already existing tension between 'Taiwanese' and 'Chinese', as doing business with the Mainland has been transformed into a question of political loyalty by both sides.

It was probably never feasible to expect anything other than a hostile reaction from Beijing to the attempt to build a new consensus over nativization inside Taiwan. Beijing never accepted the attempts to find a compromise formula that began under Lee Teng-hui. Accusations that Lee denied that Taiwan is a part of China by locating sovereignty in the people[51] and that he lacked the 'sentiments of a Chinese person' (*zhongguo ren de ganqing*),[52] only encouraged demonstrators in Taiwan to assert a distinctive ethnicity. When Beijing launched a propaganda barrage against Lee in the run-up to the 1996 presidential election, ethnic polarization became visible as demonstrators took to Taiwan's streets proclaiming 'I am Chinese', while counter-demonstrators insisted 'I am Taiwanese'.

The ratcheting up of the CCP's United Front that has characterized Taiwan policy under Hu Jintao's leadership goes some way to explaining the new salience of the argument over de-sinicization that took place under the Chen administration. Initiatives such as meeting opposition leaders Lien Chan and James Soong and targeting the DPP's core vote by providing economic concessions to Taiwanese agricultural exports to the Mainland were accompanied by a tightening of restrictions and the imposition of penalties on the activities of supporters of Chen. Generous offers were made to discuss a range of issues, including Taiwan's room for international manoeuvre, so long as 'one China' under the so-called '1992 consensus' is accepted. Those who are categorized as independence activists are isolated from this process and are to be resolutely struggled against.

Even when Beijing has adopted a relatively moderate approach to unification, it usually demonstrates a failure to comprehend just how much identity politics has shifted since its Taiwan policy was established in the late 1970s. The furthest it has managed to go in addressing the nativization issue in this respect has been Hu Jintao's recognition that it is quite understandable for the islanders to be attached to their 'native' culture, while explaining that this is the same as people in Mainland China identifying with their local cultures.[53] This equation of Taiwanese identity with that of Guangdong or Fujian is only seen as belittling by many in Taiwan, as is giving them the same status as the former colony of Hong Kong under the 'one country, two systems' formula. Faced by Beijing's growing attempts to isolate opponents of unification with China, it is not surprising that many in Taiwan respond by increasingly putting a distance between their 'native' Taiwanese identity and Chinese identity.

As political actors inside Taiwan respond to this polarization, they are often tempted to see the emotions generated by ethnic politics as a political resource. As early as a campaign speech of 2 September 1995, Lee Teng-hui could be seen giving in to this when he stressed that those who do not want to contribute their strength to Taiwan and want to emigrate, should 'quickly emigrate'.[54] By the late 1990s candidates in DPP primary elections also began to speak in the Hokkien dialect, effectively excluding Mandarin speakers from the democratic process.

Many of the key initiatives described as a process of de-sinicization under the Chen administration were also direct responses to attempts by Beijing to step up its United Front tactics and isolate the Taipei government. A clear example of this is the way in which Chen announced his doctrine of 'one country on each side of the Taiwan Strait' (*yi bian yi guo*) and his intention to implement referendum legislation after Beijing persuaded Nauru to break diplomatic relations with Taipei when he became chairman of the DPP in 2002. Similarly, Chen explained his decision to scrap the NUC on 27 February 2006 as a response to the continued arms build-up by the PLA. The way that this was used in the domestic context can be seen from the announcement of this position the day before the anniversary of the February 28 Incident. This allowed Chen to make an emotional address to a memorial ceremony the next day, during which he asked in Mandarin, 'Is A-bian wrong? Is A-bian wrong by returning the right of choosing their future to the 23 million people of Taiwan?' The rest of his speech was in the Hokkien dialect.

In some respects, then, democratization can be said to have increased the temptation to resort to the politics of ethnicity. This is most evident in election campaigns at all levels. James Soong had to spend a disproportionate amount of his time and energy on proving his loyalty to Taiwan as he campaigned to be Lien Chan's vice-president in the 2004 presidential election campaign after the DPP focused its fire on his origins in Mainland China. Even Chen seems to have realized that this was taking politics in a dangerous direction, as is evident from the candid admission in his inauguration speech that the DPP and he himself needed to undertake a degree of 'candid self-reflection' on the issues of identity and ethnicity. He also reiterated the inclusive conception of civic society, this time at somewhat greater length than in his previous inauguration speech, and even mentioning the need to incorporate 'immigrant workers who labour under Taiwan's blazing sun' for the first time into the 'New Taiwan' family.

Despite this confirmation of the consensus on an inclusive civic society, however, the continuation of the attempt to consolidate Taiwanese identity by removing vestiges of the KMT's Chinese nationalism from public spaces served to perpetuate and deepen the argument over de-sinification in Chen's second term. Moreover, the temptation to politicize identity politics has proven too strong to resist even at the level of local elections, as when Chen Shui-bian portrayed the December 2006 contest for the mayor of Kaohsiung as a struggle between Taiwan and China. A repetition of ethnic politics in the presidential election can also be seen in attempts to undermine the candidacy of the Hong Kong-born Ma Ying-jeou for the 2008 contest. It is such attempts to exclude individuals from legitimate political activity due to their 'Chinese' ethnicity that fuel the broader accusations of de-sinicization in the cultural field above all else.

Towards a new consensus

When assessing responses to identity politics by Taiwan's political elites, however, it would be wrong to propose that there is a clear-cut division between parties on the choice between ethnic and civic nationalism. As Anthony Smith points out, every nationalism does in fact contain both civic and ethnic elements in varying degrees and different forms.[55] Accusations of de-sinicization levelled against the Chen administration tend to obscure initiatives that have had a counter-impact on identity politics. The influence of the continuation of the incremental but steady liberalization of transactions between the two sides of the Taiwan Strait that began in the 1980s, for example, can be seen in phenomena such as the huge numbers of Taiwanese travelling to Mainland China for work and recreation and the growing number of Mainland spouses now in Taiwan. In the cultural field it is also evident in the penetration of the island's publishing market, with a proliferation of bookshops selling Mainland Chinese works now threatening the native industry. Rather than try to stop such tendencies, the Chen administration continued to search for an optimal balance not only through strengthening Taiwan's civic consciousness as the base, but also through initiatives such as widening the study of English language in order to facilitate Taiwan's role in the processes of globalization.

On the other side of the political divide, ethnic politics has continued to character-ize power struggles inside the KMT. This came to a boiling point when the popular mayor of Taipei, Hong Kong-born Ma Ying-jeou, competed with the Taiwanese-born parliamentary speaker Wang Jyng-pin in the contest to elect a new party chairman who would be candidate for the 2008 presidential election. Part of Wang's campaign involved claiming that many people thought it was not right for an ethnic minority to rule over the majority in Taiwan.

More optimistically, however, the continuing attractiveness of the cross-party consensus on an inclusive sense of identity that was developed under the Lee Teng-hui administration can be seen in the way that the pan-Blue camp has contributed to the exploration and articulation of the discourse on nativization. Nowhere is this clearer than in the monograph *Original Native Spirit: The Model Story of Taiwan*,[56] published by Ma Ying-jeou in June 2007 to mark out his position on identity politics in time for the March 2008 presidential election.

Ma's book is an important contribution to the argument over de-sinicization because it presents an extensive re-interpretation of nativization by emphasizing the positive contributions made by China to Taiwan's economic and political development. He thus challenges the narrative of the '400 years of tragedy' under foreign occupation that is promoted by the pro-independence movement by describing the achievements of figures from China from the reforming Qing Dynasty governor Liu Mingchuan, through key political actors in the Republican period, such as the philosopher and cultural commentator Hu Shi, the early critic of the KMT dictatorship in Taiwan, Lei Chen (Lei Zhen), and Chiang Kaishek's son, Chiang Ching-kuo. He also tackles the existence of a distinctive Taiwanese consciousness before 1945 by pointing out that many natives of the island joined the Chinese in the resistance against Japan, both in Taiwan and the Mainland. The accusation that the Taiwanese were not consulted about their future status after World War II is also challenged by Ma when he observes that the island did send delegates to take part in the National People's Congress in Nanjing when it drew up and promulgated the 1947 ROC Constitution. He even undermines the privileged ethnic position bestowed on figures such as Chen Shui-bian by reminding readers that his ancestors were colonizers from Mainland China, too.

It is important to stress, however, that Ma is not trying to revive the KMT's old version of an ethnocentric kind of Chinese nationalism that can be used to suspend democracy until unification is achieved. Instead, his deconstruction of nativization is firmly committed to reinforcing democratic principles. He differs from the DPP, however, in emphasizing that Taiwan's democratization has to be seen as part of a broader process that inevitably involves Mainland China. This argument is partly pragmatic, proposing that Taiwan is dependent economically on the Mainland market and that democratization in China is therefore the best way to ensure Taiwan's future security. Yet it is also idealistic, insofar as Ma draws attention to the potential for Taiwan to be a beacon for political transformation on the other side of the Strait, drawing encouragement from the modernizing spirit of the 4 May movement that began in the Mainland in 1919 and the democracy movement that was crushed in 1989.

Ma's commitment to unification with China under the umbrella of future democratization has thus moved a long way from the ideology of a party that once imprisoned people for speaking non-Mandarin dialects and actually censored the works of many of the Taiwanese intellectuals that he praises for having resisted Japan.[57]

This is made clear from the lengthy exploration of nativization that appears in the introduction to his book, written by Yang Tu (Yang Du), a senior journalist at the Chinese-language *China Times* newpaper.[58] Yang challenges the attempt to build an exclusive Taiwanese identity based on the ethnic characteristics of the majority of the population who came from Fujian province in Mainland China before 1949 by stressing the diversity of a society that has been formed by seven waves of immigration and that is now being shaped by the forces of globalization. In this context, he argues that the only people really entitled to call themselves 'native' are the tiny number of aboriginal peoples who have survived this colonization, and that 'nativization is inclusiveness, it is the integration of immigrant culture, it is a process of constant addition, constant rejection and constant renewal'.[59]

This commitment to the development of an inclusive civic culture might well be understood as arising from the fears of exclusion from political life on ethnic grounds faced by a figure like Ma. Moreover, the positive views of Taiwan as a pluralistic, multicultural, immigrant society can actually be found in a DPP document such as Chen Shui-bian's 2004 inauguration speech. Having said this, any critique of the dangers of exclusive ethnic politics should be considered a welcome contribution to the development of democracy and a warning to political actors tempted by populist politics to depart from the consensus on inclusiveness. When Ma and Yang reveal the fallacy of a DPP that is dominated by descendants of immigrants from China attempting to purge Taiwan of Chinese influences, they are thus consolidating the consensus on the need to build an inclusive form of civic nationalism that goes back to the days of the Dang Wai. After all, as Yang points out, real de-sinicization would mean changing the name of the island itself, because the origins of 'Taiwan' can be traced to the Hokkien dialect of China's Fujian province. To be consistent, given that people like Chen Shuibian are descendants of Han Mainlanders, they should purge the island of themselves!

The success of the KMT in the 2008 Legislative Yuan and presidential elections shows that this complex nativization of the KMT has successfully cast off its iden-tification with the authoritarian past and Chinese nationalism by stressing its own contribution to Taiwan's democratization and economic development and drop-ping the cause of unification with China. This represents a new development in the reconciliation of political loyalty to Taiwan with having an ethnic Chinese identity, encapsulated by the cultural messages delivered by the KMT's electoral campaigns. Nowhere was this clearer than in the photographic exhibition commemorating the KMT's history that was mounted in the entrance hall of the campaign headquarters. While this included sections on Sun Yat-sen and Chiang Kai-shek, the largest part focused on the contribution of Chiang Ching-kuo to Taiwan's 'economic miracle'. Even more telling was the inclusion in the exhibition of a large photo-portrait of Chiang Wei-shui (1890–1931), an iconic figure in the story of Taiwan for having led passive resistance against the Japanese occupation through establishing the Taiwan Culture Association in 1923 and Taiwan's first political party, the Taiwan People's Party (台灣民眾黨), in 1927. Bearing the large slogan 'National Righteousness' (*minzu zhengqi*) and with a biographical sketch under the title 'Taiwan's Sun Yat-sen', Chiang has clearly been appropriated by the KMT as representative of the kind of person who can be loyal to Taiwan while not denying their Chinese heritage.

What might best be called the complex nativization of the KMT that has emerged from the 2008 Legislative Yuan election is perhaps best reflected by an editorial run on polling day under the heading 'Today, Let the People Redefine Taiwan's Value' by the leading Blue-leaning newspaper, the *United Daily News*. The message of the editorial was that after eight years of bad governance following the first change of ruling party in 2000, it was now time for change again and to punish politicians for bad governance. Yet the implications for identity were not absent when the newspaper proclaimed, 'No matter how over-inflated the words of the politicians, as far as the voters are concerned, this election has only one fundamental purpose: break the present hard straits, redefine the national value and the spirit of Taiwan!'

The fact that an Executive Yuan opinion poll taken a year after the Ma administration came to power reveals that the proportion of people identifying themselves as 'Taiwanese' had risen to 65 per cent, with 12 per cent identifying as 'Chinese' and 18 per cent as 'both', shows how even deeper cross-Strait integration and a government that puts more emphasis on valuing the Chinese elements in Taiwanese culture is unlikely to slow the long-term process of nativization.[60]

Maintaining a culture fit for civic nationalism

It has been argued above that calling all changes made to the old symbols of KMT-era authoritarianism 'de-sinicization' amounts to a caricature of the complex negotiation of identity politics that has to take place under Taiwan's democratization. While many people have angrily reacted to the idea of renaming the Chiang Kai-shek Memorial Hall in central Taipei as 'Taiwan Democracy Hall', for example, this is quite different from renaming it 'CSB Hall'. The proposal to pull down the traditional-style Chinese walls that surround this monument might well jar on aesthetic sensibilities, but more is required to show that this is a deliberate policy to purge Taiwan of Chinese influences rather than just a tasteless project to create a more accessible public space.

The potential of the state to manipulate national identity should also not be exaggerated. As of writing, signposts in Taiwan remain a confusing mixture of various types of Romanization. That the government position on nativist education recognizes the complex ethnic composition of Taiwanese society and the special role played by Han culture has been spelt out on numerous occasions by a figure like Tu Cheng-sheng.[61] Yet this did not shield him from the wrath of the TSU in the summer of 2007, when 67 per cent of the content of the National Literature (*guo wen*) university entrance exam was concerned with classical Chinese literature. The very fact that the TSU was not satisfied by Tu's explanation, in his capacity as minister of education, that he had deliberately commissioned the independent Examination Centre to deal with such sensitive issues,[62] shows just how difficult it is for the state to get identity politics right. Even if the state does accelerate the building of a new Taiwanese identity with a vengeance, the failure of the KMT to instil a sense of Chinese national identity in Taiwan when it did not have to worry about the complications of democratic politics may well be the best precedent for showing why the prospects for the success of such a project are limited.

Rather than concluding that an erosion of democracy is occurring due to 'de-sinicization', therefore, it has been proposed that a consensus has in fact emerged between the main political parties on the need to develop a politics of identity that is based on an inclusive, participatory form of civic culture. This has its origins in a democracy movement that realized how destabilizing it would be to replace Chinese nationalism with an exclusive form of Taiwanese nationalism based on ethnicity.

Yet it is also worth noting that the civic culture paradigm is rather limited when it comes to dealing with the way in which identity is negotiated in Taiwan. This is because it is not directly concerned with the questions of *national* identity that are forced on the island by its relationship with China. Almond and Verba, for example, are concerned with exploring the 'balance among the parochial, subject and par-ticipant roles',[63] which can take place in a wide variety of states, some of which are highly decentralized. Putnam's work is an exploration of Italian *regional* democracy.[64] In principle, therefore, the proposition that Taiwan should have a participatory civic culture that draws its values from native traditions might be compatible with it being part of a greater entity called 'China', just as Tuscany is part of Italy. While this might fit the model of 'one country, two systems' advocated by Beijing, it would not do justice to the way in which the arguments over nativization and de-sinicization in Taiwan unavoidably involve the issue of how to consolidate the island's sovereign independence and have it recognized as such by international society.

Taiwan's identity politics thus has to be understood as shaped by the wider trans-formations of identities in Northeast Asia, too. Serious repercussions are generated in this region whenever attempts are made to address the legacies of the Chinese and Japanese versions of nationalism that moulded the island's identity in the past. In particular, it has not been possible to present the nativization project in a way that is acceptable to a Chinese government and Communist Party that still bases its unifica-tion policy on the politics of ethnic nationalism, from the appeal to the 'descendants of the Yellow Emperor' that is made in the Letter to Taiwan Compatriots sent by the National People's Congress in 1979, down to Hu Jintao's insistence that solving the Taiwan problem and realizing unification of the 'motherland' (*zu guo*) is 'the shared desire of Chinese sons and daughters at home and abroad'.[65]

In this respect, it is useful to draw on the distinction between 'ethnic' and 'civic' nationalism to explain the arguments over de-sinicization and nativization. Taiwan is certainly faced by the possibility of a contest between harshly opposed Chinese and Taiwanese versions of ethnic nationalism that would wreak both internal and external havoc. The discourse of nativization, however, presents a third possibility. This is closer to the kind of civic nationalism that has emerged as the foundation of the Western liberal-democratic state. In principle, this is participatory and inclusive, because it is based more on legal and territorial definitions and subjective loyalty than it is on predetermined culture, blood line or origins.

Despite the heated rhetoric generated by the argument over de-sinicization, encouragement should be drawn from the way in which democratization has so far constrained nativization within the participatory framework of civic nationalism. If the literature on 'civic culture' is to be useful in explaining this kind of development, it should be through reminding us how the type of democratic culture that developed as the foundation for the liberal-democratic Western state is 'neither traditional nor modern but partaking of both; a pluralistic culture based on communication and persuasion, a culture of consensus and diversity, a culture that permitted change but moderated it'.[66]

Notes

1 Almond and Verba, *The Civic Culture: Political Attitudes and Democracy in Five Nations* (New Jersey: Princeton University Press, 1963), p. 8.
2 Anthony D. Smith, *National Identity* (London: Penguin, 1991), p. 11.
3 *Taiwan Yearbook 2006–7*. Available online at http://www.gio.gov.tw/taiwan-website/5-gp/yearbook/cover.html, accessed 10 June 2007.
4 The new passport began to be issued in September 2003.
5 National History Institute (*Guoshi guan*) Available online at http://www.drnh.gov.tw/www/page/A/page-A.aspx (accessed 10 June 2007).
6 On national identity and the education reforms of the Lee Teng-hui era see Hughes, C. and Stone, R. 'Nationalism and Curriculum Reform in Hong Kong and Taiwan', *China Quarterly*, No 160, Dec 1999, pp. 977–91.
7 This system was largely devised by Dr. B.C.Yu (Yu Boquan) of the Academia Sinica and approved in 1996 by the Educational Reform Council (*jiaoyu gaige weiyuanhui*) led by the Nobel laureate Dr. Lee Yuan-tseh (Le Yuanzhe), then head of the Academia Sinica.
8 Taiwan Affairs Office, *Zhongguo Taiwan wenti waishi renyuan duben* (*Reader on China's Taiwan Problem for Non-Specialist Personnel*), (Beijing: jiuzhou chubanshe, 2006) pp. 138–47.
9 A more extensive account of the emergence of thinking about identity from the Dang Wai to the KMT can be found in Christopher Hughes, *Taiwan and Chinese Nationalism: National Identity and Status in International Society* (London and New York: Routledge, 1997).
10 Liu Feng-sung (Liu Fengsong), *Formosa*, 1979. No. 3, p. 76.
11 Peng Ming-min, *A Taste of Freedom* (Holt, Rinehart & Winst: New York, Chicago, San Francisco, 1972), p. 244.
12 Peng Ming-min, *A Taste of Freedom*, (Holt, Rinehart & Winst: New York, Chicago, San Francisco, 1972), p. 239.
13 Lucien Pye, 'Taiwan's Political Development and Its Implications for Beijing', *Asian Survey*, June 1986, pp. 618–19.
14 *Zhongguo shibao* (*China Times*), 31 December 1994.
15 Pi Hsiao-hua (Bi Xiaohua) *Taiwan minjian jiaoyu gaige yundong: guojia yu shehui de fenxi*, (*Taiwan's Civil Movement for Education Reform: Analysis of State and Society*), (Taipei, Qianwei chubanshe, 1996), pp. 128–98.
16 Pi, p. 377.
17 Pi, pp. 268–9.
18 Pi, pp. 183–90.
19 *The Taiwan Question and Reunification of China* (Beijing, Taiwan Affairs Office and Information Office State Council, 1993).
20 *There is no 'Taiwan Question' There is Only a 'China Question'* (Taipei, Mainland Affairs Council, 1993), p. 4.
21 Ibid.
22 Lee Teng-hui, 'Love and Faith', *Creating the Future*, p. 133.
23 Complete text in *China Post* (Taipei), 31 December 1994.
24 Lee Teng-hui, 'Towards the 21st Century Arm in Arm – The Republic of China and the New Asian-Pacific Situation', *Creating the Future*, pp. 121–7.

25 Lee Teng-hui, 'From Uncertainty to Pragmatism – The Shape of the Age to Come', *Creating the Future*, p. 116.
26 Lee Teng-hui, 'From Uncertainty to Pragmatism', p. 117. The term '*shengming gongtong*' is translated in English texts as 'Gemeinschaft'. Lee does not mention Ferdinand Tonnies, who is usually associated with developing the concept for sociology.
27 Speech to KMT conference held to examine performance in the elections for provincial governor and city mayors. Full text in *Zhongguo shibao* (*China Times*), 31 December 1994.
28 Complete text in *Zhongguo shibao* (*China Times*), 31 December 1994.
29 Tu Cheng-sheng, 'Bentu-zhongguo-shijie' ('Native – China – World'), *Zhongguo shibao* (*China Times*) 25 May 1994, p. 11; 'Lishi jiaoyu yao ruhe songbang' ('How to Relax History Education'), *Lianhe bao* (*United Daily News*), 23 January 1995, p. 11; 'Yi ge xin shi guan de dansheng' ('The Birth of a New Idea of History'), *Dangdai*, No. 120, 1 August 1997, pp. 20–30; 'Cong "renshi Taiwan" zuotan lishi jiaoyu' ('Discussing History Education from "Know Taiwan"'), *Dangdai*, No. 120, 1 August 1997, pp. 55–67.
30 See reports on Perry's comments to Lee on 17 January, *Free China Journal*, 23 February 1998, p. 2.
31 Available online at http://www.dpp.org.tw/ (accessed 10 August 2007).
32 'DPP China Policy Symposium'. Available online at http://taiwan.yam.org.tw/china_policy/e_bg.htm (accessed 10 August 2007).
33 Hsu Hsin-liang and Chen Chong-hsin, 'Zai guohi guanxi xin zhixu geju xia chongzhi liang an guanxi xin jiyuan' ('In the Situation of the New International Order Open Up a New Era in Cross-Strait Relations'). Available online at http://taiwan.yam.org.tw/china_policy/c_shu-c.htm (accessed 10 August 2008).
34 Lin Cho-shui (Lin Zhuoshui), 'Qiangben qian jin de Zhongguo zhengce' (Strong Base and Gradual Advance China Policy). Available online at http://taiwan.yam.org.tw/china_policy/l_lin.htm (accessed 10 August 2008).
35 'Taiwan Stands Up: Towards the Dawning of a New Era'. Available online at http://www.taipei.org/chen/chen520c.htm (accessed 10 August 2007); 'Paving the Way for a Sustainable Taiwan'. Available online at http://www.gio.gov.tw/taiwan-website/5-gp/pi2004/ (accessed 10 August 2007).
36 This was one of Chen's promises included in his 'Four Nos' formula of 'not announce independence, not include Lee Teng-hui's "two states doctrine" in the constitution, not change the name of the country, not change the status quo by having a referendum on independence'. He also added that 'the abolition of the National Reunification Council or the National Unification Guidelines will not be an issue'.
37 The official English translation 'so that Taiwan's local cultures connect with the cultures of Chinese-speaking communities and other world cultures' does not completely reflect the Chinese version, '*rang lizu Taiwan de bentu wenhua yu huaren wenhua, shijie wenhua ziran jiegui*'. This would more accurately be rendered as 'allow the establishment of Taiwan's native culture to naturally connect with the culture of the Chinese people [huaren wen-hua] and world culture'.
38 In August 1997 the National Institute of Compilation and Translation (NICT) produced three standard textbooks for 'Know Taiwan': *Renshi Taiwan lishi pian* (*Know Taiwan History Volume*), *Renshi Taiwan shehui pian* (*Know Taiwan Society Volume*), and *Renshi Taiwan dili pian* (*Know Taiwan Geography Volume*).
39 Wang Hsiao-po *et al.*, '"Renshi Taiwan" lishi pian xiuding' ('Corrections to the History Volume of "Know Taiwan"') in Taiwan shi yanjiu hui (ed.), *Renshi Taiwan jiaoke shu* (*The Know Taiwan Textbook*), (Taipei: Taiwan shi yanjiu hui, 1997), p. 9.
40 NICT, *Renshi Taiwan shehui pian*, p. 63.
41 *Renshi Taiwan: shehui pian*, pp. 11–14.
42 Wang Xiaopo *et al.*, '"Renshi Taiwan" lishi pian xiuding', p. 53.
43 NICT, *Renshi Taiwan shehui pian*, p. 63.
44 Jiaoyu bu, *Guomin zhongxue kecheng*, (1994), pp. 854–5.
45 NICT, *Renshi Taiwan shehui pian*, p. 90.
46 This point is made by Wang Chung-fu (Wang Zhongfu) of the Department of History at National Taiwan Normal University, among others, in 'Dui yu "renshi Taiwan" jiaoke shu

zhi ying you de renshi' ('Concerning What Should Be Known About "Know Taiwan"'), in Taiwan shi yanjiu hui (ed.), *Renshi Taiwan jiaoke shu*, pp. 6–7.

47 This is a liberal (but I think accurate) translation of the Chinese 'jiandu zhizheng dang shi fo zou Taiwan zhuti luxian'. TSU website. Available online at http://www.tsu.org. tw/index.php?option=com_content&task=view&id=81&Itemid=28.

48 TSU website. Available online at http://www.tsu.org.tw/index.php?option=com_cont ent&task=view&id=17&Itemid=28.

49 Sun Ch'ing-yu (Sun Qingyu), *Min jin dang de xian xiang* (*The DPP Phenomenon*), (Taipei, 1992), p.12. Senior opposition activists Lin Cheng-chieh (Lin Zhengjie) and Fei Hsi-p'ing (Fei Xiping) were singled out in particular for criticism and were subjected to what Lin described as 'Taiwan-independence fascism'. *Zhongyang ribao* (*Central Daily News*), 4 June 1991. Both eventually withdrew from the DPP.

50 The complex nature of the politicization of identity is made clear from the letters pages of the daily newspapers. A telling case is that of the 'middle class', 'floating voter' woman whose family had been in Taiwan for eight generations and whose Hakka grandmother was ejected from a taxi because she spoke Taiwanese with 'an accent' she picked up from her Mainlander husband. *Lianhe bao* (*United Daily News*), 2 December 1994. See also the revulsion felt by popular figures from the arts world towards the antagonism released by the elections, in the report 'Yi ren kan xuanju' ('Artists Look at the Elections'), *Lianhe bao*, 4 December 1994.

51 *Wenhui bao*, 16 June 1994.

52 *Wenhui bao*, 16 June 1994; *Renmin ribao* (*People's Daily*), 16 June 1994.

53 'Hu Jintao he Lian Zhan juxing zhengshi huitan jiu fazhang lian an guanxi ti chu si dian zhuzhang' ('Hu Jintao and Lian Zhan hold formal talks and propose four principles for developing cross-Strait relations'), *Renmin ribao* (*People's Daily*), 30 April 2005.

54 *Lianhe bao* (*United Daily News*), 2 September 1995.

55 Smith, *National Identity*, p. 13.

56 Ma Ying-jeou, *Yuanxiang jingshen: Taiwan de dianfan gushi*, Taipei, tianxia yuanjian chuban.

57 This point about how the KMT used to treat Taiwanese intellectuals lauded by Ma for having resisted Japan is made with reference to the debate over Lai He (1894–1943), the 'Father of Taiwanese literature, who was listed as "dangerous" by the KMT in 1958 due to his left leaning political views', in Hsu Wei-te (Xu Weide) 'Jiedu Lai He guozu rentong suo sheji de jidian zhengyi' ('Interpreting Some Points of Contention that Touch on Lai He's National Identity'), *Gonghe* (*The Republic*), 2007: 55 (June), pp. 6–13.

58 Yang Tu (Yang Du), 'Xin Taiwan ren, xiang qian xing' ('New Taiwanese, Moving Forward'), in Ma, pp. 1–38.

59 Yang, p. 27.

60 Executive Yuan, '*Minzhong de zhengzhi taidu ji zuqun guandian*'. Available online at http://www.rdec.gov.tw/public/Data/952711431071.pdf (accessed 29 June 2010).

61 On Tu's theory of education see Hughes and Stone, 'Curriculum Reform in Hong Kong and Taiwan'. For a more recent personal exposition of Tu's views see his speech 'Taiwan's Educational Reform and the Future of Taiwan' delivered on 10 January 2007 at the London School of Economics and Political Science. Available online at http://www.lse. ac.uk/collections/LSEPublicLecturesAndEvents/events/ (accessed 10 August 2007).

62 '*Zhi kao wen yan wen bilie gao tailian: dakao zhongxin zhuren mei guankong ying xia tai daoqian*' ('High Proportion of Classical Chinese in Exam TSU: University Exam Centre Director Should Stand Down and Apologize for not Controlling'). *Zhongguo shibao* (*China Times*), 4 July 2007. Available online at http://www.tol.com.tw/ (accessed 10 August 2007).

63 Almond and Verba, *Civic Culture*, p. 440.

64 Robert D. Putnam, *Making Democracy Work: Civic Traditions in Modern Italy* (Princeton, NJ: Princeton University Press, 1993).

65 'Hu Jintao tichu xin xingshi xia fazhan liang an guanxi si dian yijian' ('Hu Jintao proposes four opinions on cross-Strait relations under the new situation', *Renmin ribao* (*People's Daily* (overseas edition)), 5 March 2005.

66 Almond and Verba, *Civic Culture*, p. 8.

4

THE POLARIZATION OF TAIWAN'S PARTY COMPETITION IN THE DPP ERA

Dafydd Fell

Polarizing politics after 2000?

The Democratic Progressive Party's (DPP) victory in Taiwan's second direct presidential election in 2000 was widely acclaimed as a democratic milestone. It was the first instance of a Chinese society experiencing a change in ruling parties through a democratic election. Election rhetoric meant that the public had unrealistically high expectations of the new administration. There was an initial honeymoon period in which the president received high support levels and faced a relatively uncritical media.[1] Even within the Kuomintang (KMT), many saw the positive side of losing power, as the party embarked on its most ambitious programme of party reforms since the 1950s.[2] In short, there was a great deal of optimism at the outset of the DPP era.

By the first anniversary of the change in ruling parties, much of the initial goodwill had been dissipated.[3] The attempt by the opposition parties to recall the DPP's president Chen Shui-bian over his handling of the Fourth Nuclear Power Station construction project represents the first in a series of unprecedented political crises during the DPP era. These include the island's worst economic recession, record levels of unemployment, high levels of political violence, a series of corruption scandals involving high-ranking DPP politicians including Chen and his close relatives, huge demonstrations calling on the president to step down over corruption allegations and three votes in parliament to recall the president. A critical feature of this period was the adversarial relationship between the ruling DPP and the coalition of opposition parties (known as the pan-Blue bloc).[4] The incessant political conflicts in parliament contributed to the declining public confidence in democratic institutions. This political cynicism has been visible in falling election turnout rates and also the public sentiment to punish the parliamentarians by halving their numbers.[5]

Democratic theorists agree that democratic consolidation requires strong and institutionalized political parties. In the late 1990s, Shelley Rigger listed strengthening political parties as one of the six main challenges facing the island's democracy.[6] Ten years later, after the end of the second Chen Shui-bian administration, it is a good time to take stock of the state of party competition. Since the DPP era has the reputation as a time of party polarization, this study focuses on the ideological dimension of party politics.

The ideological distance between the main political parties has important implications for the quality of Taiwan's democracy. Only where political parties offer distinct policy packages will voters view elections as making a difference. However, if the parties completely forsake the centre ground for the poles, then political stability is unlikely. In previous works, I argued that Taiwan had a healthy state of party competition, in which 'although the main parties moved towards a moderate centre and ideological distance between parties has reduced, the parties consistently stress different issues and the public are able to distinguish between parties on core issues'.[7] I term this pattern of competition 'moderate party differentiation'.[8] Thus, this study aims to test whether Taiwan still deserves the label of a 'healthy democracy'.[9]

Moreover, an examination of the factors creating heightened polarization can offer suggestions for how such divergent politics may be ameliorated. In *Party Politics in Taiwan*,[10] I employed a framework which sought to explain changing party positions as a result of changing internal balance of power between election-orientated and ideologically conservative factions. It was hypothesized that when the party is dominated by election-orientated politicians, the party will respond to public opinion and election results by taking more popular and moderate positions. In contrast, when the party is dominated by ideologically conservative factions, the party will seek to stick to its traditional positions, even though these may be 'electoral poison'.[11] In the case of the KMT, the more ideologically conservative wing was represented by the pro-Chinese unification Non-Mainstream Faction, while the DPP's more ideological groups of the 1990s were the radical proponents of de jure Taiwan independence, such as the New Tide Faction. The election-oriented side of the KMT was the Mainstream Faction led by Lee Teng-hui, while the DPP's moderates were exemplified by the party leaders that attempted to de-emphasize national identity and broaden the party's appeal into social issues. I am interested to see whether this framework is still applicable to explain party change in the DPP era. Lastly, in the light of the KMT's landslide election victories in 2008, it is important to examine the future prospects for party politics in Taiwan, as the recent conflictual nature of party politics and apparent return to a one-party (KMT) dominant system after 2008 both represent potential challenges to Taiwan's democratic future.

Salient political issues in the second Chen Shui-bian term

I examine changing party positions on three of the most salient issues in the DPP era. The following issue areas are discussed: (1) Taiwan independence versus Chinese unification, (2) Taiwanese versus Chinese identity, (3) military procurement. In each case, the generally convergent trends of the 1990s and first Chen administration are briefly sketched. This is followed by a more detailed discussion of the party divergence after 2004.

Almost all political scientists working on Taiwan agree that national identity is the most salient issue in Taiwan's electoral politics. Questions of national identity address two central issues: who are the people and what are the boundaries of the state? In the Taiwan case, these overlap with the disputes over Taiwan independence versus unification (commonly known as the TongDu issue) and self-identification as Chinese versus Taiwanese. These disputes have permeated almost every election since the outset of multiparty elections. Overall changes in the issue structure in the post-2000 period has meant that as a number of the cross-cutting social issues have declined in salience, parties have become increasingly reliant on identity issues. The issue of military procurement has been added as it is an issue that went from being consensual in the 1990s to become highly polarized in the DPP era.

Party movement on TongDu

TongDu can be viewed as a spectrum in which the far left incorporates calls for immediate declaration of Taiwan independence and a new Taiwan constitution (I term this 'pure Taiwan independence'),[12] and the far right refers to calls for unification and the centre means maintaining the status quo. Between the two poles, the centre left (I term this 'diluted Taiwan independence') includes opposition to unification and more moderate self-determination appeals, while the centre right (termed as 'Taiwan independence: negative') includes calls to protect the Republic of China (ROC) and its 1947 Constitution and opposition to independence.

A number of studies have attested to the gradual process of convergence away from the parties' initially polarized positions of the early 1990s.[13] In 1991, the parties were truly poles apart. The DPP had just passed its Taiwan Independence Clause (TIC), which called for declaring a Republic of Taiwan (ROT) and a new constitution. Almost all DPP candidates carried the title, 'Constitution Drafting National Assembly Candidate' on their publicity material.[14] In response, the KMT promoted the National Unification Guidelines (NUG), a framework for a three-stage process towards eventual unification. The KMT argued that only minor revisions were required for the existing constitution and that a new constitution could lead to recession and PRC invasion.[15]

During the 1990s, both parties moved away from these extreme positions. Although the KMT continued to attack the DPP's Taiwan independence platform and rejected the DPP demand for a new Taiwan constitution, it steered clear of unification during subsequent 1990s campaigns. The KMT actually co-opted a number of components of the DPP independence agenda. For instance, though the official KMT position in 1991 was opposed to direct presidential elections and UN application, by 1994 the KMT had adopted these DPP proposals. Convergence was even greater in the second half of the 1990s, as constitutional reform took a more balanced, negotiated approach. In 1997 and 2000, the KMT and DPP cooperated as partners in radical

constitutional reform measures, such as effectively eliminating the provincial government structure and the National Assembly.[16]

The DPP also contributed to the convergent trend by dropping its open espousal
of 'Pure Taiwan independence'. It ceased openly calling for an ROT, and instead
repackaged its independence message with more electorally popular appeals, such as
opposition to unification. Similarly, the DPP dropped its insistence on a new constitution and agreed to promote its reform agenda through constitutional revisions. The
DPP's more moderate approach was formalized in its 1999 Resolution Regarding
Taiwan's Future, which recognized the ROC as the national title. In addition, it
made clear that there was no need to declare independence as, 'Following the 1992
general elections of the National Legislature, the 1996 direct presidential elections
and constitutional reform to abolish the provincial government, Taiwan has become
a democratic and independent country'.[17] Although the KMT gave heavy emphasis
to its terror equation of 'DPP=Taiwan Independence=CCP invasion' in the 2000
presidential election, in terms of TongDu policy, the two parties were closer than
at any time in their histories. There was little distance between Lee Teng-hui's contention that cross-Strait relations be designated as 'special state-to-state ties [*teshu
de guoyuguo de guanxi*]',[18] and the DPP's Resolution Regarding Taiwan's Future. By
the end of the Lee Teng-hui era, the parties had converged on the centre left of the
TongDu spectrum.

Despite the inter-party tensions of the first Chen term, the convergent pattern
on the TongDu spectrum did actually continue. In Chen's inaugural speech he made
his 'five noes' declaration. In other words, so long as the PRC did not use military
force against Taiwan, he would not declare Taiwan independence, would not support
changing the national title of the Republic of China, would not push for the inclusion of Lee Teng-hui's 'state-to-state' description in the ROC Constitution, would
not promote an island-wide referendum on the island's status, and would not abolish
the National Unification Council (NUC) or the NUG.[19] This was the first time that
the DPP had made such explicit declarations on moderating its cross-Strait positions.
Throughout the first Chen administration, he did stick to these pledges and generally
steered clear of TongDu in election campaigns. In 2000, DPP chairman Frank Hsieh
went even further than Chen's 'five noes' in his remark that the DPP does not rule
out unification as an option and that the party's current goal is to defend Taiwan's
status quo.[20] On occasion, Chen did make controversial statements, such as arguing
that there is 'one country on either side' of the Taiwan Strait and Taiwan should 'go
its own way'.[21] Nevertheless, the general DPP trend was moderate, exemplified by
the DPP's decision in 2001 to elevate the Resolution Regarding Taiwan's Future to
the same level as the TIC in the party charter.[22]

After 2000, the new KMT chair, Lien Chan, did make some initial attempts to
reposition the party to the centre right on TongDu. Lien dropped references to the
'special state-to-state' formula and floated a proposal for a confederacy model for
cross-Strait relations in 2001.[23] In addition, 'one China' and the '1992 consensus'
were again stressed. However, there was still some distance between the KMT and
the pro-unification New Party (NP). In 2001 the head of the KMT Mainland Affairs

Department stated that the KMT tried to steer clear of unification because, 'We know the Taiwan public is afraid of unification'.[24] By 2003 the gap on TongDu between the parties once again narrowed, as the KMT ceased stressing 'one China'. In the run-up to the 2004 presidential election, KMT vice chairman Wang Jin-ping even refused to rule out Taiwan independence as a possible future option.[25] Chairman Lien Chan took a slightly more centrist stance by commenting that, 'We are opposed to the ideas of immediate independence; we also oppose immediate unification'.[26] Unlike in 1996 and 2000, the KMT refrained from using the anti-Taiwan independence terror equation in the 2004 presidential campaign. In a mark of convergence, the KMT even allowed a referendum bill to be passed in late 2003, despite the fact that many view referendums as a component of Taiwan independence.[27]

The assassination attempt on Chen on the eve of the 2004 presidential election meant that his narrow victory was highly controversial. The KMT refused to recognize the legitimacy of the result, claiming electoral fraud and that Chen had staged the assassination attempt as a stunt to win voter sympathies. Nevertheless, Chen began his second term on a moderate note. In his 2004 inaugural address, Chen reiterated his 'five noes' pledge and called for establishing a cross-party 'Committee for Cross-Strait Peace and Development', to draft the 'Guidelines for Cross-Strait Peace and Development'.[28] Chen also talked of constitutional re-engineering rather than a new constitution. A cross-party 'Constitutional Reform Committee' was proposed to draw up the reform proposals and Chen explained that, 'consensus has yet to be reached on issues related to national sovereignty, territory and the subject of unification/independence: therefore, let me explicitly propose that these particular issues be excluded from the present constitutional re-engineering project.'[29] However, the high levels of inter-party hostility following the contested presidential election meant the KMT ignored Chen's call for a consensus-seeking conference along the lines of the 1996 National Development Conference. In early 2005, Chen also infuriated Taiwan independence extremists by signing a ten-point agreement with People First Party (PFP) leader James Soong that reiterated support for the ROC and pursuit for constitutional revision rather than a new constitution.[30]

Considering the inter-party tensions, it is quite remarkable that the next phase of constitutional reform received the support of all five relevant parties in the summer of 2004 to pass the Legislative Yuan, and in 2005 the KMT and DPP cooperated to see these reforms through the final National Assembly. This set of reforms was focused on the electoral system, replacing the multiple-member district system with a single-member district two-vote system and halving the number of legislators.

Nevertheless, after the above reforms were achieved, the parties returned to polarization on the constitution issue. A number of constitutional proposals that came out of the pan-Green camp were all roundly condemned or ignored by the KMT. Chen proposed a 'second round of constitutional reforms', in which he hoped civic groups would take the lead in drafting and promoting the creation of a new constitution. However, by attempting to bypass the KMT-dominated Legislative Yuan, such projects were doomed to failure, as constitutional changes require a three-quarters majority. The DPP's repeated linking of constitutional reform with elections and identity issues backfired, as after Ma became KMT chairman the KMT took a position opposed to any further constitutional changes; even technical revisions were ruled out.[31]

It was not until the final two years of Chen's second term that we saw a more consistent DPP move away from the centre ground on TongDu. Firstly, in January 2006, Chen Shui-bian raised the idea of scrapping the NUG and NUC.[32] This created a political storm, as such a move meant breaking one of Chen's 'five noes' pledges. Finally, on 27 February, Chen announced that the NUG would cease to apply and NUC cease to function.[33] Although the play with words was meant to appease the US, in reality both the NUG and NUC were scrapped.

Despite the storm created by Chen's abolition of the NUC and NUG, the move was more symbolic than substantive, as they had already been marginalized during Lee's second term and ceased to function or apply as soon as Chen came to office in 2000. On 4 March 2007 Chen made his most comprehensive repudiation of the 'five noes' when he declared that 'Taiwan wants independence, wants name rectification, wants a new Constitution and development'.[34] Even tougher rhetoric was employed by the DPP party chairman, Yu Hsi-kun, who stated that if he won the presidential election, he would no longer accept the 'five noes' pledge.[35]

The KMT's critical move away from the centre on TongDu came in the immediate aftermath of China's passing of its Anti-Secession Law (ASL) in February 2005, a law which formalized the threat to use force against Taiwan if it crossed certain red lines. This was an opportunity for cross-party unity in the face of the China threat, something that Taiwan did achieve for much of the Lee presidency. Although a number of KMT leaders, including Ma Ying-jeou, did openly attack the ASL, the Blue camp boycotted the one million-strong protest march against the ASL on 26 March 2005.[36] Undoubtedly, the historic visit by KMT chairman Lien Chan to China in April 2005 did help to reduce cross-Strait tensions, but it had a divisive impact on Taiwan. Lien's departure from Chiang Kai-shek International Airport for China saw the worst scenes of political violence between rival party supporters since the early 1990s.[37] Lien's promotion of the 'One China' principle, failure to mention the ROC or to condemn the ASL and his pledge to cooperate with the CCP against Taiwan independence meant that the KMT was moving even further to the right than in the early 1990s. The KMT had been fostering closer ties with the CCP since Chen's first term. However, Lien's trip was the first time any of Taiwan's major parties had held face-to-face meetings with leading Chinese government and party officials. Not only did the visit undermine the elected DPP government but it also went against the letter of the KMT-era NUG, which stipulated that official negotiations should only take place after the ending of the state of hostility.[38]

After Ma Ying-jeou replaced Lien Chan as KMT chairman in the summer of 2005, the party continued its rightward direction. Ma pledged to uphold the agreements that Lien reached in the PRC and gave Lien a free hand to continue improving cross-Strait ties.[39] To appeal to floating voters, Ma issued a newspaper ad in the *Liberty Times* to explain that independence could be an option for Taiwan, though he later clarified that it was not an option for the KMT.[40] Instead, Ma made increasingly pro-unification statements. In a December 2005 interview with *Newsweek* magazine, Ma argued that 'For our party, the eventual goal is unification'.[41] Under Ma, the KMT also revived its support and emphasis of the NUG and the 'One China principle'. During Ma's UK tour in 2006, he called for a return to the '1992 consensus' of 'One China, different interpretations'. At the same time, the KMT's deputy party whip Tsai Chin-lung called for a return to the NUG and NUC, calling them 'a safety valve in the often tense relations between Taiwan and China'.[42] In response to Chen's abolition of the NUG and NUC, Ting Shou-chung, a senior KMT legislator, even attempted to initiate a recall vote to punish Chen for taking Taiwan to the 'brink of war'.[43] In short, by the summer of 2007 the leaders of both main parties had dragged their parties to their most polarized positions on TongDu since the early 1990s.

Analysis of survey data in Table 4.1 can also offer some support for the trend towards party polarization on the TongDu issue. The survey question asks respondents to place themselves and the main parties on an issue spectrum in which the fastest independence equals 0, maintaining the status quo is 5, and immediate unification is 10. As with the qualitative review of party movement, the public viewed the main parties as moving towards the centre during the 1990s through to 2000, then the parties are seen as diverging through to 2008. The table also shows how, unlike in the 1990s when the KMT remained close to the median voter, the gap between the public and the main parties on TongDu has widened considerably since 2000. In other words, the polarization of parties has taken them out of step from median public opinion, which has remained close to the centre since the mid-1990s.

TABLE 4.1 Party image survey on the Taiwan independence versus Chinese unification spectrum

	1992	1994	1996	1998	2000	2001	2002	2004	2008
Public	7.0	5.9	5.1	5.0	5.3	5.1	4.7	4.7	4.6
KMT	8.0	6.8	6.1	6.5	6.4	7.2	7.2	7.4	7.3
DPP	2.0	3.0	2.0	2.3	3.2	2.6	2.4	2.2	1.9
NP		6.5	6.5	7.2	7.2	7.6	7.5		
PFP					7.0	7.2	7.5	7.3	7.2
TSU						2.6	2.0	1.8	2.6

Source: Figures for 1992–2001: Fell, *Party Politics in Taiwan*, 94. Figures for 2002–4 supplied by Professor Wu Chung-li, Academia Sinica, Institute of Political Science. Figures for 2008 from *Taiwan Election and Democratization Study, 2008 (TEDS 2008L): Legislative Elections, Final Report* (2008).

Notes:
a   This table shows where respondents place themselves and the main political parties on an issue spectrum in which the fastest independence equals 0, maintaining the status quo is 5, and immediate unification is 10.
b   The 2002 survey only covered Taipei and Kaohsiung City, so these figures represent the average placement for these two cities.

Party movement on Taiwan versus Chinese identity

We see a similar pattern of convergence and more recently polarization on the Taiwan versus Chinese identity spectrum. The far left of this spectrum is a form of exclusive Taiwanese identity that incorporates anti-Mainlander appeals and the tragic Taiwan appeals, the centre left includes more inclusive Taiwanese appeals, such as the 'New Taiwanese', the centre is dual identity, the centre right is ROC identity and the far right is greater Chinese nationalism.[44]

In 1991 the parties made quite contrasting identity appeals during the first full democratic multiparty election. The DPP stressed an exclusive Taiwanese identity, with anti-Mainlander attacks focusing on Premier Hau Pei-tsun, and giving heavy emphasis to the tragic Taiwan appeals such as 'White Terror' and the February 28 Incident. In contrast, the KMT still used the Chinese nationalist symbol Chiang Kai-shek in its ads and made Mandarin its primary language of political communication. However, in the 1990s the two parties moved closer on the symbolic dimensions of identity. Chinese nationalist symbols such as Chiang Kai-shek and Sun Yat-sen were dropped from the KMT's ads, and the KMT began to actively compete with the DPP over ownership of Taiwan identity. Examples of this new project include the increasing use of maps of Taiwan in KMT political advertising and Lee Teng-hui's 'New Taiwanese' discourse in 1998.[45] The DPP also adjusted its identity message from the mid-1990s, reducing use of the tragic Taiwan and anti-Mainlander appeals. By the end of the Lee Teng-hui era, there appeared little difference on questions of identification. This was highlighted in the controversy over the 'Getting to Know Taiwan' textbooks in 1997. Both the KMT and DPP were supportive of these new junior high school texts which were designed to tackle the long-term lack of coverage of Taiwan in the society, history and geography curriculum.[46]

Under the DPP, Taiwan saw a continuation and acceleration of the Taiwan consciousness policies begun by Lee Teng-hui. The Chen government was regularly denounced as promoting desinification policies. According to Chang Bi-yu, the aim of DPP's cultural policies was to 'reduce the Chinese claim on Taiwanese culture and political ownership'.[47] Nevertheless, the Taiwan identity DPP rhetoric was far greater than the actual policy implementation, thus claims of desinification were exaggerated. A good example is in language policy, where, though native language education was introduced to primary schools, it has only amounted to a couple of hours' conversation class per week and is not a language of instruction for other subjects. As Henning Klöter argues, 'Mandarin remains more equal'.[48]

In a number of other identity-related policies the DPP continued where the Lee administration left off. In the late 1990s, the KMT had cancelled the national holiday for Chiang Kai-shek's birthday; Chen did the same for Sun Yat-sen's birthday.[49] Official commemorative activities for the February 28 Incident began under Lee, and under Chen February 28 became arguably the primary national holiday, eclipsing Double Tenth National Day. Similarly, just as Lee began the practice of using the ROC and Taiwan interchangeably, Chen followed suit. The difference is that under Chen the balance was stacked heavily on the side of Taiwan. Thus in his 2000 inaugural speech he referred to Taiwan 33 times and the ROC only nine times.

The DPP was often accused of Hokklo chauvinism and stirring up ethnic tensions. For instance, Chao Chien-min talks of a process of 'Hokkloization'.[50] In the first term, the DPP had a mixed record in this area. It undoubtedly did reach out to certain minority groups, such as Hakkas and aboriginals. There was a large increase in the number of Hakka cultural centres, creation of Hakka TV and radio stations, and inclusion of Hakka as an option in the native language education project. Nevertheless, one group that was excluded from this project was the Mainlanders. Mainlanders were largely overlooked in the selection of cabinet ministers in the national government. While Mainlanders made up almost half of cabinet ministers in 1993, they accounted for just 5 per cent or only two cabinet members in 2001.[51] The DPP also fell back on anti-Mainlander appeals in some campaigns. For instance, Chen cast doubt on Mainlander Ma Ying-jeou's loyalty to Taiwan by referring to him as having 'athlete's foot' ('Hong Kong foot' in Chinese).[52] On the eve of the 2004 presidential election, the DPP organized the 'Hand in Hand' rally, in which citizens created a human chain from the far north to the far south of the island. For the DPP this was meant to be an inclusive multi-ethnic event to show a united front against the PRC missile threat; however, by holding the event on February 28, it was perceived by many Mainlanders as further proof of Chen playing the divisive ethnic card.

In 2000 and 2001, the KMT employed a far stronger Chinese identity message than it had during the latter part of the Lee Teng-hui era. After a long absence, Chiang Ching-kuo and Sun Yat-sen returned to KMT election ads. In the 2001 legislative elections, the KMT used old TV footage of Chiang Ching-kuo in its TV ads.[53] The KMT also gave greater importance to ROC nationalist rituals such as the pilgrimage to the Martyrs Shrine.[54] However, by the time of the 2004 presidential campaign, the KMT was once again competing for ownership of Taiwan identity. The most consistently used KMT slogan in the campaign was 'Change the President, Save Taiwan'.[55] Similarly, in the climax of the campaign, pan-Blue presidential candidates Lien Chan and James Soong kissed the ground to show their love for Taiwan.[56] However, by boycotting the 'Hand-in-Hand' rally, the KMT lost an opportunity to promote ethnic reconciliation. Similarly, the focus on savage personal attacks, such as likening Chen to figures such as Saddam Hussein, Bin Laden and Hitler was widely perceived among Taiwanese as playing the divisive ethnic card.[57]

In sum, by the end of the first Chen term, both the KMT and DPP had shown mixed trends in their treatment of identity issues. Nevertheless, they were further apart than they had been in the final years of the Lee Teng-hui era. In the second Chen term, the parties projected similar mixed identity messages but continued to drift apart.

The DPP began its second term in a relatively conciliatory manner. In Chen's 2004 inaugural speech, he called for ethnic reconciliation of all groups in the 'New Taiwan Family'.[58] This was followed up by the DPP's passing of its 'Multi-Cultural Resolution', which was a reworking of Lee's inclusive 'New Taiwanese' discourse. It attempts to incorporate all ethnic groups, including Mainlanders into the Taiwan consciousness project. It calls for mutual toleration of ROC or Taiwan identities, an acceptance that all ethnic groups are the masters of Taiwan, that all ethnic group languages are Taiwanese languages, ethnic harmony and, in place of previous assimilation policies, an acceptance of Taiwan as a diverse multicultural state.[59]

Despite the inclusive message contained in this resolution, the DPP's reputation for promoting exclusive Taiwan identity and desinification was actually reinforced in Chen's second term. Under Education Minister Tu Cheng-sheng, principles previously employed in the 'Getting to Know Taiwan' textbooks were extended to the senior high school history curriculum. The new Taiwan-centric approach involved separating Taiwan history from Chinese history in a course titled 'Domestic History', and placing the study of China post-1500 (including the ROC until 1949) in the course on 'Modern World History'.[60]

In the second term, the DPP first showed signs of moving away from its moderate position on symbolic identity issues in election campaigns when it began echoing the Taiwan Solidarity Union's (TSU) call for name rectification in December 2004. At an election rally, Chen called for the names of all government agencies to be changed from China to Taiwan in two years. However, it appeared that this was just a temporary shift, as soon after the election, the new Premier Frank Hsieh took a more cautious approach to name rectification in January 2005.[61] In the run-up to the 2005 National Assembly elections, Chen's speeches and DPP election ads cast doubts on the loyalty of the KMT to Taiwan. These were once again perceived as inciting ethnic tensions.[62] It was not until 2007 that the DPP actually began implementing name changes of government-owned enterprises. In February 2007 Chen's administration succeeded in changing the company names of Chunghwa Post and Chinese Petroleum Corporation to Taiwan Post and Taiwan CPC Corporation respectively.[63] In a highly symbolic move, the first postage stamp in which the ROC was replaced with Taiwan (in English and Chinese) showed the February 28 Incident Memorial Museum.[64]

The DPP's more exclusive Taiwan identity message was accelerated in 2006–7 with the campaign against the cult of Chiang Kai-shek. Although the DPP framed such moves as part of democratization and transitional justice, in some circles it was perceived as an attack on the Mainlander community. The gradual removal of Chiang Kai-shek statues and portraits had already begun quietly under Lee Teng-hui and had continued during Chen's first term. In the first step Chiang Kai-shek International Airport was renamed Taiwan Taoyuan International Airport in September 2006.[65] The anti-Chiang campaign continued into 2007 with the removal of the huge Chiang statue from the Kaohsiung Culture Centre and the Ministry of Defense pledge to remove all Chiang statues from its bases. In Taipei the central government also renamed Chiang Kai-shek Memorial Hall into Taiwan Democracy Memorial Hall.[66]

The Taiwan identity policies of the DPP since 2000 show a high degree of continuity with those practised under Lee's KMT in the 1990s. The sense of polarization is exacerbated by the hugely different reaction to these moves from the KMT. The KMT reacted to the continued Taiwanization of the education system in a similar manner to that of the NP in the late 1990s. Pan–Blue legislators' questioning of Minister Tu often verged on hysteria, with wild accusations such as 'involvement in a desinification conspiracy'.[67] During Lien Chan's speech at Beijing University, he expressed the Blue's perception of DPP desinification, arguing that things had got so bad that parents were now forced to take their own initiative to 'allow young people to receive Chinese culture'.[68]

The KMT also took a sharply different approach to the greater Chinese national-ist symbols. As in Chen's first term, Sun Yat-sen was employed in KMT election communication. On the day after the pan-Blues retained their legislative majority in December 2004, the KMT ran a full-page ad with a portrait of Sun and the slogan, 'Thank you for allowing me to continue to be the Nation's Father'.[69] However, the change in KMT party values was more apparent in its treatment of the Chiang Kai-shek statue debate. The KMT took its most pro-Chiang Kai-shek stance since the early 1990s. The KMT-run Taipei City Government attempted to block the name change of the Chiang Kai-shek Memorial Hall. On 31 March 2007, the KMT even organized a rally to protest against the anti-Chiang campaign, in which demonstrators shouted, 'Long Live Chiang Kai-shek!'[70] KMT leaders repeatedly condemned the anti-Chiang campaign as similar to the Chinese Cultural Revolution and as inciting ethnic tensions.[71] Increasingly, KMT politicians are emphasizing Chiang Kai-shek's contribution to Taiwan rather than his role in the White Terror era. For instance, in April 2007, the party organized a photograph exhibition to mark the anniversary of Chiang's death, titled 'The age of Takeoff. ... Old Chiang and Old Taiwan', which linked Chiang with the Taiwanese economic miracle.[72]

TABLE 4.2 Top ten issues in party election newspaper ads in parliamentary elections

	1990s	Post-2000
1	Political corruption 17.5	Party: positive 25.2
2	Party: positive 17.2	Taiwan nationalism 8.8
3	Uncategorizable/Others 15	Candidate: positive 7.1
4	Government competence 5.7	Taiwan independence: negative 6.8
5	Political stability 5.3	Economic growth and prosperity 6.6
6	Democracy 4.5	Political stability 4.5
7	Diluted Taiwan independence 4.3	Diluted Taiwan independence 4.2
8	Party: negative 4.1	Chinese nationalism 4.2
9	Economic growth and prosperity 4	Pure Taiwan independence 3.2
10	Taiwan independence: negative 3.2	Other parties' lack of government competence 3.2

Notes:

a This table shows the top issues stressed by the main political parties in their newspaper ads in the parliamentary elections of the 1990s, and the post-2000 period.

b The main parties included in the analysis are DPP, KMT and NP for the 1990s and the DPP, KMT, NP, TSU and PFP for post-2000.

c The elections included in this analysis for the 1990s are legislative elections in 1992, 1995 and 1998. The years included for the post-2000 period are 2001 and 2004 legislative elections.

d The figures are the average percentage of issue mentions for each issue category in the 1990s and post-2000 campaigns.

In short, in contrast with the convergence at the centre left of the identity spectrum by the late 1990s, the post-2000 period, in particular the second Chen term, saw the KMT and DPP drifting back towards the far-right and far-left positions that they had occupied in the early 1990s.

Content analysis of party election propaganda before and after 2000 in parliamentary elections offers further support for the view that the political agenda is becoming more focused on identity issues and of party polarization. Table 4.2 shows the most stressed issues in party newspaper election ads in the 1990s and post-2000 era. In the 1990s, there were only two identity-related issue categories in the top ten; in contrast, there were five in the post-2000 period top ten. Moreover, while no identity issue was in the top five in the 1990s, there were two in the post-2000 period. The polarization thesis is supported by the presence of 'Pure Taiwan independence' in the top ten and the high salience of both Chinese and Taiwanese nationalism after 2000.

Party movement on military procurement

The pattern on the question of military procurement differs greatly from the previous two case studies. Military procurement had barely featured in Taiwan's political debate in the 1990s. The DPP did occasionally raise military issues to attack the KMT in the 1990s[72] and the KMT trumpeted its success of buying advanced weaponry such as the F16 fighters from the US and Lafayette warships from France. Instead, generally there was a cross-party consensus that Taiwan needed to buy high-tech military equipment to maintain its defence against China.

The change in this pattern came in the run-up to the 2004 presidential election, as the issue was transformed into a divisive and polarizing one. The extensive arms package the US offered Taiwan in April 2001 was the largest since 1992. Although a number of more extreme pan-Blue politicians such as Ting Shou-chung were critical of aspects of the package, the KMT party centre and leaders were not initially openly opposed to the deal.[74] As Steve Tsang points out, 'the Taiwanese requests were largely drawn up before Chen came to power'.[75] In other words, much of the US package had already been on Taiwan's shopping list when the KMT was still the ruling party. Unlike when Lee was offered the F16 package in 1992, the DPP administration did not immediately put forward a special arms budget to parliament. It is quite likely that such a bill would have received sufficient cross-party support, as the Economic Development Conference of August 2001 proved that there was still scope for consensual policy-making.[76] Instead the DPP administration delayed sending the special arms budget to the Legislative Yuan until May 2004.

The inclusion of an item in the 2004 referendum on whether or not to buy anti-missile weapons to meet the challenge of the growing number of Chinese missiles directed at Taiwan transformed military procurement into a contested partisan issue.[77] It was apparent during the presidential campaign that the former consensus on arms sales had been lost, as during the first presidential debate in 2004 Lien warned of the dangers of creating an arms race with the Mainland.[78] As the pan-Blues had boycotted the referendum (that included the question on anti-missile systems) and

TABLE 4.3 Overall direction of party movement on salient issues in four political eras

	1986–91	1992–2000	2000–4	2004–8
TongDu	Divergent	Convergent	Convergent	Divergent
Taiwan vs. Chinese identity	Divergent	Convergent	Divergent, then convergent	Divergent
Military procurement	Non issue	Minor issue	Minor issue, then divergent	Divergent

the referendum did probably contribute to Chen's narrow victory in 2004, this meant that the issue was highly polarized by the time the arms bill finally reached the Legislative Yuan. At that time, in late spring 2004, the pan-Blues did not recognize the legitimacy of Chen's presidential election, and there were huge anti-Chen demonstrations, a number of which turned violent. This meant that there was little chance of the DPP's special arms bill getting approved at that time.

In the subsequent three years, the main parties continued to diverge on arms procurement. The special arms budget was rejected repeatedly in the Legislative Yuan's KMT-dominated Procedure Committee. Even after Ma replaced Lien as KMT party chair, the parties appeared equally divided. Although Ma and Legislative Yuan speaker Wang Jin-ping publicly agreed to support a revised arms bill, they were unable or unwilling to convince their fellow partisans in the Legislative Yuan to fulfil this pledge. The issue became too polarized to find a compromise, as both camps mobilized their supporters in demonstrations for and against arms procurements.[79] In an incident that highlights the strength of feeling in the pan-Blue camp on the issue, on 21 October 2006, independent legislator Li Ao sprayed tear gas in the Procedure Committee to stop discussion of the arms bill.[80] In short, what had long been a consensual non-partisan issue was transformed in Chen's second term into a polarizing partisan one.

Table 4.3 offers a simplified picture of the overall direction of party movement on the most salient issues in four political eras. As has been argued above, the parties moved from polarized positions at the outset of multiparty politics in the late 1980s into a period of convergence for most of the 1990s. While the initial post-2000 era showed a mixed picture of convergence in some policy areas and divergence in other, the second Chen administration witnessed high levels of polarization across the board.

Explaining divergence

How can we best explain the trend towards partisan divergence since 2004? Taiwan's electoral system, public opinion and the change of status from opposition party to ruling party and vice versa are all often employed to explain party issue positional changes. Although these variables can contribute to our understanding of party change, they cannot offer a satisfactory explanation for why polarization was especially serious in Chen's second term. Electoral systems do tend to have a mechanical effect on party positioning, as single-member district systems encourage parties to use more moderate appeals, while multi-member district elections offer more space for extremists. However, if this was the critical variable, then we would expect to see party convergence rather than the DPP era's polarized politics in the run-up to the new single-member district legislative elections and presidential contests. Public opinion and electoral results also have a constraining effect on the political parties. Lin Chia-long's research showed how the general public has more moderate positions on identity than party elites.[81] In the 1990s, the main parties responded to opinion that was moving towards the centre by moderating their positions. However, public opinion, at least on identity spectrums, has not shown a radical change of direction since 2000, and so cannot explain the KMT's renewed embrace of Chinese identity symbols since 2000.[82] Lastly, undoubtedly, the status of government or opposition party does affect party positions. After becoming the ruling party, the DPP was forced to take a more pragmatic stance on cross-Strait relations. Nevertheless, if this were the decisive variable, we would expect DPP moderation to persist the longer it retained central office, rather than moving back towards 'Pure Taiwan independence' in Chen's second term.

Although the inner-party balance of power framework worked for explaining party change in the 1990s, an adjustment is required for developments in the more complex multiparty environment since 2000. Here I propose a framework in which party position change can be explained as a result of fluctuations in inner-party and inner-bloc balance of power, along with a reactive element whereby parties adjust positions in response to competitors' tactics.

Explaining KMT movement since 2000

Changes in the inner KMT and pan–Blue bloc balance of power were critical in the party's shifting policy positions after 2000. After the defeat in the 2000 presidential election, Lien Chan replaced Lee Teng-hui as KMT party chairman. Under the new leadership, there was a significant shift in the factional balance of power, as the Non-Mainstream Faction grew in strength and the Mainstream Faction, previously led by Lee Teng-hui (now increasingly referred to as the Localized Faction), was weakened by Lee's departure and defections to the TSU.[83] The Non-Mainstream Faction had long taken more pro-unification and pro-Chinese identity stances. In contrast, the Mainstream Faction tended to be more ambiguous on independence and took a more Taiwan-first position. Although Lien had not previously been seen as belonging to the Non-Mainstream Faction, after becoming leader he favoured them in appointments at the party headquarters and in his inner circle of advisors.[84] Within the pan–Blue bloc, the newly formed PFP, located slightly to the right of the KMT on the identity spectrums, represented a far more serious challenge to the KMT than the NP ever had done in the 1990s. While the NP had won seats from the KMT in Northern Taiwan, the PFP appeal was island-wide. The degree that the PFP appeared to be on the verge of replacing the KMT as the most powerful pan–Blue party can be seen from the fact that the PFP's seat share in 2001 reached 20.4 per cent compared to the KMT's 30.2.[85]

These balance of power changes can help explain the KMT's early policy shifts. Lien's promotion of the Confederacy Model in 2001 was his attempt to make a clean break from Lee Teng-hui on TongDu, with his own personal policy initiative. Similarly, the revived interest in 'One China', the '1992 consensus' and Chinese identity symbols was intimately linked to the greater strength of the Non-Mainstream Faction within the KMT itself and also increased competition from the PFP. Former KMT Party Spokesman Huang Hui-chen explained the party's changing approach after 2000 in these terms: 'A group of the KMT's leadership's [Non-Mainstream Faction] ideology is close to the NP type. They have taken control over explaining the KMT's ideological power. They have some distance from localization.'[86] Similarly, the KMT's Lin Yu-hsiang explained the impact of inner-bloc competition from the PFP: 'There is an overlap of KMT and PFP supporters and the PFP is declining in support … therefore, this year the KMT has a new policy, we've arranged all the leading figures to go to the Martyrs Shrine at Yuanshan to pay respects. It's a clear move to attract those voters between the KMT and PFP.'[87]

There was also a reactive element to the initial KMT shift to the right. As the DPP moved towards the centre on TongDu after 2000, the KMT was placed in a dilemma. As political scientist Wu Yu-shan explained, 'If the KMT stays at the centre, it will sound like it is echoing the present government's positions. So the KMT moved to the right.'[88] In other words, for the KMT to remain distinguishable from the more centrist DPP, it returned to some of the Chinese identity appeals that it had abandoned under Lee Teng-hui in the 1990s.

In the second half of Chen's first term, there was a move back towards the centre by the KMT, at least on the identity spectrums. Within the pan-Blue bloc, as the relationship with the PFP became more harmonious and the PFP was seen as less of a threat, appealing to deep Blue voters became less pressing for the KMT. In addition, the KMT's more centrist line in the run-up to the 2004 presidential election may be linked to the increasing influence that the former DPP propaganda chief Chen Wen-chien had on Lien. There was also a reactive element to the changed KMT approach leading up to 2004. Chen's 'one country on either side' comments in 2002 made the DPP appear less centrist, allowing the KMT space to move back towards the centre. In addition, the KMT accepted referendum legislation to contest ownership of the referendum issue and to prevent the DPP from gaining points by accusing the KMT of being anti-democratic.

In Chen's second term, the inner-party and pan-Blue bloc balance of power and the DPP polarizing moves pushed the KMT away from the centre again. The trends in KMT factional balance of power of the first Chen term continued into his second. Under Lien Chan and then Ma as party chairman, the position of the Localized Faction continued to weaken. This was highlighted in Ma Ying-jeou's resounding defeat of Wang Jin-ping in the party chair election in 2005. Although Ma used a different set of advisors from Lien, most would also fall into the category of the Non-Mainstream KMT. The position of the Non-Mainstream was further strengthened by the defection of first NP and then many PFP politicians back to the

KMT after late 2004, as most of these figures had been part of the Non-Mainstream before they left the KMT in the 1990s.

The increased strength of the Non Mainstream Faction and the ideologically more orthodox Chairman Ma all contributed to the more centre-right stance of the KMT. As we saw in the TongDu case, soon after Ma became chairman, the KMT began to speak positively on unification for the first time since the early 1990s. The shift in positions on direct talks was also related to inner-KMT power struggles. By making the trip to China in 2005, Lien was successfully able to leave his mark and retain continued influence on KMT China policy, even after he resigned as party chair.

Despite the decline in the number of PFP legislators, the KMT still relied on the PFP for its overall legislative majority. This meant that the PFP still had black-mail potential against the KMT. For instance, the PFP threatened to ally with the DPP on party assets legislation if the KMT was prepared to allow the arms bill to be approved. Therefore, the KMT was forced to compromise with the PFP's more radical agenda. Although the PFP was declining in support, it remained a relevant party with the potential to split the pan-Blue vote until 2008. Therefore, in order to avoid losing votes to the PFP in the 2004 legislative and 2006 Taipei mayoral elections, the KMT had to take a tough line on arms procurement.

A final internal factor that contributed to the more radical messages coming out of the KMT was its increasing use of primaries for leadership and candidate selection. As party chair and presidential candidate elections both rely on a closed member primary, candidates need to pander to the dark Blue voters rather than floating voters. Thus for instance, Wang Jin-ping and Ma Ying-jeou appealed to Chinese nationalists in the leadership election, making tough statements on ROC sovereignty over the Diaoyutai Islands, and Wang even sailed out to the Islands with a group of legislators.[89]

The DPP's repeated polarizing moves in conjunction with the new power structure within the KMT also pushed the KMT further from the centre. In the 1990s, the KMT and DPP could work together on constitutional reform; however, the DPP's framing of further constitutional reform in terms of Taiwan independence meant that the KMT reached the point that it would no longer even consider necessary technical constitutional reform. By including military procurement in the unilateral referendum in 2004, the DPP polarized a formerly non-partisan issue that the KMT is now no longer able to deal with rationally. We see a similar reactive pattern in the NUG/NUC and Chiang Kai-shek. In all these cases, quiet negotiation could probably have either resolved the issues or at least kept them off the agenda. Since the early 1990s, the KMT had played down the NUG and there was little KMT objection to Chen's refusal to convene the NUC after becoming president. However, by publicly scrapping the NUC/NUG, the KMT was pushed into a position where it had to oppose Chen's unilateral move and thus position itself further to the right.

Explaining DPP movement since 2000

The framework of internal balance of power and reactions to opponents' policy moves can also explain changing DPP policy after 2000. The dominant position that election-orientated leaders and factions had held since the mid-1990s continued well into the post-DPP era. This can account for the relatively moderate stances the DPP took on the core political issues throughout Chen's first term and for much of the second term. The balance of power within the party between moderates and radicals can be seen in which side occupied the critical positions of party chair and the premier. When these offices were held by more extremist DPP figures, the party took more polarizing stances. There were internal constraints on how far the DPP could move away from party ideology due to the strength of ideologically more radical factions. Another constraining factor on convergence was the danger of the TSU siphoning off extremist voters. Prior to 2005, as the DPP was far more success-ful at setting the electoral agenda, it rarely switched positions in response to KMT strategy. However, after the Lien visit to China, a number of KMT policy moves had a polarizing effect on the DPP.

The internal balance of power within the DPP since 2000 is summarized in Table 4.4, showing the politicians occupying party chair and premier. The table also lists the principal polarizing events of those seven years that have been discussed in detail. The most common pattern is one in which the retention of powerful positions by radicals, such as Yu Hsi-kun, tended to elicit more polarizing policy stances from the DPP. For instance, the referendum on military procurement and the first name rectification campaign occurred while Yu was Premier from 2002–4. More recently, the NUC/NUG incidents, anti-Chiang campaign and attacks on the 'five noes' all took place while Yu was DPP party chair from 2006–7. In contrast, the periods of relative calm coincided with periods when the relatively moderate Frank Hsieh held positions of power in 2001 and 2005.

The presence of the TSU to the left of the DPP within the pan-Green bloc had a similar effect to that of the PFP on the KMT. The DPP needed to rely on the TSU for support in parliament and also had to be vigilant against the TSU captur-ing voters supporting independence and with strong Taiwan identity. Therefore, on occasion the DPP shifted back to the far left to hold on to voters in danger of being poached by the TSU. The best example of this was the attempt by the DPP to steal the name rectification issue in the 2004 legislative election.

Lastly, the DPP also reacted to what it viewed as KMT polarizing policy measures. For the DPP, the KMT's 2005 visits to the PRC represent a breaking of a long-standing tacit consensus against party-to-party negotiations with the CCP. These KMT visits to China appeared to be an open alliance with the CCP against the elected Taiwanese government. Therefore, the DPP responded with its own divisive accusations of the KMT selling out Taiwan. Similarly, Chen claimed that it was Ma's decision to reiterate that the KMT's eventual goal was unification that prompted him to abolish the NUG and NUC.

TABLE 4.4 DPP premiers and party chair and polarizing policy moves 2000–7

	2000	2000	2001	2002	2003	2004	2005	2006	2007
Premier	Tang Fei	Chang Chun-hsiung	Chang Chun-hsiung	Yu Hsi-kun	Yu Hsi-kun	You Hsi-kun	Frank Hsieh	Su Chen-chang	Su Chen-chang
Party chair	Lin Yi-hsiung	Frank Hsieh	Frank Hsieh	Chen Shui-bian	Chen Shui-bian	Chen Shui-bian	Su Chen-chang	Yu Hsi-kun	Yu Hsi-kun
Polarizing move		Nuclear power station decision		One country on each side	New constitution and referendum raised	Referendum held and name rectification raised		NUC and NUG scrapped, name rectification implemented, anti-Chiang campaign.	Name rectification implemented, anti-Chiang campaign, attacks on five noes.

Conclusion and prospects for the future

This study has compared the trends in party competition before and after the first change in ruling party in 2000. It is been shown that, while the convergent trends seen in the 1990s continued well into Chen's first term, since 2004 Taiwan has experienced severe partisan polarization. The term 'moderate party differentiation' is no longer appropriate for describing Taiwanese party politics. Instead, we have increasingly seen a pattern of polarized and antagonistic two-party competition. A framework that incorporates a changing inner-party and inner-bloc balance of power along with reactions to opponents' provocative issue strategies has been employed to explain the shift from convergent to divergent party politics.

In the summer of 2007 Taiwan's parties appeared to be at their most polarized state for many years. How does this bode for the future of Taiwanese democracy? It was encouraging to see that primaries were held for party nomination and leadership in both major parties, as these help voters to have a clear idea of where politicians stand on core issues. The winners of both leading parties' presidential nomination processes, Ma Ying-jeou and Frank Hsieh, can be viewed as moderate pragmatists. Both showed signs that they were trying to drag their parties back towards the moderate centre of Taiwanese politics. However, neither had sufficient authority within their own parties to resist the strength of more ideological factions. Therefore, polarizing tactics were employed by both camps in the run-up to the 2008 elections.

The fluctuations in inner-party power struggles are likely to be critical in determining future ideological distance between the main two parties in the Ma Ying-jeou era. On the part of the DPP, the victory of a relative moderate Tsai Ying-wen against more radical rivals in the DPP party chair election in 2008 suggests that the party will take a more centrist path, at least until its next major election test in late 2009. For the KMT, despite the strong Taiwan identity appeals it employed during Ma's presidential campaign, it appears that the Non-Mainstream side of the party has been highly influential in guiding policy since the KMT returned to power. There has been a range of policy moves designed to please this constituency of the party. On identity matters, the new government has renamed the Taiwan Democracy Memorial Hall back to Chiang Kai Shek Memorial Hall. There has also been a number of policy endeavours aimed at improving cross-Strait relations, such as opening regular cross-Strait charter flights, negotiating an Economic Cooperation Framework Agreement, a more low-key UN campaign, and an end to the battle for formal diplomatic allies. In short, the KMT appears to be reverting to its more centre-right stances after winning power.

At the outset of the new KMT era, Taiwan's democracy faces significant challenges but also has opportunities for further consolidation. The fact that many of the most divisive political figures have left the central political stage after 2008 should bode well for more consensual politics. Only time will tell whether the new generation of Taiwanese leaders will be able to make democracy work or will continue the recent destructive and polarizing style of politics.

Notes

1 After Chen Shui-bian's first month in office a survey found 77 per cent of respondents satisfied with his performance. See *TVBS Poll Center*. Available online at http://www.tvbs.com.tw/code/tvbsnews/poll/20010521/20010521.asp (accessed 5 April 2007).

2 This point was made by a number of KMT politicians to the author during interviews in 2001. Key reforms included a complete reregistering of party members and the introduction of a radical new nomination system that incorporated closed member primaries and public opinion polls.

3 Satisfaction with Chen's performance had fallen almost 40 per cent to only 41 per cent. See *TVBS Poll Center*. Available online at http://www.tvbs.com.tw/code/tvbsnews/poll/20010521/20010521.asp (accessed 5 April, 2007).

4 The pan-Blue bloc incorporates the KMT, People First Party (PFP) and the New Party (NP). Blue refers to the main colour on the KMT party flag.

5 In the December 2004 legislative elections the turnout fell to a record low of 59.16 per cent and in the 2005 National Assembly elections the turnout was only 23.35, compared to 76.21 in the 1996 National Assembly contest. See Wu Chung-li, 'Vote Misreporting and Survey Context: The Taiwan Case', *Issues and Studies*, 42, No. 4 (December 2006): 223–39, 229.

6 Shelley Rigger, *Politics in Taiwan: Voting For Democracy* (London: Routledge, 1999), 188–9.

7 Dafydd Fell, *Party Politics in Taiwan* (London: Routledge, 2005), 2.

8 Ibid, 143.

9 Working independently, Joseph Wong also used the medical term to describe the quality of the island's democracy in the volume *Healthy Democracies: Welfare Politics in Taiwan and South Korea* (Ithaca: Cornell University Press, 2004).

10 Fell, *Party Politics in Taiwan*.

11 The term electoral poison was often used by more moderate DPP politicians that the author interviewed in 2001 to refer to radical Taiwan independence.

12 In the DPP party charter, the section on 'Establishing a sovereign, independent Republic of Taiwan' calls for the creation of a new constitution. Available online at http://www.dpp.org.tw/ (accessed 8 April, 2007).

13 Wu Yu-shan, 'Taiwanese Elections and Cross-Strait Relations: Mainland Policy in Flux', *Asian Survey* 39, No. 4 (July–August 1999), 565–87; Fell, *Party Politics in Taiwan*.

14 See *Liberty Times*, 20 November, 1991, 1.

15 These arguments were made in the KMT's 1991 TV ad titled, 'Constitutional Revision Ad'.

16 Jean-Pierre Cabestan, 'A New Constitutional Balance and the Prospect for Constitutional Change in Taiwan', in *Presidential Politics in Taiwan: The Administration of Chen Shui-bian*, Steven Goldstein and Julian Chang, eds (Norwalk, CT: Eastbridge, 2008), 29–48.

17 See DPP website. Available online at http://www.dpp.org.tw/.

18 Cited in Richard Bush, 'Lee Teng-hui and "Separatism"', in *Dangerous Strait: The US-Taiwan-China Crisis*, ed. Nancy Bernkopf Tucker (New York: Columbia University Press, 2006), 70–92, 87. Lee made this comment in a radio interview with Deutsche Velle in July 1999. This statement is generally referred to as the 'special state-to-state relations', but is termed the 'two-state theory' (*liangguo lun*) by his detractors.

19 Biography, 'Term as ROC (Taiwan) President', ROC President website. Available online at http://www.president.gov.tw/en/prog/news_release/document_content.php?id=1105495895&pre_id=1105496225&g_category_number=154&category_number_2=143 (accessed April 6, 2007).

20 *Central News Agency*, 'DPP Does Not Rule Out "Unification" as Option for Taiwan's Future'. Available online at http://taiwansecurity.org/CNA/CNA-090600.htm (accessed April 6, 2007).

21 Lin Chieh-yu, 'Chen Raises Pitch of Anti-China Rhetoric', *Taipei Times*, 4 August, 2002, 1.

22 Joyce Huang, 'DPP Makes Minor Revisions to Stance on Independence', *Taipei Times*, 21 October, 2001, 3.
23 See 'KMT Urges Serious Consideration of Confederation', *Taipei Times*, 16 July, 2001, 3.
24 Chang Jung-kung, interview with author, Taipei, 17 October, 2001.
25 Huang Tai-lin, 'Unification Can Wait', 17 December, 2003, *Taipei Times*, 3.
26 Ibid.
27 Fiona Lu, 'Legislature passes Referendum Law', *Taipei Times*, November 28, 2003, 1.
28 President Chen Shi-bian's Inaugural Speech (2004): Paving the Way for a Sustainable Taiwan. Available online at http://www.president.gov.tw/2_special/2004_520/subject3. html#English (accessed 6 April, 2007).
29 President Chen Shui-bian's Inaugural Speech (2004).
30 Caroline Hong and Huang Tai-lin, 'Chen, Soong Sign 10-point Consensus', 25 February, 2005, *Taipei Times*, 1.
31 Ma made this point in discussions with academics in London, February 2006.
32 Ko Shu-ling, 'Scrap Unification Guidelines, Chen Says', 30 January, 2006, *Taipei Times*, 1.
33 Taipei Representative Office in the UK Press Release, 'President Chen Announces National Unification Council and Guidelines to Cease'. Available online at http://www. roc-taiwan.org/uk/TaiwanUpdate/nsl010306a.htm (accessed 6 April, 2007).
34 *China Post Online* edition, 'Chen Declares Four Wants and One Without', *China Post*. Available online at http://www.chinapost.com.tw/backnews/archives/front/200735 /103826.htm (accessed 7 April, 2007).
35 Radio Interview on Radio Taiwan International April 3, 2007. Transcript available online at http://www.rti.org.tw/RtiBroad/RtiBroadContent.aspx?bid=10&cid=34175 (accessed 7 April, 2007).
36 Caroline Hong, 'Blue Camp Calls Rally a Waste', *Taipei Times*, 27 March, 2005, 5.
37 Ko Shu-ling, 'Journey of Peace Starts Violently', *Taipei Times*, 27 April, 2005, 1.
38 The text of the NUG is available online at http://www.mac.gov.tw/big5/rpir/2nda_3. htm (accessed 7 April, 2007).
39 Since leaving the KMT headquarters Lien has continued making visits to China. During Ma's visit to London in February 2006, Ma reaffirmed his support of the agreements that Lien had struck with the PRC.
40 Mo Yan-chih, 'KMT Against Independence: Ma', *Taipei Times*, January 28, 2007, 1.
41 *Newsweek International Edition*, 'Conditions Aren't Right'. Available online at http://www. msnbc.msn.com/id/10511672/site/newsweek/ (accessed 7 April, 2007).
42 *Taipei Times*, 'Ma Tells China to Dismantle Missiles', *Taipei Times*, 13 February, 2006, 3.
43 Mo Yan-chih, 'Soong, Ma divided on recalling Chen', *Taipei Times*, 27 May, 2006, 1.
44 For the detailed list of the sub-issues included in each zone of this spectrum see Fell, *Party Politics in Taiwan*, 88.
45 For an example of the rising use of Taiwan maps in KMT ads see KMT ad, *China Times*, 12 March, 1996, 20; For details of Lee's famous New Taiwanese speech see Stephane Corcuff, 'Symbolic Dimensions of Democratization and the Transition of National Identity under Lee Teng-hui', in *Memories of the Future*, ed. Stephane Corcuff (Armonk: M. E Sharpe, 2002), 73–101, 87.
46 See Stephane Corcuff, 'History Textbooks, Identity Politics, and Ethnic Introspection in Taiwan', in *History Education and National Identity in East Asia*, ed. Edward Vickers and Alisa Jones (London, Routledge, 2005), 133–69.
47 Chang Bi-yu, 'Constructing the Motherland: Culture and the State since the 1990s', in *What has Changed? Taiwan Before and After the Change in Ruling Parties*, ed. Dafydd Fell, Chang Bi-yu and Henning Klöter (Harrasowitz, 2006), 187–206, 203.
48 Henning Klöter, 'Mandarin Remains More Equal: Changes and Continuities in Taiwan's Language Policy', in *What has Changed? Taiwan Before and After the Change in Ruling Parties*, ed. Dafydd Fell, Chang Bi-yu and Henning Klöter (Harrassowitz, 2006), 207–24.
49 See Chang, 201.

50 See Chao Chien-min, 'Reformation of a Nation: Taiwan's Mainland China Policy after the 2004 Presidential Election', paper presented at the 33rd Sino-American Conference on Contemporary China, 27–28 May 2004, Taipei, Taiwan, 8.

51 See Chao Chien-min, 'Reformation of a Nation: Taiwan's Mainland China Policy after the 2004 Presidential Election', paper presented at the 33rd Sino-American Conference on Contemporary China, May 27–28 May 2004, Taipei, Taiwan, 8.

52 Chao, 17.

53 Yi Nai-ching, 'KMT Propaganda Changes to Playing the Chiang Ching-kuo Card', *China Times*, 22 May 2001.

54 Pointed out to the author by veteran KMT politician Lin Yu-hsiang, Taipei, October 4, 2001.

55 KMT ad, *Liberty Times*, 9 March, 2004, 9.

56 *China Times*, 15 March, 2004, A5.

57 See the now infamous KMT ad likening Chen to Hitler at *Liberty Times*, March 12, 2004, 8.

58 President Chen Shui-bian's Inaugural Speech (2004). Available online at http://www.president.gov.tw/ (accessed April 8, 2007).

59 See DPP website. Available online at http://www.DPP.org.tw/ (accessed 8 April, 2007).

60 See Chang, 200.

61 *Taipei Times* Staff Reporter, 'Hsieh offers KMT, China Peace Pipe', January 29, 2005, *Taipei Times*, 1.

62 Ho Po-wen and Hsiao Hsi-chin, 'In Response to Chen's Accusation of an Alliance with the CCP Against Taiwan Independence, the Lien Camp Says Don't Paint us Red', *China Times*, 9 May, 2005, A4.

63 Shih Hsiu-chuan, 'Chen Pushes Corporate Name-Change', *Taipei Times*, 9 February, 2007, 3.

64 See *Taiwan Post* website. Available online at http://www.post.gov.tw/post/internet/w_stamphouse/stamphouse_eng.htm (accessed 7 April, 2007).

65 Jimmy Chuang, 'Chiang Kai-shek Airport Enters Dustbin of History', *Taipei Times*, 7 September, 2006, 1.

66 Flora Wang, Rich Chang and Shih Hsiu-chuan, 'CKS Statues' Removal Nears Completion', *Taipei Times*, 6 February, 2007, 1. The choice of Taiwan Democracy Memorial Hall is an odd one, seeming to imply that democracy is something Taiwan has already lost.

67 Peter Huang, 'Altered Map Caused Silly Legislative Encounter', *Taipei Times*, 6 June, 2008, 8.

68 *United Daily News*, 'Lien Chan's Question and Answer Session at Beijing University', 29 April, 2005.

69 KMT ad, *China Times*, 13 December, A11.

70 Mo Yan-chih, 'Thousands Protest Anti-Chiang Campaign', *Taipei Times*, 1 April, 2007, 3.

71 For instance, KMT legislator Shuai Hua-min made this argument, see Rich Chang, 'KMT Statue Proposal Generates Uproar', *Taipei Times*, 21 March, 2006, 1.

72 See KMT website. Available online at http://www.kmt.org.tw/category_3/category 3_1_n.asp?sn=502 (accessed 8 April, 2007).

73 In one 1992 DPP TV ad the talking head jokes that the Indigenous Defense Fighter (IDF) planes should be renamed 'I don't fly'. Also the DPP repeatedly accused the high level KMT figures of receiving kickbacks from high profile defence procurement contracts, for instance, surrounding the Lafayette warship deal.

74 For Lee Ching-hua's criticism see Brian Hsu, 'Ex-Navy Chiefs Object to Plans to Purchase Kidds', *Taipei Times*, 26 April, 2001, 3.

75 Steve Tsang, 'Taiwan's Changing Security Environment', in *Presidential Politics in Taiwan: The Administration of Chen Shui-bian*, Steven Goldstein and Julian Chang, eds (Norwalk, CT: Eastbridge, 2008), 259–88, 265.

76 Joyce Huang, 'KMT to Get Rolling on Cross-Party Meeting on EDAC', *Taipei Times*, 29 August, 2001, 2.

77 The full question asked voters, 'The people of Taiwan demand that the Taiwan Strait issue be resolved through peaceful means. Should Mainland China refuse to withdraw

the missiles it has targeted at Taiwan and to openly renounce the use of force against us, would you agree that the Government should acquire more advanced anti-missile weapons to strengthen Taiwan's self-defense capabilities?'

78 *China Times*, 22 February, 2004, A5.
79 Lin Chieh-yu, 'Thousands Protest Against Arms Deal', *Taipei Times*, 26 September, 2004, 3.
80 Shih Hsiu-chuan, 'Li Ao Gasses Legislative Meeting', *Taipei Times*, 25 October, 2006, 1.
81 Lin found far greater support for Taiwan independence among political elites than was found in mass surveys. See Lin Chia-long, 'Paths to Democracy: Taiwan in Comparative Perspective', (PhD Dissertation, Yale University, New Haven, 1998), 508.
82 In response to the question of self-identification as Chinese, Taiwanese or both, National Chengchi University's Election Study Centre surveys show a decline in Chinese self-identification from 13.1 per cent in June 2000 to 6.2 per cent in June 2006. See 'Changes in Taiwanese/Chinese Identity of Taiwanese as Tracked in Surveys by the Election Study Center (NCCU): 1992–2006'. Available online at http://esc.nccu.edu.tw/eng/data/data03-2.htm (accessed 10 April, 2007).
83 The terms Mainstream and Non-Mainstream Faction have ceased to be fashionable among political analysts, but they are useful for explaining change and continuity in the KMT's internal power structure before and after 2000.
84 During interviews in 2001 a number of KMT politicians claimed that Lien's inner circle included Yu Mu-ming, Chao Shao-kang and Kuan Chung. All were once key figures in the Non-Mainstream KMT. The first two were by 2001 leading members of the NP, while Kuan had been marginalized in the KMT since 1989.
85 In contrast, even at the NP's peak its seat share was only 12.8 per cent compared to the KMT's 51.8 in 1995.
86 By localization Huang is referring to the Taiwan first rhetoric used by the KMT for much of the 1990s. Cited in Fell, *Party Politics in Taiwan*, 120.
87 Fell, *Party Politics in Taiwan*, 119.
88 Fell, *Party Politics in Taiwan*, 119–20.
89 Mac William Bishop, 'Wang Leads Charge in Diaoyutais Show', *Taipei Times*, 22 June, 2005, 1.

PART II

Economic restructuring in the global context

5

IS THE TAIWAN MODEL OF GROWTH, HUMAN RESOURCE DEVELOPMENT AND EQUITY SUSTAINABLE IN THE TWENTY-FIRST CENTURY?

Anne Booth

The achievement

Taiwan's remarkable progress from the shattered former colony of a defeated power in 1945 to an 'Asian tiger' in the 1960s and 1970s, and a formidable producer and exporter of medium- and high-technology products after 1980, is well known, and has been much studied. Even among the fast-growing Asian economies, Taiwan stands out for its success in achieving both rapid growth and an equitable distribution of income. In the early 1950s, few observers would have predicted this success story. At that time, Taiwan was still struggling to regain levels of per capita output that had been reached in the final phase of the Japanese colonial era, and living standards for many people were well below their pre-war peak. In the last two years of the Pacific War, allied bombing of Taiwan had been intense and it was estimated that, by VJ Day in August 1945, three-quarters of the island's industrial capacity and two-thirds of the power generating capacity had been destroyed. At least half of the railway rolling stock and track was not functioning (Hsing 1971: 149).

Furthermore, the dynamic agricultural export economy, which had been built up under the Japanese mainly to supply Mainland Japan with rice, sugar and other products, was facing severe problems. Rice production had fallen to only 64 per cent of the pre-war peak in 1946, while sugar-cane production was less than 10 per cent of that in 1938–9 (Hsing 1971: 150). Japan was no longer in a position to supply vital inputs such as chemical fertilizers, and neither could it supply a market. Taiwan would have to look for new markets for its agricultural exports or find new export products. After retrocession to Mainland China, a decision which was taken by allied leaders without consulting the Taiwanese people, it was no doubt hoped that Mainland China would provide a market for Taiwanese exports. But the Mainland was in the grip of a savage civil war, and when the Communist forces finally prevailed in 1949, the defeated Republican government fled to Taiwan and re-established the

Republic of China on the island. All trade and investment ties between Taiwan and the Mainland were severed.

After 1950, there was some progress in re-establishing a stable growth trajectory. Inflation was brought under control, and by 1953 it was estimated that real national income per head had returned to the maximum achieved in the 1930s, in spite of the substantial increase in population which had taken place (Hsing 1971: 152). The KMT government had the advantage of not being beholden to powerful vested interests on Taiwan, and was able to push through an effective tenancy reform, which meant that most agricultural land was operated by small owner-cultivators. By 1960, it has been estimated that real per capita GDP (in 2005 prices, adjusted for changes in the terms of trade), was about 11 per cent of that in the US (Table 5.1). This was about the same as in South Korea, although less than in the Philippines, Malaysia or Singapore. The Philippines, which had been an American colony in the first four decades of the twentieth century, recovered from the Japanese occupation and reoccupation by allied forces in the last phase of the Pacific War, and in 1960 was viewed by many as the most promising economy in East and Southeast Asia.

But it was Taiwan, along with South Korea and the city states of Hong Kong and Singapore, which were to achieve the fastest rates of economic growth and structural change in the three decades from 1960 to 1990. By 1996, it was estimated that real per capita GDP in Taiwan had reached 56 per cent of that in the US, and about 66 per cent of that in Japan (Table 5.1). Singapore had achieved even faster growth since the 1960s, although, with virtually no agricultural sector, the Singapore economy was not strictly comparable with that of either Taiwan or South Korea. But there were common factors in the success story of Singapore, Hong Kong, Taiwan and South Korea, which have been much discussed. Most observers agree that a key element of their success was the emergence of new, export-oriented manufacturing industries that rapidly increased their world market share. In the 1960s and 1970s, many of these industries were labour-intensive and used fairly simple production technologies, but increasingly over the 1980s all four economies moved into new, technologically more sophisticated export industries that demanded more skilled labour.

TABLE 5.1 Per capita GDP in Taiwan and South Korea as a percentage of per capita GDP in the US and Japan, 1953–2007*

Year	Taiwan/ USA	South Korea/ USA	Taiwan/ Japan	South Korea/ Japan	China/ USA	Singapore/ USA
1953	8.9	10.6	36.7	43.9	4.0	n.a
1960	10.5	10.8	27.9	28.9	4.5	26.6
1970	16.4	14.3	23.0	20.0	3.9	31.8
1980	27.6	22.0	36.2	28.9	4.4	55.4
1996	55.6	55.2	65.7	65.2	10.2	91.8
2007	61.2	54.5	87.1	77.5	18.2	104.8

Source: Heston, Summers and Aten (2009).

Note:

* 2005 constant prices, adjusted for changes in the terms of trade.

Crucial to this transition were educational policies. It has often been argued that the Japanese colonial government in Taiwan was unusual, at least in comparison with most other colonial territories in East and Southeast Asia, in the emphasis it placed on increasing school enrolments. By the late 1930s, the ratio of enrolments to total population in Taiwan was higher than in any other colony except the Philippines (Booth 2007: 138). But, in contrast to the Philippines, the emphasis in Taiwan was almost entirely on basic education. Secondary and tertiary facilities were limited in number and enrolments were usually dominated by Japanese students. The one university, Taihoku Imperial, was established mainly for research purposes and few Taiwanese students were accepted. The ten specialized middle schools were open to most Japanese boys but only a small number of Taiwanese. This was also true of other high schools for both boys and girls (Kerr 1942: 53; Barclay 1954: 68; Wyndham 1933: 154). As Tsurumi (1984: 308) has pointed out, it was never the intention of the Japanese to replicate their own educational system in Taiwan, but rather to fashion only the 'lower track of the two-track Meiji education system'.

After 1949, the government's first aim was to achieve universal primary education and expand enrolments at higher level in line with national needs. In spite of the achievements under the Japanese, a high proportion of the population in the early 1950s (over 80 per cent) had at most primary education, and the high birth rate meant that more and more children were coming into the education system. To cope with this, government expenditures on education increased rapidly between the early 1950s and the early 1970s and, after a fall in the middle part of the 1970s,

TABLE 5.2 Indicators of educational development, 1952–2005

Year	Expenditures (% of GDP)*	Net enrolments in HE†	Vocational enrolments as % of senior HS	Percentage of population over 15 with:	
				Primary‡	HE
1952	2.0	n.a	47	n.a	n.a
1965	3.3 (2.7)	n.a	40	n.a	n.a
1976	4.0 (3.3)	10.0 (20.8)	66	54.7§	8.4§
1981	5.0 (4.1)	11.5 (21.5)	71	49.6	9.5
1991	6.7 (5.6)	21.0 (23.7)	73	35.1	14.1
1996	6.5 (5.1)	29.1 (21.1)	70	28.0	19.3
2005	6.1 (4.4)	57.4 (40.3)	48	19.8	31.6

Sources: Expenditures/GDP: Ministry of Education (2006: 53); Net enrolments: Ministry of Education (2006: 30, 39); Vocational enrolments: 1952 and 1965, Cheng (1993: 62), 1976 onwards, Ministry of Education (2006: 36); Percentage of the population over 15 by educational attainment: Republic of China (2006: 26).

Notes:
* Figures in brackets refer to public expenditures only.
† Figures in brackets show expenditures on university and college education as a percentage of total expenditures.
‡ Includes no education and incomplete primary.
§ Figures refer to 1978.

increased again until they reached 5.6 per cent of GDP in 1991 (Table 5.2). Numbers of teachers and schools also increased, although class sizes remained high until the 1970s, especially at the primary level (Ministry of Education 2006: 31). Influential technocrats initiated surveys of labour requirements and manpower plans in the late 1950s; an important consequence of these exercises was the emphasis on vocational education at the upper secondary level. By 1970, it was estimated that half the enrolments at the senior high school level were in vocational schools, and this proportion increased until the early 1990s (Table 5.2).

It has been argued that Taiwan's manpower policy and especially the vocational build-up failed in that the actual labour demand, driven by exceptionally rapid economic growth, far outstripped the planners' estimates, and 'the gap between disciplinary training and job requirements remained wide' (Cheng 1993: 62). In the mid-1970s, rates of unemployment among both senior vocational and college/university graduates were fairly high at over 6 per cent (Young 1976: 723). At the same time, the government faced enormous pressures from parents for more places in the academic secondary and tertiary institutions. Enrolment rates in universities grew fast, even in those disciplines where it was far from obvious that there was demand in the labour market. By the early 1980s, analysts were arguing that there was a growing mismatch between what the educational system was providing and what the economy needed. In particular, there appeared to be an oversupply of liberal arts graduates and a lack of graduates in science and technology (Lucas 1982: 218–19). But demand for tertiary places continued to grow, and increasingly private colleges and universities provided places for those students who could not get into the government institutions. By 2005, over 70 per cent of all students enrolled in junior colleges, colleges and universities in Taiwan were in private institutions, and over 67 per cent of graduating students came from private institutions (Ministry of Education 2006: 107, 125). This expansion also explains the very rapid increase in the share of total educational expenditures accounted for by higher education after 1995 (Table 5.2).[1]

Labour market pressures do seem to have led to a very rapid growth in enrolments in technical subjects, including maths, computer sciences and engineering. Taiwan's success in expanding production of electronics, information and communications products since the 1980s has been due in part to government initiatives, including the establishment of science-based industrial parks, which have attracted foreign investors, and also encouraged overseas Taiwanese talent to return from the US to start up businesses in a supportive environment.[2] The government gave generous tax incentives to research and development (R&D) activities and directly subsidized some forms of research in targeted sectors. Tax incentives were also used to promote venture capital activities, while various deregulation measures were used to facilitate the listing of high-technology companies which could draw capital from the booming stock market (Chu 2006: 131). All these measures created more jobs for well-qualified young graduates and also sent a strong signal to students and their parents that the IT sector was where the glamorous and well-paid jobs were likely to be in the future.

The IT sector in Taiwan experienced a severe downturn in 2001, but by then most firms were sufficiently well established to deal with the adverse international conditions. Certainly the indicators of Taiwan's relative standing in international scientific and technological league tables looked very encouraging in the early years of the twenty-first century. Between 1998 and 2007, numbers of researchers almost doubled, and spending on research and development by both government and private institutions increased from 1.9 to 2.6 per cent of GDP (Table 5.3). By 2003, expenditure on research and development by public and private institutions as a percentage of GDP was above the OECD average, and above all other non-OECD countries except Israel (OECD 2005: 21). A higher proportion of Taiwanese businesses was connected to the internet and had a website in 2004: than either Singapore or Hong Kong (OECD 2005: 121). Taiwan also achieved a more rapid growth of numbers of US-registered patents over the 1990s than any other country except South Korea (Chu 2006: Table 4.12). As the chapter by Chu and San in this volume points out, by the early twenty-first century, Taiwan outclassed several of the smaller advanced OECD economies such as Ireland and the Netherlands on a number of educational and technological indicators; only Finland was ahead.

In the Asian context, it has been argued that Taiwan's path towards high-technology industrialization has been different from that pursued in both South Korea and Singapore (Shin and Chu 2006: 58–9). Singapore has chosen the internationalist path, with foreign multinationals accounting for a very high share of total equity in the electronics sector, while South Korea has tended to take the 'techno-nationalist path', with the emphasis on establishing internationally competitive Korean firms in sectors such as semiconductors. Taiwan's 'semi-internationalist' approach has also promoted internationally competitive local firms, while at the same time seeking alliances with foreign multinationals in order to access new technologies. Keller and

TABLE 5.3 Research and development (R&D) indicators and growth in labour productivity

	R&D expenditures (% of GDP)	Numbers of researchers* ('000)	Annual growth of labour productivity
1998	1.9	53.5	3.4
1999	2.0	54.8	4.8
2000	2.0	55.5	4.6
2001	2.1	59.7	-1.0
2002	2.2	69.9	3.9
2003	2.3	75.1	2.2
2004	2.4	81.2	3.9
2005	2.5	88.9	2.6
2006	2.6	95.2	3.1
2007	2.6	103.5	3.9

Source: Republic of China (2007: 125); Republic of China (2009: Tables 2-c, 6-1).

Note:

* Data refer to full time equivalents.

Pauly (2003: 138) have suggested that Taiwan's 'more flexible and pragmatic approach' enabled Taiwan to weather the various storms at the end of the twentieth century more successfully than South Korea. They pointed to Taiwan's success in attracting back skilled engineers and technical staff from the US to work in the rapidly developing semiconductor industry, and argued that the close government-business partnership which built up the semiconductor industry over the 1980s and 1990s would serve Taiwan well in the future.

It has frequently been pointed out that foreign direct investment (FDI) accounted for only a small percentage (less than 2 per cent) of total capital formation in Taiwan during the 1970s and 1980s. This was a much lower percentage than in Hong Kong, Singapore and Malaysia, or indeed in several European economies (Yoshida *et al.* 1994: Table 4.4). In 1986 it was estimated that FDI inflows amounted to only 0.43 per cent of GDP, although this ratio did increase over the 1990s to around 1 per cent of GDP in 1999. But by then outward flows of FDI exceeded inward flows (Aw 2006: 224–6). In the early 1990s, less than 20 per cent of outward investment from Taiwan went to China; most went to other Asian countries, the US and Europe (Chen, Chen and Ku 1995: Table 4.1). The motivations were mixed; much of the FDI flows to other Asian countries represented Taiwanese companies searching for cheaper production platforms. But FDI flows to Europe and the US were in part at least motivated by the need to forge strategic alliances with European and American companies in order to obtain new technologies. There was also an incentive to establish plants in both Europe and the US in order to circumvent trade barriers.

By the early twenty-first century, Mainland China had become the principal recipient of Taiwanese FDI outflows. Much of this outflow has been motivated by the search for low-wage production locations for industries such as electronics, textiles and garments. But, in addition, many Taiwanese firms are seeking to establish themselves in the rapidly growing Chinese market; this includes both IT firms and firms producing plastics, precision instruments, transport equipment and food and beverages. Firms in these sectors accounted for a high proportion of all Taiwanese FDI on the Mainland by 2000 (Kao and Lin 2004: Table 11.5). The impact of this capital outflow on industrial production and employment within Taiwan will be examined further in the following section.

Taken together, the evidence might suggest that Taiwan can face the economic challenges of the twenty-first century with confidence, and can expect sustained economic growth in coming decades. But before making such predictions, we need to examine some warning signals that have become more visible over the past decade. While no single problem is sufficiently serious to derail Taiwan's continued progress, it is not impossible that a combination of economic and political factors could have serious consequences for the Taiwanese economy in coming decades.

Emerging challenges

Slowing economic growth and de-industrialization

While Taiwan has experienced an impressive degree of catch-up with both the US and Japan over the second part of the twentieth century, the gap between Taiwan and the US in terms of real per capita GDP in 2007 remained considerable (Table 5.1). Furthermore, the evidence indicates that the rate of GDP growth in Taiwan is slowing, so that catch-up with both the US and Japan in the future may well be slower than in past decades. Although Taiwan was dealt only a glancing blow by the Asian crisis of 1997–8, growth rates have exceeded 6 per cent per annum in only one year between 1998 and 2008 (Table 5.4). In the decade from 1995 to 2005, GDP grew by around 54 per cent, so the average annual growth rate over the decade from 1995 to 2005 has been slightly above 4 per cent per annum. This is higher than the OECD average, but much slower than what was achieved in the decades between 1960 and 1990. After 1995, growth rates have also slowed, and have become more erratic, in South Korea, Singapore and Hong Kong, as well as in Malaysia, Thailand and Indonesia. While there are different explanations for slowing growth in all these countries, there are also some common factors. The economies that were important exporters of electronics and IT products were all affected by the global slow-down in these sectors in 2001, with Taiwan and Singapore experiencing negative growth (Table 5.4).[3] And all economies have had to compete with China, both in attracting inward FDI, and in competing with Chinese products in export markets of third countries.

The global financial crisis which erupted in 2008 slowed growth in most parts of Asia. In Taiwan GDP growth was only 0.1 per cent in 2008, which was slower than in South Korea or Malaysia (Table 5.4). Estimates indicate that GDP will contract by between 3 to 4 per cent in 2009, which is a more severe contraction than that

TABLE 5.4 Annual average rates of real GDP growth, and growth index: Taiwan and other Asian economies: 1998–2008

Year	Taiwan	Hong Kong	South Korea	Malaysia	Singapore
1998	4.6	−5.5	−6.9	−7.4	−1.4
1999	5.7	4.0	9.5	6.1	7.2
2000	5.8	8.0	8.5	8.7	10.1
2001	−2.2	0.5	4.0	0.5	−2.4
2002	4.6	1.8	7.2	5.4	4.1
2003	3.5	3.0	2.8	5.8	3.8
2004	6.2	8.5	4.6	6.8	9.3
2005	4.2	7.1	4.0	5.3	7.3
2006	4.8	7.0	5.2	5.8	8.4
2007	5.7	6.4	5.1	6.3	7.8
2008	0.1	2.5	2.2	4.6	1.1

Source: Republic of China (2007: 1); Republic of China (2009: 1).

predicted in several other small open Asian economies. The main reason for the 2009 contraction was a steep decline in exports; government stimulus packages appear to have had only modest success in counteracting the sharp fall in export demand. Most analysts predict some recovery in economic growth in 2010, as demand for exports recovers; the Taiwan Institutue for Economic Research (TIER) has predicted growth of 4.2 per cent for the calendar year.[4]

Slower growth since the 1990s also affected employment growth, and growth in labour productivity. Increases in employment were positive between 1997 and 2005, with the exception of 2001, but growth in labour productivity more than halved over these years, falling from 5.4 per cent in 1997 to 2.5 per cent in 2005 (Table 5.3). This suggests that, while open unemployment (at around 4.4 per cent of the labour force in 2004) was still quite modest, much of the employment creation over the decade from the mid-1990s to 2005 was in sectors of the economy where output per worker was relatively low. The growth slow-down in 2008 and negative growth in 2009 has inevitably affected unemployment; the open unemployment rate edged up to six per cent in 2009, although fell slightly in 2010.

Since the 1980s, both agriculture and industry has accounted for a falling proportion of GDP, while the share of the service sector grew to 73 per cent in 2008. There has also been a substantial increase in the share of the labour force in services. As a result, there has been a fall in service sector labour productivity relative to the national average between 1981–5 and 2001–5, although it was still, in 2001, 21 per cent higher than the national average (Table 5.5). There has also been a decline in output per worker in manufacturing, relative to the national average, which indicates that the decline in the share of employment in this sector has not been as rapid as the decline in the share of output.

As in other parts of the OECD world, the decline in the percentage share of manufacturing in GDP and the labour force in Taiwan since the mid-1980s can be explained by both internal and external factors (Baldwin 2006: 15–16). Externally, as Taiwan liberalized its trade, many labour-intensive manufactures which were previously produced locally have been imported, as have a growing number of parts and

TABLE 5.5 Percentage breakdown of GDP and the labour force by sector and relative labour productivities, 1981–5 and 2001–5

Sector	As % of GDP		As % of the labour force		Relative labour productivities	
	1981–5	*2001–5*	*1981–5*	*2001–5*	*1981–5*	*2001–5*
Manufacturing	30.7	23.9	32.9	27.3	93.2	87.7
Services	55.7	69.9	40.0	57.6	139.2	121.2
Other	13.6	6.2	27.1	15.1	50.4	41.0

Source: Republic of China (2006).

Note:

Other includes agriculture, construction, mining and utilities. Relative labour productivities refer to output per worker in each of the sectors as a percentage of average output per worker for the whole economy.

components, from China and other parts of Asia. Internally, as incomes have increased, Taiwanese consumers have tended to spend a higher proportion of their disposable income on non-traded services, including sport and other leisure activities, medical services and education. Prices of these services tend to increase with growing domestic demand, and resources are pulled in to their production from other sectors of the economy. A second internal factor that tends to lead to a decline in employment in manufacturing is increased productivity in manufacturing industry globally, which reduces the number of workers needed to produce a given quantity of output.

But why the slower growth since the early 1990s? Some economists argue that the shift from a manufacturing-based to a service-based economy must lead to a slow-down in GDP growth because services tend to be non-traded, and therefore production is constrained by domestic demand. In the Taiwanese context, slower growth has also been attributed to the slow pace of domestic liberalization, particularly of the financial sector. While the cautious approach to financial reform may well have protected Taiwan from the financial crisis that affected other parts of Asia in 1997–8, it has been argued that in the early twenty-first century, Taiwan has a financial sector which in several respects is still 'out of date' and lagging behind those of the dynamic regional finance hubs such as Singapore and Hong Kong (Wang 2004: 186; Wu 2004: 147). These critics point to a rather opaque regulatory climate, which does not encourage full disclosure of information to outside investors on the part of listed corporations or financial institutions, including banks. While the Taiwan government may have ambitious plans for the country's emergence as a key financial centre in the Asia-Pacific region, there is little evidence that it will be able to compete effectively with the more developed centres in the immediate future.

Rising income inequalities?

It has been argued that, as a result of the hollowing out of manufacturing industry and the increasing role of the service sector, inequalities in earnings and in household income have widened in Taiwan since the 1970s, as indeed has happened in economies such as those of the US and the UK. The official figures confirm this: they show that the ratio of incomes accruing to the top and bottom quintiles in the household income distribution have widened from 4.4 in 1974 to 6.03 in 2004 (Republic of China 2006: 80–1). But these figures relate to households and do not allow for changes over time in household size. An analysis of the household survey data by Schultz (1997: Table 2) has shown that, when inequality is measured in terms of incomes per capita (that is household incomes divided by the numbers in the households), both the Gini coefficients and the variances of logs of income fell slightly between 1976 and 1995.

On the other hand, there is evidence that wage inequality has increased in Taiwan between 1978 and 1996 (Lin and Orazem 2004). This is partly the result of rising returns to college education, especially for the older and more experienced college-educated cohorts, both male and female. Lin and Orazem argued that changing trade patterns have tended to raise labour demand in sectors that use educated labour more intensively, which is what would be expected from trade theory. They also point out that, in the fifteen years from 1981 to 1996, there has been an increase in the share of university-educated workers in traded services and a decline in their participation in production of non-tradables, both goods and services. The finding that wage inequality has risen is not necessarily inconsistent with that of Schultz, that household income inequalities in per capita terms have remained more or less stable. It is possible that changing household composition has cancelled out the effect of greater earnings inequalities, although this might not persist in the future.[5]

Increased reliance on migrant workers

In Taiwan, as in Japan and in most other OECD economies, increased outward flows of FDI have been accompanied by increased inward flows of migrant workers. The upward revaluation of the Taiwanese dollar, together with the increase in real wages that occurred in the latter part of the 1980s, pushed many Taiwanese manufacturers of labour-intensive products to relocate to other parts of Asia. But some industries found it difficult to relocate, and those producing non-tradables (construction, trade, transport, personal and leisure services) were forced to find other means of holding down costs. Increasingly many firms began to employ illegal immigrant labour. There are no reliable estimates for numbers of migrant workers prior to 1991, but they may well have exceeded 100,000 (Tsay and Tsai 2003: 16). In 1992, the government passed the Employment Service Act, which introduced a work permit system. It was stressed that foreign workers were to be imported only to supplement native workers in those sectors of the economy where labour shortages were acute. It was assumed that migrant workers would mainly take the so-called 3-D jobs (demanding, dirty and dangerous), in manufacturing, construction and services. Work permits would only be issued on a temporary basis; the maximum stay was three years. They would not be permitted to bring families or to marry in Taiwan, and would be promptly deported if they committed any crime, however trivial (Lee 2002: 46).

These rather strict conditions were imposed to allay fears that the government was opening the flood gates to large numbers of foreign workers who would be used to hold down the wages and working conditions of local workers. Even so, numbers coming in legally increased rapidly, from under 20,000 in 1992 to 326,500 by 2000 (Tsay and Tsai (2003: 33). These authors suggested that the work permit system did have some effect in curbing outward flow of FDI, as some producers of traded goods decided to keep production in Taiwan and use imported labour. But after 1995, it was clear that 'the major function for the foreign workers in Taiwan was gradually shifting from alleviating the labour shortages in the labour-intensive industries, towards the promotion of the high-tech and rapidly expanding industries' (Lee 2002: 47). In manufacturing industry, many migrant workers were employed to carry out the less skilled jobs in sectors such as electronics and machinery; in addition, many migrant workers, especially women, were recruited to work as maids and carers. This was intended to free up Taiwanese women for work outside the home.

The system of legal work permits has meant that numbers of illegal workers have probably declined, although it is argued that some workers who had worked for three years illegally moved to other employers rather than return home (Lee 2002: 57). A further incentive to migrant workers to return home at the end of their contract was the measure enacted in 1998 that employers could deduct up to 30 per cent of monthly earnings to be placed in a savings account, which workers could only claim back when they were ready to depart. By 2000, the great majority of legal migrant workers in Taiwan came from Thailand, Indonesia and the Philippines, although numbers from Vietnam were growing quite rapidly. By 2002, Indonesian workers, many of them women, were largely concentrated in personal and social services, while Thai workers were mainly in manufacturing and construction. Workers from the Philippines were mainly in manufacturing and services, as were the Vietnamese (Tsay and Tsai 2003: Table 3).[6]

At around 326,500, legal migrants were only around 3.4 per cent of the labour force in Taiwan in 2000, and to the extent that they were occupying jobs that the locals did not want, their presence would not have had a serious impact on either the number of jobs or the wages available to local Taiwanese workers. Nonetheless, the issue of migrant workers featured in the 2000 presidential election with the DPP candidates promising stricter controls. The newly elected DPP government pledged to reduce migrant workers by at least 15,000 per year, and numbers did fall in 2001, although that may partly have been due to the contraction in GDP. Since 2001, numbers appear to have stabilized, in spite of some increase in unemployment. From time to time the local and international press reports describe outbreaks of rioting by guest workers unhappy with their conditions, but the majority seem quite content.[7] The wage differential between migrant and local workers is not very large; certainly there can be little doubt that their wages are much higher than what they could expect to earn at home. Thus demand for work permits from ASEAN countries is likely to grow.

In addition to the legal migrants, there are an unknown number of illegal workers from the Chinese Mainland who are presumably much harder to detect, given their racial and linguistic similarities to the locals. Increased numbers from this source, many of whom probably wish to stay long term, could lead to opposition from both politicians and the broader public. Certainly, increased reliance on migrant workers, whatever their provenance, will create tensions in Taiwanese society of the kind that are already familiar in Western Europe and North America. As an island, it is easier to impose border controls in Taiwan than in other parts of Asia, and migrant workers from countries such as the Philippines and Indonesia are easy to identify in a largely Chinese-speaking society. Thus, imposing strict controls might be feasible. The impact of such controls on Taiwan's longer-term economic development is more controversial, and will be explored in the last part of the chapter.

Education and employment

It was pointed out in the first part of the chapter that Taiwan is well known for having educated 'ahead of demand' and invested heavily in formal schooling at an early stage of the development process. Already by 1980, gross secondary enrolment ratios were around 80 per cent of the secondary age group, which was higher than either Singapore or South Korea, or indeed in several OECD countries. The ratio of tertiary students to population was also much higher than in other parts of East and Southeast Asia (Booth 2003: Table 8.1). Thus, when the currency revaluation of the latter part of the 1980s forced manufacturing industry to move towards higher value-added products, there was a ready supply of skilled workers that manufacturers could draw on.[8] But by the end of the century, the disparities between Taiwan and other high-income Asian countries such as Singapore in terms of educational attainment of the labour force were eroding. In 2001, around 20 per cent of the labour force in Singapore had at most primary education, compared with 17 per cent in Taiwan (Table 5.6). At the other end of the educational spectrum, almost 17 per cent of the Singapore labour force had degree-level qualifications, compared with 12.3 per cent in Taiwan. This change reflected both the improved educational attainment of the Singapore labour force since the 1980s, and the government policy of encouraging highly qualified foreign workers to move to Singapore to work in the financial sector, higher education and research.

There was also some evidence of mismatches between educational attainment in Taiwan and the needs of the labour market. In 2008, unemployment rates were highest for university graduates, and for junior high school graduates (Table 5.7). The proportion of employed workers with tertiary qualifications (both junior college and university) had increased sharply to over 40 per cent in 2008. Demand for tertiary places had increased so much relative to vocational school places that many vocational schools and professional colleges converted themselves into regular high schools and universities. These changes no doubt reflect a perception on the part of students and their parents that old-style vocational skills are in diminishing demand in the rapidly changing labour market, where the need is much more for the kinds of skills required in high-technology industry, and in the service sector. It probably

TABLE 5.6 Employed persons by highest level of education attained

Level of education*	1996		2001	
	Singapore	Taiwan	Singapore	Taiwan
Primary	24.9	23.9	19.9	16.9
Junior H. S.	14.0	19.4	14.2	18.5
Senior H. S.	30.5	8.7	28.0	9.2
Vocational	11.5	25.6	10.4	27.0
Junior college	7.4	12.9	10.6	16.2
University	11.6	9.5	16.9	12.3
Total	100.0	100.0	100.0	100.0

Sources: Ministry of Manpower (2002: Table 1.2); Republic of China (2005: Table 28).

Note:

* The Singapore data refer to all economically active people. Educational levels refer to post-secondary rather than vocational, and diploma rather than junior college.

also reflects a desire on the part of many young Taiwanese to seek jobs in service occupations where working conditions are less onerous and the pay better than in traditional manufacturing.

But as Chu (2004: 115) has argued, these trends have added to the problems of small and medium-size firms in the more traditional industries, which increasingly will have to depend on migrant workers to fill many of the jobs that in the past were taken by vocational school graduates. This reliance will increase as the supply of workers with vocational and technical qualifications falls. In 2008 vocational school graduates still accounted for 27 per cent of the employed labour force, and the lower unemployment rates among these workers than for university graduates might indicate that their skills are still in demand, although it is also likely that they are older workers with considerable work experience (Table 5.7). As they leave the labour force, it is probable that the percentage of workers with vocational training will fall. Since the 1980s, many young Taiwanese progressing to post-secondary education have elected to study engineering, mathematics, natural sciences and medicine; over 40 per cent of tertiary enrolments were in these subjects in 2003–4 (Howe 2006: 227). While this is to some extent the result of government direction, it also reflects perceptions of both parents and students that these disciplines offer the most attractive career paths in a rapidly changing labour market. Whether in the future all these graduates can be absorbed in employment appropriate to their qualifications remains to be seen.

The role of women workers in the Taiwanese economy

Have women been an under-utilized resource in the Taiwanese economy? International comparisons for 2003–4 indicate that, compared with most other East and Southeast Asian economies, female labour force participation rates are rather low in Taiwan, at just over 50 per cent (Table 5.8). This is in spite of the evidence that

TABLE 5.7 Percentage distribution of employed persons by highest level of education attained, and unemployment rates by educational attainment: 1989 and 2008

Level of education	1989		2008	
	Employed	% Unemployed	Employed	% Unemployed
Illiterate	5.6	0.3	0.5	1.1
Primary	29.9	0.6	9.7	2.7
Junior H. S.	19.9	1.6	14.4	4.5
Senior H. S.	8.1	2.5	8.5	4.4
Vocational	21.1	2.4	26.8	4.3
Junior College	8.6	2.3	17.2	3.4
University	6.9	1.9	23.0	4.8
Total	100.0	1.6	100.0	4.1

Sources: Republic of China (2005: Tables 28 and 29); Department of Manpower Planning (2009: Tables 10 and 12).

the share of women aged 15 to 65 who are in the labour force has steadily increased since 1976 (Schultz 1997: 29). The fact that participation rates are still rather low might suggest that women workers have not participated in the labour force as fully as men, at least in the high growth decades of the 1960s to the early 1990s.[9] But it should be noted that by 2003, male participation rates in Taiwan were also quite low by Asian standards. This suggests that young Taiwanese, both male and female now stay in the educational system longer than in many other parts of the region. It is also possible that they retire earlier.

But whatever the situation in the early twenty-first century, it is probably set to change in coming decades. The increased female participation rates mean that the supply of women workers has been growing relative to men over the years from 1978 to 1996; it has also been claimed that the educational attainment of women has also been improving relative to that of men (Lin and Orazem 2004: 297). The rapid growth in women entrants to the labour force since the 1980s can be attributed to higher ages of women at marriage, lower fertility within marriage, the greater availability of service-sector jobs which educated women find congenial, and the greater availability of home help and childcare, much of it supplied by migrant workers.

These factors are likely to continue to encourage more women to enter and stay in the labour force in coming years. Another factor encouraging greater female labour force participation is the continuing improvement in female access to education. It is striking that girls now outnumber boys in both secondary and tertiary education, and that the female enrolment rates at the tertiary level in Taiwan are much higher than in any other country in Asia (Table 5.8). These educated women appear to be able to compete quite successfully in the labour market even in times of economic downturn. The Council of Labour Affairs (a cabinet-level body) reported in March

TABLE 5.8 Labour force participation rates and female enrolment rates at secondary and tertiary levels for Taiwan and other Asian countries, c. 2003

Country	Labour force participation rates		Female enrolment rates	
	Male	Female	Secondary	Tertiary
Taiwan	76.2	51.2	100 (102)	93 (106)
South Korea	79.9	59.7	93 (100)	69 (63)
Hong Kong	85.6	57.7	83 (97)	32 (97)
China	88.8	79.2	73 (100)	17 (81)
Singapore	81.7	54.5	73 (97)	40 (85)
Thailand	89.7	77.7	74 (103)	45 (110)
Malaysia	81.4	51.9	81 (114)	38 (141)
Philippines	82.6	52.0	90 (110)	32 (128)

Sources: Asian Development Bank (2005: 8); Asian Development Bank (2006: Table 2).

Note:
Labour force participation rates for Taiwan are for 2001. For other countries they refer to 2003. Educational enrolment figures refer to 1997 for Singapore, 2003 for Taiwan and Malaysia, 2004 for Hong Kong, China and the Philippines, and 2005 for Thailand and South Korea. Figures in brackets show female enrolment rates as a percentage of male rates.

2010 that female labour force participation rates rose from 46.6 per cent in 2002 to 49.6 per cent in 2009, while male participation rates fell over the same period from 68.2 to 66.4 per cent. The reasons given for these trends was that women tend to be less choosy about the jobs they take up, while many male workers have either retired or been laid off because of the recession.[10]

But, in spite of the obvious improvements in female participation in both higher education and the labour force since the 1970s, it would appear that women are still under-represented in many professional and technical occupations. In 2004, they accounted for around 18 per cent of all R&D personnel (in FTE terms). Although the numbers of women in R&D jobs had increased since 1998, the rate of increase was less than that of male workers, so that their share of total jobs had fallen (Republic of China 2006: 125). Does this reflect discrimination against women in R&D occupations? Or that women graduates do not have the necessary qualifications for these occupations? More research on this issue would seem to be needed.

Towards a knowledge-based economy?

In Taiwan, as in other parts of Asia over the past decade, there has been much talk of creating a knowledge-based economy (KBE), where a large part of national output would be generated in high-technology industry and in the modern service sector, including financial, educational and management services.[11] This reflects the rise in international awareness of the importance of knowledge as 'the central element of competitiveness and the driving force behind long-term economic growth' (Chen 2004: 2). Of particular importance in triggering the international debate was the emergence of the so-called new economy in the US over the 1990s, which led to considerable improvements in both economic growth and labour productivity. It is hardly surprising that economies such as South Korea, Taiwan, Singapore and Malaysia have sought to emulate the American example by encouraging the development of new industries based on information technology, biotechnology, pharmaceuticals, telecommunications and aerospace, as well as knowledge-based services, including financial services.

What proportion of total national product is generated in knowledge-based industries and services? Estimates using the OECD definitions indicate that only around 13 per cent of manufacturing in 2001 was 'knowledge-based' and 23 per cent of services (Chen 2004: 3). These proportions might look quite modest, given the growth of sectors such as computers and chemicals over the past two decades, and given the relatively high spending by both the government and the private sector on research and development. R&D spending increased rapidly in the decade from 1994 to 2004, both in absolute terms and relative to GDP, so that by 2004 it was estimated to be around 2.4 per cent of GDP (Republic of China 2006: 125). While this is lower than in Japan and Korea, or the US and Germany, it is higher than in most other parts of Europe and Asia, and higher than the OECD average. In addition, Taiwan generated a remarkable growth in patent applications in the US; it has been estimated that, in 2000, more patents from Taiwan were registered in the

US than from any other country except Japan and Germany (Yusuf 2002:Table 5; see also Chu 2006:Table 4.12).

On the other hand, it has been argued that most of the patents generated in Taiwan are based on process technology and few were related to basic research. In spite of the large number of patents, Taiwan's 'technology balance of payments' remains negative; the imbalance between receipts and payments was particularly large vis-à-vis the US, the UK and Japan (Chu 2006: 163–4). Critics such as Chu have also pointed out that 'the high-calibre R&D personnel have been concentrated in the non-market, non-competitive academic sector and government agencies' (Chu 2006: 171). In spite of various efforts by the government to sponsor collaboration between university researchers and industry, Chu argued that little has been achieved, and that much of the scientific research in Taiwan has little to do with the needs of industry. While these criticisms are hardly unfamiliar in other parts of the OECD world, they have to be taken seriously in Taiwan, where many of the supposedly 'high tech' export industries such as notebook computers and mobile phones face declining profit margins and much tougher international competition, not least from China.[12] New export industries will have to develop in sectors such as information technology, biotechnology and pharmaceuticals, which will depend on the successful application of research to the development of new products.

Population ageing

Will Taiwanese grow old before they grow rich? Behind the brave rhetoric about creating a knowledge-based economy, based on cutting-edge science and technology, lies the uncomfortable fact that population growth is now very low, and that, given current low levels of fertility, and only modest increases in life expectancy and in-migration, the increase in the size of the population over the next 50 years will be tiny. Indeed, some recent projections indicate that population size in 2050 will be 18.9 million compared with 22.7 million in 2005.[13] The average age of the population is likely to increase rapidly, and the proportion of the population in the prime working age groups will fall. In 2002, 70.5 per cent of the population was in the 15–64 age groups, and only 9 per cent were over 65. It is likely that by 2050 more than 25 per cent of the population will be over 65, and a relatively small proportion will be under the age of 30.

Because population ageing is a relatively new problem for most human societies, the literature in the OECD countries, especially Western Europe and Japan, has tended to focus on the implications for savings and pension provision, as well as the cost of health care for the frail aged. Given the rapid demographic change in China and some other Asian countries, these issues are now attracting attention in Asia as well. It has become widely accepted that, over the decades from 1960 to 2000, the high-growth economies of East and Southeast Asia reaped a 'demographic bonus' in terms of the falling demographic dependency ratio and the growing proportion of the population in the prime age groups (Bloom and Williamson 1998). This meant that numbers in the labour force grew faster than total population. The demographic bonus is inevitably transitory, and in East Asia it will gradually erode over the next 50 years. Not only could the absolute size of the labour force start to decline, but a much higher proportion of the population will be elderly and requiring greater care, either within the extended family or from other sources, both state and private.

A second type of demographic bonus relates to the 'powerful incentive to accumulate assets', which people will experience towards the end of their working life, when facing perhaps 20 years or more of retirement (Lee and Mason 2006: 16). In the East and Southeast Asian context, it has been argued that the combined effects of these two bonuses has accounted for over 40 per cent of growth per capita in the last three decades of the twentieth century. But as the proportion of the population that is producing more than it consumes starts to decline, both forms of the demographic bonus will erode.[14] The effects on total economic growth rates are likely to be adverse, even if workers stay longer in the labour force. Older workers are less capable of hard physical labour, usually prefer to work shorter hours and are probably less intellectually creative, although as life expectancies continue to increase, it is quite possible that many workers will remain active and productive into their 60s and beyond.

Given that growth rates in Taiwan have slowed over the past decade, even while the net contribution of the demographic bonuses is still positive, it seems likely that in future growth rates will slow even further. On the other hand, the costs of supporting an increasing number of elderly people may be less in Taiwan than in Western Europe or Japan. There is evidence that the extended family still acts as a support for the elderly in Taiwan. Mason and Lee (2004: 225) have found that 'those who reached 60 in 1998 were somewhat less likely to live with their adult children than those who reached 60 in 1978, but the cohort trend is quite modest'. To the extent that families still care for their older relations, the burden on government may be less. The ability of families to cope will in turn depend on the availability of home help, much of which will be supplied by migrant workers.

The impact of population ageing on economic growth rates is in part determined by changes in savings behaviour. This has also received empirical investigation in Taiwan. Heller and Symansky (1998: 41) concluded that an ageing population is unlikely to have much effect on savings in Taiwan, South Korea, Hong Kong or Singapore before 2010, but after that the impact will be negative. Just how negative depends on a number of factors including the rate of growth of the economy and exogenous changes in savings behaviour. They cited several studies which produced very different results (Heller and Symansky 1998: Table 5). Deaton and Paxson (1999: 22) also argued that the savings rate in Taiwan will decline after 2010, but 'the effects are modest, and the aggregate household savings rate in 2030 will be only a point or two lower than it is now'. This result does however depend on what assumptions are made about rates of economic growth. The authors caution that if 'Taiwan's growth rate falters, the combination of lower growth and the aging of the baby boom generation is capable of sharply reducing the rate of saving' (Deaton and Paxson 1999: 23). If economic growth does slow, then it is possible that the lower savings rate will adversely affect investment, which in turn may reduce growth rates further, leading to even lower savings and so on.

The end of the developmental state?

Taiwan and South Korea, together with Japan, have long been regarded as the archetypal 'East Asian developmental states', possessing strong technocratic bureaucracies that are insulated from short-term political pressures and able to make decisions that facilitate the achievement of long-term economic goals. Such states are characterized by close cooperation between public and private interests, and heavy investment in both physical and human capital formation. Their authoritarian approach to government means that non-government organizations such as trade unions, environmental and human rights groups, and even religious institutions, are usually not tolerated or are only allowed to operate within narrow limits. Such states are distinguished from Communist regimes by their reliance on the price mechanism to allocate scarce resources and their willingness to give private enterprise space to operate, although state enterprises have historically been important in both Japan and its two former colonies, and at times, all these governments have resorted to non-market means of allocating scarce resources such as foreign exchange and credit.

By the 1990s, it was clear that the 'strong developmental state' model was no longer able to generate rapid economic growth, either in Japan or in Taiwan and South Korea. In Japan the collapse of the bubble economy of the late 1980s caused a long recession, the consequences of which the political and bureaucratic institutions built up over the previous four decades were painfully slow to deal with. In both Taiwan and South Korea, the advent of greater political democracy meant that non-state institutions such as trade unions exercised far more power. Increasingly assertive electorates demanded 'jam today' even at the expense of long-term economic growth. By the early twenty-first century, it was argued in the Taiwan case that the developmental state had 'mutated into something different' (Chu 2006: 147). The Taiwanese state continued to play a crucial role in the economy as the largest, or only, shareholder in many enterprises, as the largest landowner and as a key player in science and technology policy. But it appeared to have largely lost its capacity to direct economic policy in order to achieve goals laid down by an insulated technocracy.

To a considerable extent these changes are the result of growing economic affluence, and a greater desire, especially among the educated middle classes, for a political system which is more responsive to their perceived needs. But the question inevitably arises, if the Taiwanese developmental state is mutating into something else, what kind of mutant will emerge? Will it be able to respond effectively to the challenges, both economic and political, which Taiwan will face in the twenty-first century? The final part of the chapter addresses this question.

What of the future?

In the early 1990s, Maddison (1994: 56) argued that 'countries such as Korea and Taiwan seem likely to converge to slower growth paths within the next two decades'. Certainly the experience of the decade from 1998 to 2008 in both countries bears out this prediction. Given that there was still, in 2007, a considerable gap in per capita GDP between Taiwan and the US, slower economic growth implies that the process of catching up will take longer, if indeed it occurs at all. Whether Taiwan will catch up with the US and the other leading OECD economies, including Japan, will depend on Taiwan's ability to grow faster than these economies over coming decades. That in turn will depend on Taiwan's capacity to absorb new technologies in both industry and services, and to exploit new niches in the regional and world economies for exports of both goods and services.

Taiwan's development path since the 1960s, and especially its success over the past two decades in moving into high-technology industry and modern services might suggest that the economy is now well positioned to meet new challenges over the next two decades and beyond. Government and private expenditures on research and development, relative to GDP, are high in world terms, and an extremely high percentage of young people are completing secondary education, and entering tertiary institutions. The very strong performance of Taiwanese students in international tests in mathematics and science indicates that the quality of student achievement is high. A much higher percentage of tertiary students in Taiwan enrol in science, engineering and technology courses than in most Western countries. While it is futile to try to predict the directions in which both pure science and applied technology will move in the next two to three decades, a country with a labour force which possesses solid training in mathematics and basic science will be better able to cope with new demands than one where the great majority lack these skills.

But the problems outlined in the previous section must be factored into any assessment of the Taiwanese economy's medium-term economic prospects and its ability to stay competitive in those markets where it has already established a global presence, as well as to develop new goods and services which will compete in new markets in Asia and elsewhere. On the one hand, given the very high level of attainment that has already been reached in Taiwan in terms of educational enrolments and spending on research and development, the returns to further investment in education may be quite low. Indeed, given the huge expansion of higher education in Taiwan in recent years, some scholars are casting doubt on whether the labour market can continue to absorb the additional supply of educated workers, and it appears that many Taiwanese workers consider themselves overeducated for the jobs they are doing.[15] On the other hand, the forces of demographic change and falling savings rates will probably impact negatively on economic growth in the medium term. Of course, other factors can intervene to influence both demographic change, and savings rates and economic growth. If the female labour force in Taiwan were to rise even to the levels reached in South Korea in 2003 over the next decade, there would be an appreciable increase in the total size of the labour force and in household incomes.

In addition, the government could take a more proactive approach to immigration, which would allow greater numbers of foreign workers to enter for varying lengths of time to take up both unskilled and skilled jobs in key sectors. The Taiwanese government may not be prepared to go as far as Singapore in encouraging immigration, but there are lessons to be learned from the Singapore experience. The 2000 Population Census for Singapore enumerated 754,500 non-residents out of a total population of just over four million. While some of these workers were unskilled or semi-skilled, many were also in top-end occupations in financial and legal services and in research positions in the universities and in the private sector.

Taiwan has not embraced the 'full-on' global approach of Singapore in attracting international staff into sectors such as financial services, or in encouraging the use of English. But Taiwanese firms have other important strengths, including staff fluent in Mandarin and several important dialects. It has been argued that, given the size and sophistication of the IT sector in Taiwan, the emphasis should be on providing 'integrated service packages encompassing a wide range of value-chain activities', especially to China. Already many Taiwanese companies are moving well beyond standard OEM manufacturing and 'also engage in product design and interact intensively with OEM customers to strengthen their learning and innovation capabilities' (Chen and Liu 2003: 97). Given the fact that Taiwan's integrated circuit industry is the fourth largest in the world and many workers in that sector have close connections with counterparts in the US, Taiwanese firms in this sector would seem ideally placed to build bridges between world leaders and the rapidly growing IT industries in China.[16]

Indeed Taiwan in the early twenty-first century is in the rather strange position of having caught up with many economies in both Asia and Europe in terms of educational achievement and in research indicators, in spite of the gap in per capita GDP that still exists between Taiwan and economies such as Singapore, Hong Kong, the Netherlands and Ireland, let alone the US. In this sense, it could be argued that human resource development should not be the main focus of future development strategy. The education system, both public and private, should now be able to cope with whatever demands the economy places on it. The main future challenge will be to deploy the existing large stock of highly educated people, both male and female, more effectively so as to further increase productivity in both manufacturing and services. In addition, the Taiwanese government, like many other governments in the OECD countries, will have to fashion a strategy for using migrant workers efficiently, especially in the context of an ageing domestic labour force. How the government deals with these challenges is likely to have an important influence on growth rates in coming decades.

Notes

1 Between 1971 and 1991, 83 per cent of the total increase in expenditures on education came from the public sector. Between 1991 and 2005, only 61 per cent of the increase came from the public sector and the balance from private funds (Ministry of Education 2006: 51 3).

2 As early as 1964, key technocrats such as K.T. Li were concerned about the outflow of young scientists and engineers from Taiwan, mainly to the US (Greene 2007: 136–7). But effective strategies to lure back brain workers took time, and it was only in the 1990s that numbers of returning scientists began to grow rapidly. Howe (2006: 227) has argued that over the 1990s, the numbers of returning Taiwanese averaged between 3,000 and 6,000 per year, many of whom had gained valuable work experience in the US and elsewhere.

3 Manufacturing output declined by 5.7 per cent in 2001 (Chu 2006: 147).

4 See 'Taiwan's GDP Growth May Reach 4.21% for 2010:TIER'. Available online at http://www.thefreelibrary.com/.

5 The study by Schultz makes it clear how dramatically family size has changed in Taiwan in the three decades from 1966 to 1995. Whereas in 1976, 72 per cent of people were living in households with six or more people, by 1995 that proportion had fallen to only 26 per cent. While single-person households still appear to be relatively rare in Taiwan compared with parts of Europe, by 1995 almost half the population were living in families of four or less (Schultz 1997: Table 1).

6 Another form of migration relates to foreign females marrying Taiwanese citizens. It has been estimated by Wang (2005) that these numbers exceed those of legal migrants entering with work permits. Around half come from the Chinese Mainland, and it is likely that most of those coming from Thailand, Vietnam and Indonesia are of Han Chinese origin. Wang estimates that in 2003 more than 13 per cent of all births in Taiwan were to foreign-born mothers. Given the overall declining birth rate, over time this will change the demographic profile of Taiwan in favour of families where the mother is foreign-born.

7 Tsay (2002) argues that most Thai workers in Taiwan feel that they are being paid fairly for their work, although construction workers in particular complain about their working conditions.

8 This contrasted with the situation in Thailand where under investment in education meant that many manufacturers had great difficulty recruiting skilled workers in the early 1990s (Booth 2003: 180–1).

9 Young (1976: 723) argued that unemployment rates for female high school and tertiary graduates were consistently higher than for boys in the mid-1970s. It is likely that many unemployed females married and dropped out of the labour force altogether.

10 See 'Female Labour Force Participation Rate Rises', dated 9 March 2010. Available online at http://www.taiwantoday.tw/. It should be noted that the Council of Labour Affairs gives estimates of participation rates that are lower than those given in Table 5.8. They are derived from official figures published by the Department of Manpower Planning in their annual publication *Manpower Indicators*. The 2009 edition of this publication showed that female labour force participation rates rose from 45.6 per cent of the population to 49.7 per cent over the decade 1998–2008. The increase was most rapid for the 25–44 age groups. See Department of Manpower Planning (2009), Table 4.

11 A useful collection of studies on the emergence of knowledge-based economies in East and Southeast Asia can be found in Masuyama and Vandenbrink (2003). An historical perspective on the evolution of the knowledge-based economy in Taiwan can be found in Greene (2007).

12 Chu (2006: 158) has estimated that, in the late 1990s, total sales effects accounted for nearly 90 per cent of the total growth in manufacturing value-added, while growth in value-added accounted for only 14 per cent. (Other effects were negative.) He concluded that this was not an encouraging finding for those who argue that Taiwan must seek to expand new, higher value-added sectors in manufacturing.

13 See Population Reference Bureau (2007: 9).

14 Lee and Mason (2006) point out that the period when workers produce more than they consume tends to be shorter than the normal working span. In Taiwan it is estimated to cover ages 26 to 55, after which the average worker is consuming more than she or he is producing even if still working.

15 Concern focuses on the problem of 'overeducation' in Taiwan, which is usually defined as a situation where a worker's actual education exceeds the required education for his or

her occupation. Hung (2008) examines the problem in Taiwan, and finds that, according to one definition, based on the worker's own assessment of his or her qualifications, 65 per cent of the younger workers feel that they are overeducated for the job they are doing.
16 Chen (2004: 252) argues that many Taiwan-based IT firms operating in China are doing at least part of their R&D in China.

Bibliography

Asian Development Bank (2005), *Key Indicators of Developing Asian and Pacific Countries*, Manila: Asian Development Bank.

Asian Development Bank (2006), *Key Indicators of Developing Asian and Pacific Countries*, Manila: Asian Development Bank.

Aw, Bee-Yan (2006), 'Firm-Level Productivity and FDI in Taiwan', in Shujiro Urata, Chia Siow-Yue and F. Kimura (editors), *Multinationals and Economic Growth in East Asia*, London: Routledge.

Baldwin, Richard (2006), 'Globalisation: The Great Unbundling(s)', paper prepared for the project, *Globalisation: Challenges for Europe and Finland, Helsinki*, Economic Council of Finland.

Barclay, George (1954), *Colonial Development and Population in Taiwan*, Princeton: Princeton University Press.

Bloom, David E. and Jeffrey G. Williamson (1998), 'Demographic Transitions and Economic Miracles in Emerging Asia', *World Bank Economic Review*, Vol 12 (3), 419–55.

Booth, Anne (2003), 'Education, Equality and Economic Development in the Asia-Pacific Economies', in Martin Andersson and Christer Gunnarsson (editors), *Development and Structural Change in the Asia-Pacific*, London: RoutledgeCurzon.

Booth, Anne (2007), *Colonial Legacies: Economic and Social Development in East and Southeast Asia*, Honolulu: University of Hawaii Press.

Chen, Shin-Horng (2004), 'Knowledge Intensification in Taiwan's IT Industry' in Tain-Jy Chen and Joseph S. Lee, *The New Knowledge Economy of Taiwan*, Cheltenham: Edward Elgar, pp. 228–55.

Chen, Shin-Horng and Meng-chun Liu (2003), 'Taiwan's Transition from an Industrialising Economy to a Knowledge-based Economy', in Seiichi Masuyama and Donna Vandenbrink (editors), *Towards a Knowledge-based Economy: East Asia's Changing Industrial Geography*, Singapore: Institute of Southeast Asian Studies and Tokyo: Nomura Research Institute.

Chen, Tain-Jy (2004), 'The Challenge of the Knowledge-based Economy' in Tain-Jy Chen and Joseph S. Lee, *The New Knowledge Economy of Taiwan*, Cheltenham: Edward Elgar, pp. 45–81.

Chen, Tain-Jy, Yi-Peng Chen and Ying-Hua Ku (1995), 'Taiwan's Outward Direct Investment: Has the Domestic Industry Been Hollowed Out?' in *The New Wave of Foreign Direct Investment in Asia*, Singapore: Nomura Research Institute and Institute of Southeast Asian Studies.

Cheng, Tun-jen (1993), 'Dilemmas and Choices in Educational Policies: the Case of South Korea and Taiwan', *Studies in Comparative International Development*, Vol 27 (4), pp. 54–79.

Chu, Yun-Peng (2001), 'Liberalization Policies since the 1980s' in C. C. Mai and C. S. Shih (editors), *Taiwan's Success since 1980*, Cheltenham: Edward Elgar, pp. 89–121.

Chu, Yun-Peng (2004), 'The Transformation of Traditional Manufacturing Industries' in Tain-Jy Chen and Joseph S. Lee, *The New Knowledge Economy of Taiwan*, Cheltenham: Edward Elgar, pp. 82–102.

Chu, Yun-Peng (2006), 'The Political Economy of Taiwan's Industrialisation: The "Developmental State" and its Mutinous Mutation', in Yun-Peng Chu and Hal Hill (editors), *The East Asian High-Tech Drive*, Cheltenham: Edward Elgar, pp. 119–81.

Deaton, Angus and Christina Paxson (1999), 'Growth, Demographic Structure and National Saving in Taiwan', working paper, Research Program in Development Studies, Princeton University.

Department of Manpower Planning (2009), *Manpower Indicators ROC. (Taiwan)*, Taipei: Department of Manpower Planning, Council for Economic Planning and Development, August.

Greene, J. Megan (2007), 'Taiwan's Knowledge-Based Economy: A Historical Perspective on Higher Education, Manpower Planning and Economic Development' in Robert Ash and J. Megan Greene (editors), *Taiwan in the 21st Century: Aspects and Limitations of a Developmental Model*, Oxford: Routledge.

Heller, Peter S. and Steven Symansky (1998), 'Implications for Savings of Aging in the Asian "Tigers"'. *Asian Economic Journal*, Vol 12 (3), 219–52.

Heston, Alan, Robert Summers and Bettina Aten (2009), *Penn World Tables Version 6.3*, Center for International Comparisons of Production, Income and Prices at the University of Pennsylvania.

Howe, Christopher (2006), 'Taiwan's Scientific and Technological Development: A Newly-industrializing Economy Experience of Institutional Evolution' in Lok Sang Ho and Robert Ash (editors), *China, Hong Kong and the World Economy: Studies on Globalization*, London: Palgrave.

Hsing, Mo-Huan (1971), 'Taiwan: Industrialization and Trade Policies' in Ian Little, T. Scitovsky and Maurice Scott (editors), *Industry and Trade in Some Developing Countries: The Philippines and Taiwan*, London: Oxford University Press.

Hung, Chia-Yu (2008), 'Overeducation and Undereducation in Taiwan', *Journal of Asian Economics*, Vol 19(2), 125–37.

International Monetary Fund (2007), *International Financial Statistics, March*, Washington: International Monetary Fund.

Kao, Charles H. C. and Chu-Chia Steve Lin (2004), 'The Changing Economic Matrix between Taiwan and China' in Tain-Jy Chen and Joseph S. Lee, *The New Knowledge Economy of Taiwan*, Cheltenham: Edward Elgar, pp. 256–74.

Keller, William W. and Louis W. Pauly (2003), 'Crisis and Adaptation in Taiwan and South Korea: The Political Economy of Semiconductors' in William W. Keller and Richard J. Samuels (editors), *Crisis and Innovation in Asian Technology*, Cambridge University Press.

Kerr, George H. (1942), 'Formosa: Colonial Laboratory', *Far Eastern Survey*, 23 February, pp. 50–5.

Lee, Joseph S. (2002), 'The Role of Low-skilled Foreign Workers in Taiwan's Economic Development', *Asia Pacific Business Review*, Vol 8 (4), 41–66.

Lee, Ronald D. and Andrew Mason (2006), 'What Is the Demographic Dividend?', *Finance and Development*, September, pp. 16–17.

Lin, Chun-Hung A. and Peter F. Orazem (2004), 'A Reexamination of the Time Path of Wage Differentials in Taiwan', *Review of Development Economics*, Vol 8 (2), 295–308.

Lucas, Christopher J. (1982), 'The Politics of National Development and Education in Taiwan', *Comparative Politics*, Vol 14 (2), 211–25.

Maddison, Angus (1994), 'Explaining the Economic Performance of Nations: 1820–1989' in William Baumol, Richard Nelson and Edward Wolff (editors), *Convergence of Productivity*, New York: Oxford University Press.

Mason, Andrew and Sang-Hyop Lee (2004), 'Population Aging and the Extended Family in Taiwan: A New Model for Analyzing and Projecting Living Arrangements', *Demographic Research*, Vol 10 (8), 197–230. Available online at http://www.demographic-research.org/.

Masuyama, Seiichi and Donna Vandenbrink (editors) (2003), *Towards a Knowledge-based Economy*, Singapore: Institute of Southeast Asian Studies and Tokyo: Nomura Research Institute.

Ministry of Education (2006), *Education Statistics: The Republic of China 2006 Edition*, Taipei: Ministry of Education.

Ministry of Manpower (2002), *Singapore Yearbook of Manpower Statistics*, Singapore: Ministry of Manpower, Manpower Research and Statistics.

OECD (2005), *Science, Technology and Industry Scoreboard*, Paris: OECD.

Population Reference Bureau (2007), *2007 World Population Data Sheet*. Washington: Population Reference Bureau. Available online at http://www.prb.org/.

Republic of China (2005), *Statistical Yearbook of the Republic of China 2004*, Tapei: Executive Yuan, Directorate General of the Budget, Accounting and Statistics.

Republic of China (2006), *Taiwan Statistical Data Book 2006*, Taipei: Council for Economic Planning and Development, Executive Yuan.

Republic of China (2007), *Taiwan Statistical Data Book 2007*, Taipei: Council for Economic Planning and Development, Executive Yuan.

Republic of China (2009), *Taiwan Statistical Data Book 2009*, Taipei: Council for Economic Planning and Development, Executive Yuan.

Schultz, T. Paul (1997), 'Income Inequality in Taiwan 1976–1995: Changing Family Composition, Aging and Female Labour Force Participation', *Center Discussion Paper 778*, Economic Growth Center, Yale University.

Shin, Jang-Sup and Yun-Peng Chu (2006), 'Three Paths for High-Technology Catch-Up: Singapore, Korea and Taiwan' in Yun-Peng Chu and Hal Hill (editors), *The East Asian High-Tech Drive*, Cheltenham: Edward Elgar, pp. 57–87.

Tsay, Ching-lung (2002), 'Labour Migration and Regional Changes in East Asia: Outflows of Thai Workers to Taiwan', Paper presented to the IUSSP Conference, Southeast Asia's Population in a Changing Asian Context, Bangkok, June.

Tsay, Ching-lung and Pan-Long Tsai (2003), 'International Labour Migration and Foreign Direct Investment in East Asian Development: Taiwan and Japan Compared', Taipei: Academica Sinica.

Tsurumi, E. Patricia (1984), 'Colonial Education in Korea and Taiwan' in Ramon H. Myers and Mark R. Peattie (editors), *The Japanese Colonial Empire, 1895–1945*, Princeton: Princeton University Press.

Wang, Hong-zen (2005), 'Social Ties in the Transnational Movement of Labour between Taiwan, Vietnam and China', paper presented at the conference Remaking Economic Strengths in East Asia, University of California, Berkeley, April.

Wang, Jiann-chyuan (2004), 'Taiwan's Knowledge-based Service Industry' in Tain-Jy Chen and Joseph S. Lee, *The New Knowledge Economy of Taiwan*, Cheltenham: Edward Elgar, pp. 256–74.

World Bank (2008), *2005 International Comparison Program: Tables of Final Results*, Washington: World Bank, February.

Wu, Ho-Mou (2004), 'The Road to Financial Globalisation' in Tain-Jy Chen and Joseph S. Lee, *The New Knowledge Economy of Taiwan*, Cheltenham: Edward Elgar, pp. 256–74.

Wyndham, H. A. (1933), *Native Education: Ceylon, Java, Formosa, the Philippines, French Indo-China, and British Malaya*, London: Oxford University Press.

Yoshida, Masami, Ichiro Akimune, Masayuki Nohara and Kimitoshi Sato (1994), 'Regional Economic Integration in East Asia: Special Features and Policy Implications' in Vincent Cable and David Henderson (editors), *Trade Blocs? The Future of Regional Integration*, London: The Royal Institute of International Affairs.

Young, Frank J. (1976), 'Problems of Manpower Development in Taiwan', *Asian Survey*, Vol 16 (8), 721–8.

Yusuf, Shahid (2002), 'Remodelling East Asian Development' *ASEAN Economic Bulletin*, Vol 19 (1), 6–26.

6

TAIWAN'S INDUSTRIAL POLICY AND THE ECONOMIC RISE OF THE PRC

Opportunities and challenges

Yun-Peng Chu and Gee San[1]

Introduction

Toward the end of the 1980s, Taiwan's currency appreciated substantially. Meanwhile its labor cost kept rising. Many labor-intensive firms in the manufacturing sector lost their competitive advantage and began their relocation to the PRC and other Asian countries. At that time, people frequently talked about the "hollowing out" of manufacturing in Taiwan and thought that the era of Taiwan being heavily dependent on manufacturing was beginning to end. The service sector, they said, should be developed instead. But they were worried that because of the low productivity in the long-protected service sector and because of the limited scale of the domestic market, the overall performance of the economy would not be satisfactory – certainly not something that could be compared to the level seen in the days of the rapid expansion of manufactured exports.

To many people's surprise, the worry did not come true. Between 1992 and 1995, manufacturing began to bounce back, and grew at an increasing rate until the year 2000. Many consider this nothing short of a "miracle."

If we look at the changes in the structure of exports, it is very clear that there was a shift from low-end consumer to information technology-related goods. More specifically, from 1981 to 2002, items such as garments, footwear and toys were still important in the early 1980s, but by the end of the 1990s, their shares had become negligible. By 2002, the largest share went to electronic products, information and communication products, basic metals, non-garment textiles (mostly man-made fiber raw materials), and machinery. All of these new exports were capital- or skill-intensive or both.

Therefore, it seems that one of the reasons for the continuous expansion of Taiwan's manufacturing sector in spite of the currency appreciation and rising labor costs is that there had been a transformation in that sector itself. The capital- and skill-intensive industries rose in that sector, and the productivity in these industries was high enough to be internationally competitive. This chapter will analyze how this came about, how the rise of China has changed the competitive environment for Taiwan and what Taiwan needs to succeed in the next phase of development in the global context.

Contributing factors to the transformation of manufacturing

What made the transformation of Taiwan's manufacturing sector possible in the 1990s? In particular, what caused the miraculous rise of the electronic, information and communication industries, which became Taiwan's most important exports?

The history of the development of the electronics and the artificial fiber industry are presented in greater detail in Chen *et al.* (2001b) and Chen *et al.* (2001a), respectively. Overall both international environment and public policies mattered. As Agrawal *et al.* (2000) point out correctly, "sequencing" is important. According to them, in both Taiwan and Korea, downstream exports developed first. As these exports expanded, there was a virtuous backward-linkage effect as the newly rising domestic upper-stream raw materials industries had to be competitive internationally; otherwise their downstream manufacturers, which faced international competition, would not buy from them.

For Taiwan's information and communication technology (ICT) sector, the growing global demand for consumer electronics products enabled the expansion of the downstream sector, and a network of upper-stream suppliers mushroomed. All of the latter was subject to international competition.

But this is the general rule. What was particular to Taiwan was the rise of the IBM PC-compatible computer-related products toward the end of the 1980s in the US. What happened was a rapid rise in the personal computer market, with most products manufactured according to the original architecture of IBM design. Such an open architecture environment gave Taiwan's manufacturers a chance to expand their business. They were very good at producing standardized products on a large scale with standardized components, which could also be supplied locally. The crackdown on illegal gambling video game machines in 1996 further forced many of Taiwan's manufacturers, which were producing those machines illegally, to enter the business of producing motherboards for US buyers.

Other public policies of a more general nature also mattered. We will first mention the set of fundamental conditions which made possible the rise of the ICT industries in Taiwan.

1. Basic education has been a focus of the administration since long ago. In 1968, the mandatory basic education was extended from six to nine grades. In the 1970s and 1980s, the government developed "dual education systems" in Taiwan, somewhat modeled on the German system. The academically more successful students are allowed to enter regular middle and high schools, and the others

are allocated to vocational schools that give students practical training in skills ranging from manufacturing to various kinds of services. The system has been highly competitive.

2. Some of the best students studied abroad. Many of them would stay abroad and work there for the ICT industries. In the 1980s, with the establishment of science-based industrial parks, the government tried to attract back talent experienced in the ICT sector. Many of them responded to the call.

3. The entry requirements for the listing of ICT companies were deregulated. These companies could then readily draw a large amount of capital from the booming capital market, which hit record highs during 1988–90 amidst an asset inflation triggered by the inflow of short-term capital chasing the sharply appreciating local currency. At that time, if all of the hot money was invested in the zero-sum game of real-estate speculation, it is doubtful Taiwan would have had its status in ICT manufacturing today. It can be said that Taiwan "used" the occasion of asset inflation to expand its investment in large-scale manufacturing in the ICT industries, thus the flood of hot money was diverted into productive activities.

4. The government also promoted venture-capital activities by granting tax incentives. These venture-capital companies were happy to be involved in ICT investment as later on the stocks could be sold in the open market ("the exit") and they could then move on to the next target.

5. The government allowed companies to give stock dividends to employees and give technical shares to engineers in return for the core technologies they possessed. As these stocks could be later sold in the open market with a substantial profit, there emerged a useful incentive system.

These were the general policies. There were also sector-specific policies:

1. The government consolidated industrial technology centers into the ITRI (Industrial Technology Research Institute) in 1973 and then expanded its research spheres into machinery, electronics, energy and resources, chemicals and materials. The ITRI and its subsidiaries were involved in the development of integrated circuit manufacturing technologies by transferring them from the RCA company in the US.

2. From 1992 to 2000, the government targeted "ten emerging industries," including communication, information, consumer electronics, aerospace, medical and health care, pollution control, high-grade materials, semiconductors, special-purpose chemicals and pharmaceuticals, and precision machinery and automation. Beginning in 2001, these were changed to 18 industries with the following adjustments: (i) the further division of information industry into software and hardware, (ii) high-grade materials were further divided into special alloy, high-grade plastic, high-grade fiber materials, electronic materials, high-grade ceramic materials, and high-grade composite materials, and (iii) bio-tech and pharmaceuticals were added (see Chu, 1994, 2001, 2002).

While some of these policies might have been necessary, they were by no means sufficient, because not all of the industries the government promoted actually succeeded later. For example, while integrated circuit manufacturing later blossomed into the wafer fabrication industry, hard disk manufacturing (also vehemently promoted) never really took off. Among the targeted "emerging industries," some lagged behind while others, e.g. pharmaceuticals, never took off either.

Throughout the 1980s and 1990s a noticeable trend was that, while more of Taiwan's firms became larger, and as the capital markets became more mature, the market gradually played a larger role in the determination of the allocation of resources, while the government gradually shifted its focus from direct intervention to coaching as well as creating a better general environment. However, during the process, the priority of government policies has been the same: to develop the economy. It is just that the government adopted different ways to achieve this perceived high-order mandate over time.

Slower growth in the post-2000 period

Following the structural transformation in the 1990s, growth generally followed a descending trend coinciding with the Democratic Progress Party (DPP) taking power as a result of the general election. Since its inauguration, the DPP president Chen Shui-Bian (May 2000–May 2008) adopted many controversial policies. His move to stop the construction of the Fourth Nuclear Power Plant in late 2000 sent a shock wave through the international business community. Although that decision was later reversed, the perception of Taiwan's administration's unpredictability had taken hold among many of the business leaders.

In August 2002, ex-president Chen announced that there was one country on either side of the Taiwan Strait. That made the businessmen nervous again, as the statement hinted at de jure independence. Many mass media programs, most with the government's blessing, openly endorsed the formal announcement of Taiwan's independence, and the mood of Taiwanese nationalism was further stimulated.

As these and many other events signifying rising political populism unfolded, Taiwan's economy went through a recession during 2001–2. Recession had come to Taiwan before but, in all previous cases, Taiwan had managed to register a non-negative growth. It was different in 2001, when growth was −2.18 percent as shown in Table 6.1. The same table reveals that growth in investment by the private sector declined substantially after 2000. During the 1970s, 1980s and 1990s, average growth was 13, 7 and 10 percent respectively. From 2000 to 2007, the average rate was less than 5 percent and in 2001 alone it was an appalling negative 27 percent.

The increase in GNP per capita and in unemployment showed a similar picture. It is no wonder that by 2005 South Korea had overtaken Taiwan in terms of GDP per capita in US dollars. This was the case even though South Korea had suffered a great deal from the Asian financial crisis in the late 1990s but Taiwan did not.

TABLE 6.1 Economic growth and private investment

	Private sector investment (in 2001 prices)		Real GDP annual growth %	Unemployment Rate %	GNP per capita US$
	NT$million	Growth %			
1970–9 av.	84,399	13.39	9.83	1.61	2,344
1980–9 av.	320,455	7.23	7.96	2.07	8,111
1990–9 av.	982,393	10.13	6.42	2.04	14,188
2000	1,670,365	15.61	5.77	2.99	14,721
2001	1,218,604	–26.83	–2.17	4.57	13,348
2002	1,284,430	6.68	4.64	5.17	13,604
2003	1,335,921	3.65	3.50	4.99	14,012
2004	1,826,755	33.05	6.15	4.44	15,156
2005	1,817,190	0.31	4.16	4.13	16,113
2006	1,917,790	2.96	4.89	3.91	16,494
2007	2,044,360	3.39	5.70	3.91	17,294
2000–7 av.	1,639,427	4.85	4.08	4.26	15,093

Source: Directorate, General of Budget, Accounting and Statistics (DGBAS), Taiwan, ROC.

The rise of the Chinese economy leads to stronger ties across the Strait

After the Kuomintang (KMT) government allowed Taiwan's citizens to visit relatives in the People's Republic of China (hereafter referred to as Mainland China or China) in the late 1980s, it opened the door for cross-Strait investment. The statistics for Taiwanese investment in Mainland China can be seen in Table 6.2. Annual investment from Taiwan to China increased from US$1,092 million in 1995 to US$6,007 million in 2005. In fact, in 2003, it reached an all-time high at US$7,698 million. If we sum all the investment for the 1995–2005 period, the figure is well over US$47 billion. In addition, it is commonly believed that these statistics are substantially lower than the real number since there was a lot of private investment that failed to appear in the government statistics. From Table 6.2, we can also see that Mainland China accounted for over 71 percent of Taiwan's total outward investment. In addition, in terms of investment by industry, from Table 6.3 it is seen that the electronics industry, basic metals and metal product manufacturing, chemical product manufacturing, plastic product manufacturing, and precision instruments industries were the top five industries investing in Mainland China from Taiwan's manufacturing sector. In addition, Table 6.3 shows that the service industry also registered over US$4 billion over these years.

As Taiwan's investment intensified in Mainland China, it also changed the comparative advantage of the two economies. Based on the Taiwan Institute of Economic Research's (TIER's) computations, it is shown in Table 6.4 that over the 1999–2005 period, Taiwan's shares of the product markets in the US, Europe and Japan shrank from 3.43 percent, 1.02 percent, and 4.03 percent in 1999 to 2.08 percent, 0.84 percent and 3.30 percent, respectively, in 2005. By contrast, however, the corresponding

TABLE 6.2 Taiwan's outward investment statistics, by major investment country

Year Country/region	1995	1996	1997	1998	1999	2000	2001	2002	2003	2004	2005
	US$ millions										
Hong Kong	99.6	59.9	141.6	68.6	100.3	47.5	94.9	167.1	641.3	139.7	107.6
Singapore	31.6	165.0	230.3	158.2	324.5	219.5	378.3	25.8	26.4	822.2	97.7
China	1092.7	1229.2	4334.3	2034.6	1252.8	2607.1	2784.1	6723.1	7698.8	6940.7	6007.0
America	787.1	1443.0	1915.9	2637.0	2267.7	3946.0	3460.9	2475.6	2731.3	1881.4	1618.2
USA	248.2	271.3	547.4	598.7	445.1	861.6	1092.7	577.8	466.6	577.0	314.6
Europe	59.9	11.9	58.5	33.8	61.0	62.2	45.6	123.4	77.4	62.1	299.4
	(%)										
Hong Kong	4.1	1.8	2.0	1.3	2.2	0.6	1.3	1.7	5.5	1.4	1.3
Singapore	1.3	4.9	3.2	3.0	7.2	2.9	5.3	0.3	0.2	8.0	1.2
China	44.6	36.2	60.0	38.2	27.7	33.9	38.8	66.6	66.0	67.2	71.1
America	32.1	42.5	26.5	49.5	50.2	51.4	48.2	24.5	23.4	18.2	19.1
USA	10.1	8.0	7.6	11.2	9.8	11.2	15.2	5.7	4.0	5.4	3.7
Europe	2.4	0.3	0.8	0.6	1.3	0.8	0.6	1.2	0.7	0.6	3.5

Source: Ministry of Economic Affairs, ROC.

TABLE 6.3 Cumulative statistics for Taiwanese outward investment in Mainland China: 1991–2005; *Unit: US$million and (%)*

Industry	Cum. Amount	Share (%)
Agriculture, forestry, fishing and animal husbandry	217	0.46
Mining	127	0.27
Food and beverage manufacturing	1987	4.21
Textile mills	1583	3.35
Apparel, clothing accessories	627	1.33
Leather, fur and allied product manufacturing	373	0.79
Wood and bamboo, rattan products manufacturing	873	1.85
Paper manufacturing, printing	1064	2.25
Chemical products manufacturing	3,165	6.70
Rubber products manufacturing	1,026	2.17
Plastic products manufacturing	2,841	6.01
Non-metallic mineral products manufacturing	2,324	4.92
Basic metal, fabricated metal products manufacturing	4,348	9.20
Machinery manufacturing	1,636	3.46
Electronic products, electrical appliances manufacturing	16,440	34.79
Transport equipment manufacturing	1,762	3.73
Precision instruments manufacturing	2,576	5.45
Construction	144	0.31
Wholesale and retail trade	902	1.91
International trade	457	0.97
Eating and drinking places	142	0.30
Transportation	235	0.50
Warehousing and storage	111	0.23
Finance and insurance	450	0.95
Services	1,645	3.48
Others	202	0.43
Total	47,256	100.00
Manufacturing	42,624	90.20
Services	4,144	8.77

Source: Ministry of Economic Affairs.

shares for China increased from 7.89 percent, 2.60 percent and 13.93 percent in 1999 to 14.57 percent, 4.56 percent, and 21.21 percent in 2005.[2] Clearly, the vast Taiwanese investment in Mainland China has not only boosted Chinese export performance but has also hampered Taiwan's own export performance in the major markets.[3]

The Chinese export drive is also backed up by Taiwan's technological support and supply of intermediate goods and materials. The statistics complied by TIER from trade data show that in 2005 industries such as the electronics parts, precision instruments, chemical materials and basic metals industries each experienced a significant growth rate. More specifically, their growth rates in 2005 were: 23.85 percent (electronic parts), 24.13 percent (precision instruments), 17.22 percent (chemical materials), and 16.39 percent (basic metals), respectively (Table 6.5). If we analyze

TABLE 6.4 Market shares in major markets; *Unit: %*

	Taiwan			China		
	USA	Europe	Japan	USA	Europe	Japan
1999	3.43	1.02	4.03	7.98	2.60	13.93
2000	3.33	1.11	4.64	8.22	3.00	14.61
2001	2.92	1.00	3.96	8.96	3.21	16.71
2002	2.77	0.90	3.89	10.76	3.49	18.50
2003	2.51	0.86	3.61	12.10	4.02	19.83
2004 (B)	2.36	0.84	3.50	13.38	4.56	20.88
2005 (A)	2.08	–	3.30	14.57	–	21.21
(A)–(B)	-0.28	-0.02	-0.20	1.19	0.54	0.33

Source: Taiwan Institute for Economic Research (TIER) (2006).

these statistics from the intensity of different levels of manpower, or different levels of capital intensity, or different levels of technologies, we can obtain an in-depth understanding of this growing trend. The statistics from Table 6.6 show that among all different categories, industries characterized as lowest labor intensity, highest capital intensity, highest high-skilled labor intensity, high-tech industry, high-tech and high-capital intensity were the industries that experienced the highest growth rates in 2005. In other words, it is the industries that had the highest technology or capital content that really experienced the highest growth in China.

This phenomenon can also be examined from the Chinese side. As shown in Table 6.7, China relies on Taiwan disproportionately in those industries that are characterized as having high-capital and high-technology intensity, high-capital and low-technology intensity, high-tech, and high-skill intensity.

TABLE 6.5 Export growth rates for Taiwan's ten major industries in 2005; *Unit: %*

Type of industry	Export growth rate in 2005
Food and beverage manufacturing	45.96
Other industrial products manufacturing	29.55
Non-manufacturing industry	24.70
Precision, optical, medical equipment, watches and clocks manufacturing	24.13
Electronic parts and components manufacturing	23.85
Wood and bamboo products manufacturing	17.55
Chemical materials manufacturing	17.22
Basic metal industries	16.39
Non-metallic mineral products manufacturing	10.48
Fabricated metal products manufacturing	8.44

Source: TIER (2006).

TABLE 6.6 Export growth rates for Taiwanese goods in the Mainland Chinese market; Unit: %

Type of industry	Export growth rate in 2005	Type of industry	Export growth rate in 2005
Total	12.88		
High-labor intensity	7.61	Mid-low-tech	14.79
Mid-labor intensity	15.14	Low-tech	-3.58
Low-labor intensity	15.28	High-capital high-tech	21.77
High-capital intensity	18.71	High-capital mid-tech	13.67
Mid-capital intensity	1.33	High-capital low-tech	-0.12
Low-capital intensity	-5.85	Mid-capital high-tech	0.90
High-tech human intensity	17.48	Mid-capital mid-tech	2.89
Mid-tech human intensity	8.30	Mid-capital low-tech	-3.15
Low-tech human intensity	-1.99	Low-capital high-tech	-17.34
High-tech	17.26	Low-capital mid-tech	-0.04
Mid-high-tech	8.64	Low-capital low-tech	-4.18

Source: TIER (2006).

TABLE 6.7 China's import growth rates for Taiwanese goods, by type of industry; Unit: %

Type of industry	China's import growth rate in 2005	Type of industry	China's import growth rate in 2005
Total	15.29		
High-labor intensity	14.16	Mid-low-tech	11.99
Mid-labor intensity	17.37	Low-tech	-1.88
Low-labor intensity	12.77	High-capital high-tech	26.83
High-capital intensity	21.66	High-capital mid-tech	10.91
Mid-capital intensity	2.46	High-capital low-tech	2.70
Low-capital intensity	-3.47	Mid-capital high-tech	1.79
High-tech human intensity	21.79	Mid-capital mid-tech	4.46
Mid-tech human intensity	7.64	Mid-capital low-tech	-2.97
Low-tech human intensity	-0.80	Low-capital high-tech	-7.63
High-tech	22.39	Low-capital mid-tech	-1.01
Mid-high-tech	8.96	Low-capital low-tech	-4.19

Source: TIER (2006).

The Taiwan government also commissioned the Chung-Hua Institution for Economic Research (CIER) to conduct an in-depth survey of those Taiwanese firms investing in China in order to facilitate a comparison regarding the investment environment across the Taiwan Strait. CIER's 2005 survey report shows that, among the ten major factors, Taiwan was superior to Mainland China in all of these categories except for the taxation incentive category (see Table 6.8). In addition, it is also noted that in terms of the efficiency of the government, regulations on the environmental protection law and the feasibility of attracting highly skilled foreign talent, Taiwan was still superior to China in each of these three categories.

As for the major motivations for Taiwan firms to invest in Mainland China, the CIER (2005) survey showed that the low labor costs, vast domestic market, cheap land, the clustering effect for those Taiwanese firms investing in China and utilizing local resources were the top five reasons (Table 6.9). In terms of their future plans, the CIER survey indicated that over 55 percent of the firms surveyed planned to increase their investment in China, while 58 percent of the firms surveyed planned to receive their orders directly from their overseas customers, and only 3.4 percent of the firms surveyed planned to invest back in Taiwan (see Table 6.10). Finally, in terms of their operating model, Table 6.11 shows that most of the firms surveyed located their headquarters in Taiwan and Taiwan also served as their R&D and financial management center.

Based on the above statistical evidence, in terms of the manufacturing industries, Taiwanese investment in Mainland China may be characterized as capital intensive and made up of capital-intensive industries. The accumulated total amount

TABLE 6.8 Comparison of the investment environment between Taiwan and China; *Total firms surveyed: 691*

Items of comparison	Which one is better?	(%)
Availability of R&D personnel	Taiwan is better	81.19
	China is better	5.07
	Indifferent	10.27
Infrastructure	Taiwan is better	73.23
	China is better	5.07
	Indifferent	18.23
Feasibility of attracting foreign talents	Taiwan is better	51.81
	China is better	10.56
	Indifferent	27.93
Transparency and stability of policies and laws	Taiwan is better	87.26
	China is better	1.45
	Indifferent	7.81
Feasibility of getting financial support	Taiwan is better	88.28
	China is better	1.59
	Indifferent	5.64
Efficiency of the government	Taiwan is better	56.73
	China is better	11.29
	Indifferent	24.75
IPR protection	Taiwan is better	81.77
	China is better	0.58
	Indifferent	9.99
Taxation incentives	Taiwan is better	22.14
	China is better	48.77
	Indifferent	19.39
Environmental protection regulations	Taiwan is better	44.86
	China is better	18.38
	Indifferent	26.48

Source: Chung-Hua Institution for Economic Research (CIER) (2005).

TABLE 6.9 Motivation for making investment in China; *Total firms surveyed: 730*

Motivations	%	Motivations	%
Cheap labor	73.97	Taxation and other preferential treatment	20.68
Cheap land cost	40.41	Request by the foreign buyers	23.42
Can utilize local resources	26.44	Clustering effect by the migrating Taiwanese firms in China	37.95
Vast domestic market	55.21	Poor investment environment in Taiwan	12.74
Can utilize China's export quota	2.60	Can fully utilize the firm's capital and technology	11.78
Can utilize China's export preferential treatment	7.12	Others	4.38

Source: CIER (2005).

TABLE 6.10 Business in next year; *Total firms surveyed: 615*

Business plan in 2006	%
Increase investment in China	55.12
Will be able to receive orders from abroad directly	58.86
Try to become public-listed company in China	3.41
Try to become public-listed company in Taiwan	1.79
Try to make investment back in Taiwan	3.41

Source: CIER (2005).

TABLE 6.11 Current business arrangements in China and Taiwan, by department; *Total firms surveyed: 704*

Department	Business arrangement	%
Headquarters	Parent company in Taiwan	73.01
	Firm in China	14.77
Manufacturing base	Parent company in Taiwan	58.10
	Firm in China	74.29
R&D department	Parent company in Taiwan	72.30
	Firm in China	26.85
Marketing department	Parent company in Taiwan	78.13
	Firm in China	55.68
Financial department	Parent company in Taiwan	83.24
	Firm in China	37.22
Purchasing department	Parent company in Taiwan	76.70
	Firm in China	53.13
Others	Parent company in Taiwan	3.41
	Firm in China	4.69

Source: CIER (2005).

of investment exceeded US$42 billion. Most of these investments have long-term development plans in China, and only a few of them plan to invest back in Taiwan. As such, this has become a serious challenge to Taiwan, for many of the policy-makers worry that this huge investment from Taiwan may in turn escalate into an "industrial hollowing-out" effect. In 1997, former president Lee Teng-Hui openly stated that those planning to invest in China should "slow down and be patient." After the DPP came to power in 2000, more restrictions on Taiwanese investment in Mainland China were imposed. One of the notable restrictions was that for some designated high-tech industries, the government required that, for their investment in Mainland China, they needed to obtain government approval and that the total amount of their investment in Mainland China should not exceed the 40 percent upper-bound limit of their total amount of investment in Taiwan.

The above policy may look reasonable but it gives rise to a very strong side effect that may in turn adversely affect the development of industry in Taiwan. For example, one of the major air-conditioning (AC) manufacturers in Taiwan invested in an AC manufacturing plant in China so as to capture the vast growing market in China.[4] As the entrepreneur actively engaged in his investment in China, he fell into the "trap" of the 40 percent upper-bound limit as set by the administrative rule. When the government wanted him to return to Taiwan and clarify his investment in China, he refused, and now he has become a criminal wanted by the law. As a result, his huge investment in China ceases to be connected to his firm's operation in Taiwan. The possible positive cross-Strait interactions of the air-conditioning production for this firm were cut off entirely. This is one typical example of the situation faced by entrepreneurs in Taiwan.

Besides advocating an independent Taiwan, one of the myths that former president Lee and the succeeding DPP government have subscribed to about China is that China may fall into some serious economic or political crisis in the near future and, as such, Taiwan has all the more reason to keep itself away from China. This myth has so far proved to be false. If it is the case that Taiwan is rapidly losing its comparative advantage in its industrial development as well, then this is an alarming sign for Taiwan.

International comparisons

One question concerning Taiwan's development stage is how it compares with other small countries. San *et al.* (2006) selected three small European countries with a GDP per capita of over US$27,000 in 2005 as the yardstick for Taiwan's future development plan. These three small European countries are Ireland, the Netherlands and Finland (hereafter abbreviated as the INF countries). The San *et al.* comparison can be summarized as follows.

The R&D input

By examining various R&D indices of the INF countries (see Table 6.12), it is found that Finland is ranked first and has a significant lead over the other two countries. The Netherlands ranks second. To be specific, Finland's R&D expenditure to GDP ratio (3.44 percent) is almost twice as high as the 1.80 percent of the Netherlands, while its ratios of R&D expenditure to industrial and manufacturing value-added are 3.55 percent and 2.75 percent, respectively. These are more than twice those of the other two INF countries, as is its R&D expenditure per thousand employed persons. By contrast, Ireland ranks the lowest in all the R&D aspects, its values being roughly only approximately one-third of those of Finland. As such, the economic development strategy of Finland can be identified more in terms of a science- and technology-oriented model, with a greater concentration on R&D activities that have gained it a leading position in high-tech development (TIER, 2005).

Attracting foreign direct investment (FDI)

According to the Inward FDI Potential Index of 2001–3 (UNCTAD, n.d.), Ireland is ranked tenth in the world, while the Netherlands and Finland are ranked eleventh and thirteenth, respectively (Table 6.13). With regard to the FDI flow to total capital formation, Ireland is still ranked first. Ireland's average rate of FDI flow to total capital formation during the years 2000 to 2004 was surprisingly as high as 70.32 percent, and was almost twice as high as that for the Netherlands, which was 36.79 percent, while that for Finland was the lowest at only 21.73 percent. Based on the potential index and the performance in terms of attracting foreign firms to invest, both Ireland and the Netherlands were quite well known as investment locations. However, relatively speaking, Ireland has developed itself more successfully as the gateway for many of the non-EC member countries' high-tech manufacturing bases into Europe. The successful attraction of FDI in the high-tech industry can be regarded as a major development strategy for Ireland.

TABLE 6.12 Statistics on various R&D indices of the INF

	Finland	Netherlands	Ireland
R&D exp. /GDP (%)	3.44	1.80	1.12
	(2002)	(2002)	(2002)
R&D exp. /industrial value-added (%)	3.55	1.54	1.02
	(2002)	(2002)	(2001)
R&D exp. /value-added (manufacturing) (%)	2.75	1.17	0.71
	(2002)	(2002)	(2001)
R&D per employed person (US$)	2,088	1,095	819
	(2002)	(2002)	(2002)

Sources: *LABORSTA* Internet (ILO). Available online at http://laborsta.ilo.org/cgi-bin/brokerv8.exe); *Indicators of Science and Technology, Taiwan* (edited 2005), National Science Council, Taiwan. Available online at http://www.nsc.gov.tw/tech/book/data_main/data_main.pdf.

Comparing Taiwan with the INF

Taiwan is located across the Taiwan Strait about two hours' flying time from Shanghai. Therefore, if Taiwan can refer to the Netherlands' development model to develop itself into a regional hub, it will surely have great development potential. In addition, the high-tech industry is also well developed in Taiwan, and, therefore, with Taiwan's sound high-tech industrial base, the Finland model that focuses on the high-tech industry can also serve as a good model for Taiwan. In terms of Ireland's FDI model, Taiwan used to enjoy vast amounts of inward FDI. In recent years, however, the sharp decline in FDI has become a serious concern to Taiwan. Ireland's development model can thus be contrasted with Taiwan's experiences of failure in this regard in recent years. We shall explicitly compare the performance of Taiwan with the performances of the INF countries in terms of the quantity and the quality of their human resources, R&D and FDI, as well as some other important output performance indices. It is hoped that such a comparison can shed some light on the future development strategies for Taiwan.

The quantity and quality of human resources

We shall begin by comparing the ratio of college students to the total number of enrolled students, since this ratio can be used to gage the quality of a nation's human resources. Table 6.14 shows that among the four countries, Finland ranks the highest, followed by Taiwan, the Netherlands and Ireland (row 1). Both the number of R&D personnel per 1,000 employed and the number of R&D personnel per million people show that Taiwan ranks second among these four countries. In addition, Table 6.14 shows that Finland and Taiwan have the highest rates for college-educated employed workers, followed by the Netherlands and Ireland. These statistics all clearly suggest that Taiwan's labor quality is in no way inferior to that of the INF countries.

In Table 6.15 we compare the relevant R&D statistics for these four countries. The statistics on various R&D indices show that Taiwan ranks after Finland as the second highest R&D-investing country. The relevant indices compared in Table 6.15 include R&D expenditure/GDP, R&D expenditure/industrial value-added, R&D expenditure/manufacturing value-added and R&D expenditure per thousand employed persons. Even with the smallest R&D input among the four countries, Ireland's per

TABLE 6.13 Statistics on various FDI indices of the INF

	Finland	Netherlands	Ireland
Inward FDI potential index (rank) (2001–3)	13	11	10
The average ratio of (inward FDI flow/total capital formation, %) (2000–4)	21.73	36.79	70.32

Source. UNCTAD Inward FDI Potential Index – Results. Available online at http://www.unctad.org/Templates/WebFlyer.asp?intItemID=2472&lang=1.

TABLE 6.14 The quality of the human resources of Taiwan and the INF

	Taiwan	Finland	Netherlands	Ireland
College students/total students (%)	62.96	85.66	56.97	49.89
	(2001)	(2001)	(2001)	(2001)
No. of R&D personnel per 1,000 employed	7.1	16.4	5.5	5.1
	(2003)	(2002)	(2001)	(2001)
No. of R&D personnel per million population	3,990	7,110	2,826	2,315
	(2001)	(2001)	(2001)	(2001)
% of employed with college education	28.46	31.60	23.50	25.80
	(2001)	(2001)	(2001)	(2001)
	Ranking: *Finland > Taiwan > Netherlands > Ireland*			

Sources: *World Development Indicators* (2005), The World Bank; *Indicators of Science and Technology, Taiwan* (edited 2005), National Science Council, Taiwan. Available online at http://www.nsc.gov.tw/tech/book/data_main/data_main.pdf; *Statistical Yearbook of the Republic of China*, Directorate-General of Budget, Accounting and Statistics, Executive Yuan, ROC., 2005, December; *Yearbook of Manpower Survey Statistics*, Directorate-General of Budget, Accounting and Statistics, Executive Yuan, ROC., 2002.

TABLE 6.15 The R&D inputs of Taiwan and the INF

	Taiwan	Finland	Netherlands	Ireland
R&D exp./GDP (%)	2.20	3.44	1.80	1.12
	(2002)	(2002)	(2002)	(2002)
R&D exp./industrial value-added (%)	1.95	3.55	1.54	1.02
	(2003)	(2002)	(2002)	(2001)
R&D exp./value-added (manufacturing) (%)	1.82	2.75	1.17	0.71
	(2003)	(2002)	(2002)	(2001)
R&D per employed persons (US$)	1,295	2,088	1,095	819
	(2002)	(2002)	(2002)	(2002)
	Ranking: *Finland > Taiwan > Netherlands > Ireland*			

Sources: *Indicators of Science and Technology, Taiwan* (edited 2005), National Science Council, Taiwan. Available online at http://www.nsc.gov.tw/tech/book/data_main/data_main.pdf; *Yearbook of Manpower Survey Statistics*, Directorate-General of Budget, Accounting and Statistics, Executive Yuan, ROC., various issues, *LABORSTA* Internet (ILO). Available online at http://laborsta.ilo.org/cgi-bin/brokerv8.exe.

capita GDP reached US$34,280 in the year 2004. By contrast, with the top two of the technology and R&D inputs among the four countries, Taiwan's economic performance measured in terms of GDP per capita was only about half of the corresponding figures for the INF countries.

Output performance indices

Table 6.16 summarizes the related indices with regard to science and technology performance for the four countries. In terms of the SCI- and EI-listed research publications and the relevant statistics, Taiwan ranked after the Netherlands and performed fairly well, but in terms of the number of SCI and EI papers per researcher, Taiwan's ranking dropped to third.

The share of high-tech industry in manufacturing as well as of the high-tech industry exports to R&D expenditure ratios are illustrated in Table 6.17. The statistics show that in 2003 Taiwan had the highest high-tech industry to manufacturing ratio of 42.86 percent. In addition, among the four countries, Ireland had the highest high-tech industry exports value to R&D expenditure rate (22.07 percent), and Taiwan was ranked second (4.55 percent). Furthermore, Taiwan obtained substantially more patents from the US than any of the INF countries, and this ranking remains unchanged when it is compared in terms of US-granted patents per researcher (rows 3 and 4). As shown in Table 6.17, in terms of the high-tech industry's export value per worker, Ireland had the highest ranking followed by the Netherlands. Ireland's corresponding figure (US$96,089) was far higher than those of each of the other countries. The above statistics clearly imply that even with the lowest R&D input (as shown in Table 6.15), the fewest publications of scientific papers (as shown in Table 6.16), and the lowest patents obtained from the US (as shown in Table 6.16), the successful role played by FDI in Ireland seems to have made up for all of the deficiencies in Ireland's high-tech development.

In contrast to Ireland's development performance, the above comparison clearly shows that in terms of science and technology performance, Taiwan is not inferior to any one of the INF countries, but in terms of the high-tech industry export value per worker, or the value-added per worker (as shown in Table 6.18), its performance is far inferior to that of Ireland and the Netherlands. Clearly, this comparison shows that the real challenge for Taiwan is how to convert its good science and technology knowledge into high value-added products and it is this that will be the key for Taiwan to transform itself into a developed economy.

TABLE 6.16 The science and technology performance of Taiwan and the INF

	Taiwan	Finland	Netherlands	Ireland
No. of SCI papers (1)*	12,939 (2004)	7,421 (2004)	19,982 (2004)	3,151 (2004)
No. of EI papers (2)	10,980 (2004)	2,953 (2004)	6,020 (2004)	1,075 (2004)
(1) + (2)*	23,919 (2004)	10,374 (2004)	26,002 (2004)	4,226 (2004)
(1)+(2)/total no. of research personnel	0.301 (2003)	0.230 (2002)	0.512 (2002)	0.373 (2002)

*Ranking: Netherlands > Taiwan > Finland > Ireland

Source: *Indicators of Science and Technology, Taiwan* (edited 2005), National Science Council, Taiwan. Available online at http://www.nsc.gov.tw/tech/book/data_main/data_main.pdf.

TABLE 6.17 The performance of high-tech industry in Taiwan and INF countries

	Taiwan	Finland	Netherlands	Ireland
Share of high-tech industry in manufacturing (%)	42.86 (2003)	23.75 (2003)	30.89 (2003)	34.47 (2003)
	Ranking: Taiwan > Ireland > Netherlands > Finland			
Export value of high-tech industry/total R&D exp. (all in US$)	4.55 (2002)	1.83 (2002)	3.87 (2002)	22.07 (2002)
	Ranking: Ireland > Taiwan > Netherlands > Finland			
Patents granted by the US (1)	5,431 (2002)	809 (2002)	1,391 (2002)	132 (2002)
(1)/total no. of research personnel	0.078 (2003)	0.021 (2002)	0.032 (2002)	0.014 (2002)
	Ranking: Taiwan > Netherlands > Finland > Ireland			
Export value of high-tech industry per no. employed in manufacturing (US$)	23,812 (2003)	23,615 (2003)	30,972 (2002)	96,089 (2003)
	Ranking: Ireland > Netherlands > Taiwan ≈ Finland			

Sources: TIER calculations from the tapes for Taiwan's international trade; *World Development Indicators* (2005), The World Bank; *Indicators of Science and Technology, Taiwan* (edited 2005), National Science Council, Taiwan. Available online at http://www.nsc.gov.tw/tech/book/data_main/data_main.pdf.

TABLE 6.18 The value-added per worker in Taiwan and the INF countries

	Taiwan	Finland	Netherlands	Ireland
Product value per manufacturing worker (US$)	26,020 (2003)	82,761 (2003)	54,973 (2002)	110,630 (2003) (Manufacturing & Construction)
Product value per service sector worker (US$)	38,805 (2003)	65,085 (2003)	50,477 (2002)	65,868 (2003)
	Ranking: Ireland > Finland > Netherlands > Taiwan			

Sources: *National Income Statistics Yearbook* (2004), Directorate-General of Budget, Accounting and Statistics, Executive Yuan, ROC.; *World Development Indicators* (2005), The World Bank; *Labour Force Survey*, International Labour Organization. Available online at http://www.ilo.org/public/english/bureau/stat/portal/index.htm.

Policy implications

Based on the above discussions, as compared with the INF countries, Taiwan does not lag behind in terms of its inputs measured both in quantity or quality terms in almost all respects, but rather lags behind these countries in terms of its output performance. That is, Taiwan is not inferior to INF countries in terms of the quality of its high-tech manpower, R&D input, publications of academic papers, and certainly not in terms of patents granted by the US. The problem has nothing to do with its insufficiency in relation to inputs but rather with its poor performance in terms of value-added per capita. The superior output efficiency of the INF countries illustrates that something related to the INF countries could serve as valuable reference for Taiwan.

As we discussed above, Ireland, the Netherlands and Finland have adopted different models/strategies in promoting their own development. More specifically, the FDI attraction model adopted by Ireland, the regional hub policy of the Netherlands and the high-tech technological development in Finland are the most noticeable policies in these countries. Nevertheless, it is found that these countries have one thing in common, namely, that they all focus on the EC market and take full advantage of their nation's respective comparative advantages. Along with each country's specific development strategy, the openness of the INF provides an excellent platform or opportunity for their high-tech/high-quality manpower to apply their expertise. However, Taiwan in recent years has adopted policies that have tended to shy away from the rapidly growing Chinese market, which sharply contrasts with the strategies adopted by the INF countries in relation to the EC. In addition, Taiwan's current trade and investment policies toward Mainland China also exhibit much more self-restraint as compared with those adopted by neighboring countries such as Japan and Korea. In fact, nowadays, Japan and Korea are endeavoring to fully utilize China as their production base as well as their new product market.

As to the specific strategy adopted by each INF country to develop its economy, Ireland is an example of a country that has successfully developed itself into a gateway for non-EC member countries' high-tech manufacturing bases in Europe, and this has also led to a reversal of the brain drain in Ireland since the late 1990s. As such, whether or not Taiwan can successfully integrate itself into the emerging Asian market will be critical to its ability to utilize the high-level manpower and, in turn, attract more skilled workers from abroad.

Furthermore, based on the INF experiences (especially the experiences of Ireland and the Netherlands), attracting more foreign direct investment is surely very critical to economic development. However, Taiwan's poor performance with regard to attracting FDI in recent years is a major cause for concern, and also sharply contrasts with its own trend just a few years ago. The picture is quite clear now: if Taiwan fails to meet the international community's expectations and does not fully engage in the rapidly growing market on the Chinese Mainland, it will cease to be attractive to foreign investors as well as to multinational enterprises. Should Taiwan "voluntarily" choose to give up its strategic locational advantage in Asia, it is likely that it will encounter a new wave of brain drain and this will surely hinder the country's overall competitiveness.

Furthermore, with regard to Finland's experience, it is advisable for the Taiwan government to strengthen the R&D efforts of private enterprises. As mentioned in the previous section, Taiwan ranks just after the Netherlands and has performed fairly well in terms of its SCI- or EI-listed scientific publications, while it also ranks first in obtaining US patents. As such, how to effectively channel the R&D effort from both government sponsored technology research institutions and universities to private enterprises so as to incorporate it in commercial applications could be the key for Taiwan. This close cooperation between agencies will be particularly important to enable the numerous Taiwanese small and medium-sized enterprises (SMEs) to strengthen their export competitiveness, since most of the SMEs in

Taiwan are relatively small but account for at least 95 percent of all the enterprises in Taiwan. In addition, in-service training as well as the promotion of the worker's general skill training have been shown to have a significant impact in terms of enhancing the quality of labor as well as the flexibility of labor supply (San *et al.* 2006). Other related policies, such as improving the quality of college and vocational education, intensifying vocational training for the fast-growing service sectors, and encouraging highly educated females to enter (and/or reenter) the labor force by having more flexible labor market regulations, are some of the policies that can be considered.

Last, but not least, in this chapter we have used Taiwan as an example to show that, in light of its ambitious policy goal to double its GDP per capita by 2015, relevant policies must be implemented so as to fully utilize the country's domestic comparative advantage as well as its locational advantage in the region. In addition, the introduction of a policy to attract FDI could play a critical role in promoting the country's technological capability, but such a policy will not succeed unless the country has a stable business environment, and a consistent government policy. An international comparison of Taiwan and the INF countries as discussed in this chapter can serve as valuable reference to other developing or newly developed countries if they wish to identify their policies or options.

Summary and conclusions

The companies in Taiwan's business sector are very competitive. They have had extensive experience with international production and marketing, and they have benefited from the research and development activities encouraged by the government's policies. Our analysis also shows that the quality of the various inputs used in Taiwan's production including labor has been quite high even when compared with the Western European countries.

However, oddly enough, Taiwan's *business sector* has increasingly become a concept that is distinct from the Taiwan *economy*. The companies in this sector first moved their production abroad, mostly to Mainland China, and now they are moving some of their other activities abroad, given the stringent restrictions on cross-Strait transportation and travel. One famous example is Hsinchu Commercial Bank. It was acquired by the Standard Chartered Bank in 2006 and therefore delisted from the Taiwan stock exchange. However, as a part of the Standard Chartered Bank, it is now free to seek business opportunities in the PRC, given that many of its customers in the Hsinchu area have already moved there. Had it remained a part of the Taiwan economy, it would not have had the freedom to do so. By becoming un-Taiwanese, it could take off the straitjacket imposed upon it by the government.

There will be more such examples in the future. The paradoxes will intensify, as the economic trend runs contrary to the political trend. Such a situation is unlikely to be sustainable. Which side will "blink" first? We do not know. So far the political side has not blinked. The latest (2006) edition of the White Paper of the American Chamber of Commerce in Taipei says:

Since the early 1990s, the Taiwan government's plans and pronouncements have invariably positioned the island as a gateway to the China market, leveraging its proximity to the mainland and the close linguistic and cultural affinities between the two sides of the Taiwan Strait. The underlying premise was that Taiwan's significant competitive advantages would bring substantial profits to all concerned – a "win-win-win" approach that would simultaneously benefit domestic companies, multinationals invested on the island, and China-based business. But *the government never fully implemented that strategy. Instead it moved in the contradictory direction of tightening the regulations governing many aspects of economic activity with China.* [italics added]

Similar views can be found in the 2006–7 Position Papers published by the European Chamber of Commerce in Taipei or ECCT. The American Chamber of Commerce has repeatedly sounded its concerns but to no avail. One such report reads:

Last year, the theme of the ECCT Position Papers was to "Keep Taiwan dynamic and relevant!" This slogan was intended to encourage Taiwan not to lose its global competitiveness by further deregulating industries, by lifting cross-Strait restrictions, by complying with its WTO obligations and by accelerating the upgrading of its service industries. *Twelve months later, however, the European Chamber concludes that the Taiwan economy has not gained in competitiveness by making the necessary reforms that should have led to the necessary economic transformation.* [italics added]

One opinion advocated by the Taiwanese nationalist fundamentalists is that if the Taiwan economy were increasingly integrated into China's economy, the prospects for ultimate de jure independence would be slim, while the chances of political unification might increase. On the other hand, many political leaders adhere to the view that with increased economic interactions, Taiwan's economic strength could be best safeguarded as capable Taiwanese businessmen could use the PRC as leverage both in terms of production and markets. Restrictions on integration would conversely hurt Taiwanese businesses, forcing them to migrate and in the end would make it hard for Taiwan to maintain its economic might, which alone is arguably the best defense against possible political or military ambitions launched by the PRC to unilaterally unify Taiwan with itself.

Notes

1 The authors are professors at National Central University in Taiwan. This paper was presented at the US-Taiwan-Europe Conference: "Taiwan's Democracy and Future: Economic and Political Challenges," Georgia Institute of Technology, April 13–14, 2007.
2 The statistics for Europe are based on statistics for 2004.
3 TIER Commissioned Research Report (2006).
4 It is estimated that annual sales of air-conditioners in China can be as high as 50 million units, which contrasts sharply with total annual sales of roughly 500,000 units per annum in Taiwan.

Bibliography

Agrawal, Pradeep, Subir V. Gokarn, Meena Mishra, Kirit S. Parikh and Kunal Sen (2000), *Policy Regimes and Industrial Competitiveness: A Comparative Study of East Asia and India*, London: Macmillan.

Chen, Been-Lon, Tain-Jy Chen and Yun-Peng Chu (2001a), "The Role of Textiles and Man-made Fiber in the Process of Industrialization: The Case of Taiwan," in Wong and Ng (eds.), *Industrial Policy, Innovation and Economic Growth: The Experience of Japan and the Asian NIEs*, Singapore: Singapore University Press, pp. 283–321.

Chen, Tain-Jy, Been-Lon Chen and Yun-Peng Chu (2001b), "The Development of Taiwan's Electronics Industry," in Wong and Ng (eds.), *Industrial Policy, Innovation and Economic Growth: The Experience of Japan and the Asian NIEs*, pp. 245–82.

Chu, Yun-Peng (1994), "Taiwan's External Imbalance and Structural Adjustment: A General Equilibrium Analysis," *Asian Economic Journal*, 8, pp. 85–114.

Chu, Yun-Peng (2001), "Markets Grew and Matured as a Result of State Actions: The Taiwan Experience," *International Journal of Development Planning Literature*, 1, pp. 204–34.

Chu, Yun-Peng (2002), "The Development of Newly Emerging Industries and their Knowledge Content: How to Release the Bottlenecks to the Enhancement of Industrial Value-Added," in Lin (ed.), *Knowledge Economy and Research and Development: Proceedings of the Seventh Conference in Memory of K.-S. Liang*, Taipei: Department of Economics, National Taiwan University, pp. 1–14.

Chu, Yun-Peng (2006), "The Mutinous Mutation of the Developmental State in Taiwan," in Hill and Chu (eds.), *The East Asian High-Tech Drive*, Cheltenham, UK: Edward Elgar.

Chung-Hua Institution for Economic Research (2005), *Commissioned Research Report: Surveyed Report for Taiwanese Investment in Mainland China*, CIER, Taipei (in Chinese).

Johnson, Chalmers (1987), "Political Institutions and Economic Performance: The Government-Business Relationship in Japan, South Korea and Taiwan," in Deyo (ed.), *The Political Economy of the New Asian Industrialism*, Ithaca and London: Cornell University Press, pp. 136–64.

San, Gee, Li-Hsuan Huang and Tung-Chun Huang (2006) (in Chinese), "Establishing a Sound and Competitive Labor Market to Cope with Taiwan's Economic Development in 2015," paper presented at The 26th STAG Board Meeting, April 2, 2006, Taipei, Taiwan.

Taiwan Institute for Economic Research (2006), *Commissioned Research Report: Analysis on Cross Strait Comparative Advantage on Industrial Development* (in Chinese).

The American Chamber of Commerce in Taipei (2006), *The White Paper*.

UNCTAD (n.d.) *Inward FDI Potential Index, 2001–2003*, Geneva: UNCTAD. Available online at http://www.unctad.org/sections/dite_dir/docs/Potential_Index_2001 2003_en.pdf (accessed February 17, 2011).

Woo-Cumings, Meredith (1999a), "Introduction: Chalmers Johnson and the Politics of Nationalism and Development," in Woo-Cumings (ed.), *The Developmental State*, Ithaca, NY: Cornell University Press, pp. 1–31.

Woo-Cumings, Meredith (ed.) (1999b), *The Developmental State*, Ithaca, NY: Cornell University Press.

Yang, Ai-Li (1989) (in Chinese), *Sun Y.-C.: A Biography*, Taipei: Commonwealth.

7

TRADE, INVESTMENT, AND TECHNOLOGICAL UPGRADING

Opportunities and challenges facing Taiwan

Barry Naughton

Over the past forty years, Taiwan has developed and prospered in tandem with the restructuring of the global economy. The remarkable ascent of Taiwan that has transformed it from a poor, agriculture-based economy into a knowledge-based economy has been part of a broad set of changes often labeled as "globalization." Taiwan entrepreneurs and scientists have been important drivers of the process of globalization, and the Taiwan economy has naturally been one of its largest beneficiaries. Two major interpretive frameworks have been developed to understand the coevolution of Taiwan firms and the global economy. Both of these interpretive frameworks command significant respect today and consciously or unconsciously structure most discussions of firm strategy and economic development in East Asia. In this chapter I argue, however, that both of these frameworks are obsolete and provide little guidance for policy and little insight into future developments. Instead, deeper restructuring of global networks of production, trade, and especially innovation require an even greater degree of flexibility and adaptability than in the past. This is particularly true given that the next stage of Taiwan's prosperity must involve the launch of an even more creative knowledge-intensive economy that stays a step ahead of the emerging giants of China and India.

The two existing paradigms that I discuss each has good descriptive capability for past developments in the Taiwanese, Chinese, and global economies. The first paradigm, the "international subcontracting" model, accurately described how Taiwan (and other East Asian firms) moved from simple manufacturing subcontracts to increasingly sophisticated activities. The second paradigm, the "slicing the value chain," or what might for Taiwan be called the "global hi-tech factory" paradigm, accurately described how Taiwan businesses profited from the extension of their production networks across the Taiwan Strait, relocating low-skill and labor-intensive stages of the value chain in China in accordance with principles of comparative advantage. However, both these models suggested ongoing and future directions of change that have not, in fact, been realized. As recognition has spread that the predictions of these models have not been fulfilled, the feeling has grown that Taiwan is in danger of becoming trapped in its current arrangements and at its current stage of development.

In this chapter I examine the current state and challenges of development and upgrading facing Taiwan and China. I begin with an overview of a few selected aspects of the China and Taiwan economic relationship. I then discuss the two existing paradigms, taking examples from the computer, integrated circuit (IC), and cell phone industries. I go on to discuss the relationship between innovation, markets, and production, and argue that three changes have created significant new opportunities for Taiwan firms: the rise of the China market, the redistribution of R&D capabilities, and moves toward reintegration of selected modules of the value chain. I argue that a new model, which I label "strategic re-assembly of the value chain," better describes the economic opportunities of the future. In this model a key competitive advantage is proximity to a large market. Taiwan has an enviable degree of proximity to the emerging China market, but so far economic policy has significantly hampered the ability of Taiwanese firms to fully leverage this proximity. From an economic and business standpoint, this shortcoming can be relatively easily remedied, if the political obstacles to doing so can be removed. It remains to be seen whether the advent of the Ma Ying-jeou administration will facilitate the removal of this constraint.

Patterns of growth and interaction between China and Taiwan

Since 2001, the Chinese economy has entered a new cycle of rapid economic growth. New types of economic integration are taking place, integration that is reducing the degree of duality in the Chinese economy, opening certain sectors wider to external participation, and accelerating the pace of economic growth. Already, these processes have led to a new phase of China's long economic boom. As a result, even after cautious adjustments are made to China's official statistics, it is now apparent that China has grown faster, and for longer, than any previous economy.

These processes have led to many complex changes in China's relations with outside economies. They have led to the sudden emergence of a large global trade surplus for China – to the surprise of many – as rapid domestic industrialization has led to an equally rapid process of import substitution. Equally surprising, foreign direct investment (FDI) inflows have not kept pace with economic growth, despite the market-opening provisions of WTO membership. FDI inflows to China as a share of GDP declined from 5.2 percent of GDP in 1995 to only 2.5 percent in 2006. Yet at the same time, exports, as a share of GDP, have continued their powerful, inexorable rise, reaching 36.9 percent in 2006. And yet, despite these two simultaneous trends, the dependence of this mighty export machine on foreign invested enterprises (FIEs) has not diminished: in 2006, FIEs accounted for 58 percent of total exports, and 86 percent of the crucial high-tech export sector (Ministry of

Commerce 2007). To be sure, we may be seeing a turning point of sorts. In 2006, for the first time ever, the share of FIEs in China's exports did not increase, and in fact slipped, albeit infinitesimally, from 58.3 percent to 58.2 percent (in 2007 the corresponding figure declined by a more significant, but still very small, margin to 57.1 percent!). China is becoming more open, indeed, but the patterns are not, and will not be, as linear as in the past.

When we examine Taiwan's relationship with China, we also see increasingly complex trends subject to conflicting interpretations. By some measures, Taiwan's involvement with China has decreased: Chinese figures show Taiwan investment declining from its peak of 0.6 percent of Chinese GDP in 1994 to just below 0.1 percent in 2006. But a further look at data on Taiwan-sourced FDI, in the context of the total, provides a rather different picture. As Figure 7.1 shows, the only real growth component among FDI sources in China in recent years has been investment from "tax havens and free ports." While Hong Kong investment has held steady in absolute dollar terms, investment from both the US and Taiwan has declined since 2002, and investment from Korea and Japan has declined in the past year or so. Tax haven investment, meanwhile, approached US$16 billion in 2006, with the Virgin Islands by far the largest source ($11.2 billion), followed by the Cayman Islands ($2.1 billion) and Samoa ($1.5 billion). A large portion of this investment comes from Taiwan. It is difficult to provide precise estimates of the share of tax haven investment in China that comes from Taiwan, because the tax havens have many uses, such as lowering tax, disguising ownership, and providing needed property rights services not available in China. For example, Beijing-based hi-tech entrepreneurs will often incorporate in the Cayman Islands in order to utilize venture capital funds, including domestic funds. Some of this shows up as FDI from a tax haven. Despite these

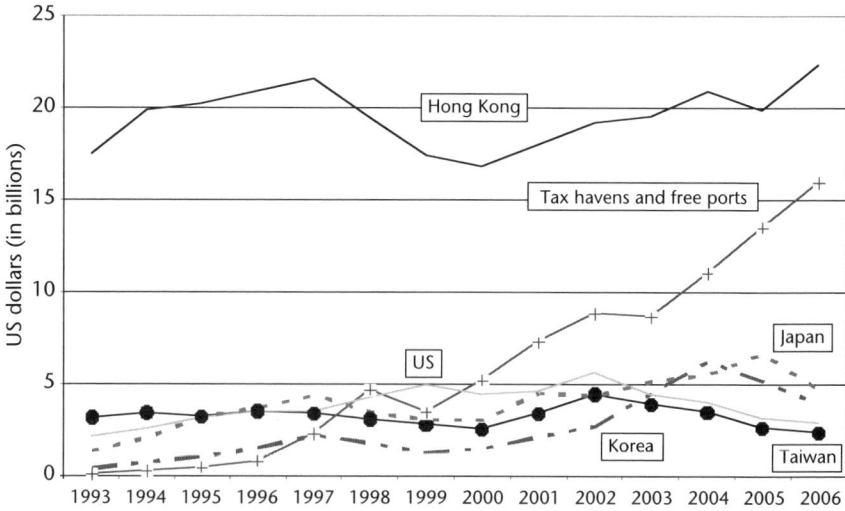

FIGURE 7.1 Main sources of FDI in China.

Source: Author.

complications, a conservative estimate would be that a third of tax haven investment comes originally from Taiwan. In fact, the Chinese Ministry of Commerce estimated that in 2005, US$3.7 billion of Taiwan investment transited through tax havens. If this is added to $2.15 billion registered Taiwan FDI (not including "other" direct investment), total Taiwan FDI in that year is found to have been $5.85 billion. While that figure is actually slightly below FDI from Japan in 2005 (when Japanese investment temporarily surged), it implies that in nearly all years since 1993 Taiwan has been the second largest investor in China, after Hong Kong, with close to $6 billion invested annually in recent years. Next in importance were Korea and Japan, which both invested around $6 billion in their peak years of 2004 and 2005 respectively.

Paradigms of development

The "international subcontracting" model arose to explain the emergence of Japanese, Korean, and Taiwan firms in the global production system. Firms in "late-comer" countries began manufacturing for international markets by subcontracting for global firms headquartered in developed economies. Early-stage firms did not have the capability to enter into global markets on their own and, in exchange for the opportunity of sourcing low-cost manufactured goods, global firms were willing to transfer manufacturing technology. These relationships were formalized into "original equipment manufacturing" (OEM) in which Asian firms produced goods according to specifications provided by global firms, which were sold under the brand names of the global firms. In this model, upgrading occurred as Asian firms developed capabilities beyond simple manufacturing and began to provide a more complex bundle of services. A key stage in upgrading came with the move to "original design manufacturing" (ODM), in which Asian firms were given general product attributes and took over the design of specific products. With widespread success in migrating design capabilities to Asian firms, many anticipated that the next step of upgrading would be the launch of successful Asian brands incorporating product designs developed on Asian soil. This next step was sometimes labeled "own-brand manufacturing" (OBM). Early experience of Japanese firms was widely adduced as evidence that this process was occurring. The key feature of these companies – such as Sony and Samsung – was that they retained their core manufacturing capabilities while adding marketing and brand building.

In Taiwan, this transformation never happened. Taiwanese firms developed enormous sophistication in manufacturing and creative design and technological capabilities. But no firm successfully repositioned itself as a global firm directly selling into the US market. Moreover, even today, there is virtually no significant Taiwan brand equity in the US consumer market.[1] Nor was this unexpected outcome the result of lack of trying. Several companies attempted the transformation to global firm status, none more energetically than Acer Computer, which lost an estimated $3 billion in its effort to establish its brand in the US marketplace (Dean and Spencer 2007). More recently, a similar dynamic seems to have played out in the cell phone handset industry. Since around 2003, a number of Taiwan OEM handset makers have made big plans to bring their own brands to market. The most dramatic move came when BenQ purchased Siemens' handset business as a platform to launch its own-brand business. But by the end of 2006, the Siemens purchase had become a fiasco, and almost all the other handset makes had scaled back their efforts to be own-brand manufacturers. In spite of this nearly uniform record, one frequently hears students, businessmen, economists, and policy-makers argue that the crucial next step is for Taiwan – as well as China and other Asian countries – to establish their own brands in developed country markets.

Instead, a very different process was in evidence. Taiwanese firms built upon their outstanding capability in manufacturing, and leveraged it by incorporating the China Mainland into their production networks. Taiwan developed its own particular, and very profitable, version of the global trend to outsourcing. Taiwanese companies deepened their comparative advantage in manufacturing, but restructured manufacturing operations by locating labor-intensive and low-skill manufacturing stages in China. The paradigm shifted: the focus of productivity improvement and comparative advantage was slicing up the value chain into increasingly narrow slices. The firms that moved along this route most quickly gained competitive advantage. Taiwanese firms seized on their comparative advantage in one particular link of this global process, namely the transfer of labor-intensive production processes to the Mainland, while maintaining control of logistics and more sophisticated manufacturing on the island. In this new paradigm, Taiwan was set to become, and perhaps remain, the "global hi-tech factory." These changes set off an explosive new phase of growth, launched China's export economy and (later) high-tech economy, and propelled Taiwan into a new phase of prosperity.

This phase of development is now history, and it has been well described by many analysts. We can, however, make three quick observations. First, the rapid restructuring that occurred during these twenty years (1985–2005) corresponded very closely to the economist's definition of comparative advantage. The difference in factor endowments between Taiwan and the Mainland created the economic opportunities, and businesses responded. The difference between China's labor-abundant, skill- and capital-scarce economy, and the increasingly skill- and capital-intensive Taiwan economy drove the process. Indeed, in an extended sense, the model applied to several tiers of skill- and capital-intensiveness, ranging from developed countries (US and Japan), to second-tier manufacturing centers (Taiwan and Korea), to third-tier but experienced manufacturing locales (ASEAN), to China's abundant but inexperienced labor. The logic of the restructuring led not only to rapid profit growth but also to some enthusiastic theorizing about mutually beneficial ladders of upgrading, new "flying geese" patterns, etc. (Naughton 1997; Kojima 2000). In retrospect, these theories took for granted relatively large differences among cooperating economies; that is, they assumed a regional hierarchy of skills (Kasahara 2004). The theories described a "maquiladora" connection, in which it is the difference among contiguous economies that drives rapid development.

The second observation is that these theories focused overwhelmingly on factor endowments in production, subordinated demand-side considerations and did not directly address innovation. Implicitly, these theories assumed a continuing reliance on external markets in developed countries such as the US.

Third, and finally, these theories did not directly examine the actual global production networks (GPNs) that implemented restructuring, leaving them in the background. Global corporations were, in the phrase of Ozawa (1995: 2), mere "agents of comparative-advantage recycling." While there was sometimes controversy about the degree of hierarchy in emerging East Asian systems, most of this focused on the role of Japanese corporations (Bernard and Ravenhill 1995; Kasahara 2004). Taiwanese firms were already affiliated with GPNs, but during this period they greatly increased their integration into global production networks. As Ernst and Kim (2002) stress, integration into these networks is highly asymmetric. Developed country "flagship firms" have the predominant power to structure the GPNs themselves, and thus serve as the architect of the overall value chain. Shin-Horng Chen (2004) calls these firms "brand marketers." Taiwan firms, even as they expanded their own logistic operations, and became "mini-flagships" running sub-networks in China, also became even more closely tied to the global brand marketers. Thus, in a sense, Taiwan firms became squeezed into an increasingly narrow niche in the overall production process. Taiwan firms exemplified the global factory.

But overall, this configuration prevailed because it was overwhelmingly the most efficient and lowest-cost strategy. As Borrus (1997) pointed out, this pattern of restructuring raised the profile of Taiwan firms enormously and, in the process, saved US firms (which adopted it quickly) from the competitive challenge created by Japanese firms (which were slow adopters). This process is perfectly exemplified by the notebook computer industry. In 2001, the government in Taiwan first gave Taiwanese notebook computer producers permission to set up assembly operations in China. The share of notebook computers produced by Taiwanese firms operating in China jumped from almost nothing to 71 percent by 2003, and has continued to climb since (Yang 2006). The relocation of notebook production was explosively rapid, and involved the displacement of billions of dollars of trade flows (creating, at one stroke, the impression that China's exports were driven by high-technology products). But what is even more remarkable is the fact that this configuration of production has since driven virtually all competing configurations out of the global market. As Figure 7.2 shows, Taiwan OEM/ODM producers, manufacturing predominantly in China, have steadily increased their share of global notebook production to over 80 percent (Yang 2006; updated MIC 2006). Only a few integrated Japanese firms still produce their own laptops, plus a few ODM operations in Korea.

This was an astonishing outcome. It implies that the "failure" of Taiwan firms to develop into integrated companies with famous name brands was really not a failure at all. Or rather, if it was a failure, it was one shared with every other company in the world. Once we shift our attention from generalizations about economies to observations about specific companies, we see that the "failure" of brand name development was actually only a surface reflection of a deeper contest between business strategies. In that contest, regardless of nationality, one strategy dominated: the strategy of radical delocalization of value chains. In the case of notebook computer

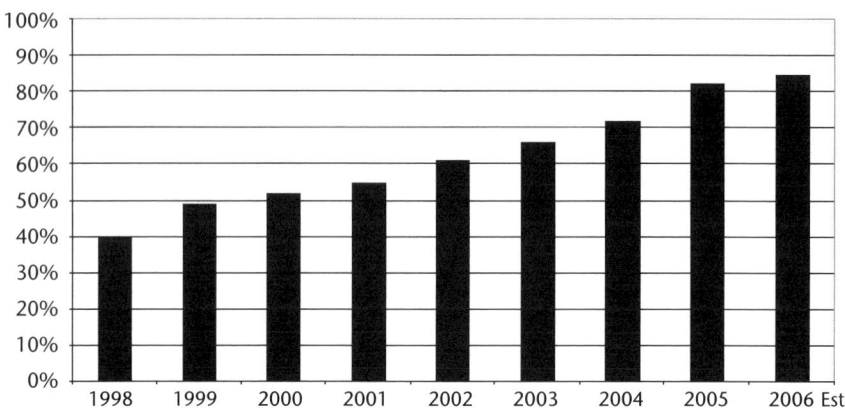

FIGURE 7.2 Notebook computers: global market share of Taiwan OEM/ODM manufacturers.

Source: Calculated from Yang Yung-kai (2006) and Market Intelligence Center (2006).

production, this implied its concentration in the territories on both sides of the Taiwan Strait. In trying to establish itself as a brand leader, Acer could not compete with this model; but nor could any other company in the world. Overall, Taiwan was one of the biggest beneficiaries of this change in production location. In a way, Acer had the last laugh. Wistron, the manufacturing assets of Acer, spun off into a separate company in 2000, is the third largest notebook manufacturer, after Quanta and Compal, and thus one of the main companies that implemented this "both sides of the Taiwan Strait" solution.

Similar patterns are observable in a range of industries from running shoes (Nike and Pou Chen) to cell phones. In all these cases, Taiwan firms became managers of manufacturing systems that extended across both sides of the Taiwan Strait. In that sense, Taiwan became the best exemplar of one of the core processes of globalization, the disaggregation and relocation of global production networks. The astonishing competitiveness of the Taiwan–China notebook computer complex can be traced, paradoxically, in the strategies of two of the most interesting "brand marketers." First, Acer Computer, in the years since its failure to transform itself into an own-brand manufacturer, has reinvented itself as a focused brand marketer, and has achieved substantial success in Europe. Indeed, in 2006, Acer was the fourth largest computer vendor in the world (by number shipped), just behind Lenovo. However, to achieve this success, Acer had to completely adopt the model of the leaders (Dell and HP), and separate out its manufacturing arm. The Acer that is rising in the global rankings is a firm that subcontracts all its production to the same Taiwanese OEM/ODM firms that make Dell and HP computers. Acer's success in Europe seems to show that it can become a successful brand marketer, not that it has become an own-brand manufacturer (OBM). Surprisingly, a related story can be told with respect to Lenovo, the global number three producer. Contrary to much that has been written, Lenovo has never really been a manufacturing powerhouse. Rather, Lenovo demonstrates the importance of strategic flexibility in the Chinese context. The company started out primarily as a reseller of foreign computers, and gradually moved into assembly. Its founder espoused a model he dubbed "mao-gong-ji," or moving from trade, through manufacturing, to technology development. In fact, Lenovo developed a strong domestic brand and good design, distribution, and supply networks. But in 2003, Lenovo outsourced 100 percent of its laptops (and 40 percent of its motherboards) to Taiwanese contract manufacturers, thus turning the "international subcontracting" model on its head (Xie and White 2004; Jiang 2004). Indeed, this inversion is true more generally: the absolute competitive dominance of disaggregated manufacturing networks turned the entire international subcontracting model on its head. Instead of ODM being a transition to a "developed" style OBM, it turned out to be part of a stable long-run division of labor.

Tensions

Despite the enormous successes, tensions have been building around Taiwan's position in global production networks. Most of these tensions can be traced to the dramatic rise of China, combined with Taiwan's relatively narrow insertion into global production networks. As intense competition continues unabated throughout Asia, no model can take its predominance for granted. Large-scale structural changes throw aspects of the "global factory" model into question.

- Decreased salience of skill hierarchy across economies: China's rise has led to a rapid increase in the supply of skilled workers and engineers. More of the tasks that had been reserved in Taiwan can now potentially be moved to China. Logistics, most back-office functions and, crucially, many research and development (R&D) tasks can be performed at lowest cost on the Mainland.
- Increased weight of Chinese production and final markets: The GPNs that initially structured globalization "end" in developed country markets. However, China's rapid growth is beginning to overturn the hierarchy of market size. Now the third largest overall market (by GDP), China has an even larger presence in some categories of electronic goods. Because of the concentration in export-oriented production in China, a huge volume of demand is created for upstream products, including ICs. Moreover, in some markets where population size is an important determinant of overall market demand, such as that for cell phones, China has already emerged as the largest world market.
- Relatively closed networks in China: Taiwanese manufacturers in China continue to source virtually all their inputs from other Taiwanese and foreign-invested firms. While it is true that there has been a massive shift to local procurement, that shift has been made possible by the wholesale transplantation of component suppliers and subcontractors to the Mainland from Taiwan and other countries. For example, Yang (2006) in his study of the notebook computer industry found that *none* of the components to notebook computers were supplied by Chinese companies in 2003, and in his follow-up interviewing found that in only a few

cases did notebook producers rely on Chinese firms even for the cardboard boxes in which computers are packed. There are many reasons for this slow transfer of supply relations, some of which are discussed below. However, it clearly indicates that a potential source of cost-saving is not yet being realized.

- Narrow innovation profile: Taiwan has already become an innovative society. Taiwanese scientists and engineers receive the third largest number of patents from the US Patent Office, after the US and Japan. There is no gainsaying this astonishing achievement. Not surprisingly, most of these patents arise in areas where the energy and intellect of Taiwan scientists are concentrated, which is on the operation of the global hi-tech factory. As a result, these patents are highly concentrated in a few industrial fields, and are dominated by a few outstanding companies (e.g. Taiwan Semiconductor Manufacturing Company [TSMC] and Hon Hai). Reflecting this practical specialization, Taiwan patents score relatively lower in terms of their impact across sectoral and functional categories, and have relatively lower impact in terms of new product creation and new standard definition (Ernst 2006a and the sources cited there). As I will discuss in the following section, most of the innovation is "incremental," within the structure of products and processes defined elsewhere in the GPNs.

- Vulnerability to aggressive intellectual property (IP) strategies being adopted by US companies: As Tain-Jy Chen (2004) argues, developed-country companies, particularly those in the US, are increasingly focused on exploiting the value of their IP portfolios. They are charging more for use of IP, and erecting IP barriers to block entry by emerging industries into lucrative sectors.

- Asymmetric opening by China: Two economic initiatives by China may have negative consequences for Taiwanese firms. The Closer Economic Partnership (CEP) accords firms from Hong Kong and Macau nearly unfettered access to the China market. This special provision, combined with efforts elsewhere to unify tax rates on foreign and domestic firms in China, may give Hong Kong firms an advantage over Taiwanese firms. Similarly, the China-ASEAN Free Trade Agreement, as it gradually takes effect over the next decade, may also marginalize Taiwan to a certain extent. None of these are immediate threats, but they may gather force over the next few years (East Asia Economy 2007).

As a result of all these factors, there has been substantial pressure on the profitability of Taiwanese manufacturers. For example, despite their astonishing competitive success, notebook computer producers experienced dramatically declining profit margins from 1998 through 2004, when average margins declined from about 16 percent to only 6 percent (Yang 2006). Other companies are feeling the pressure as well. The tepid recent performance of the Taiwan stock market is of course due to multiple factors, but one contributing factor has certainly been the relatively slow growth of firm profits.

All of these challenges are directly related to the specific character of Taiwanese companies' integration into global production networks. Such companies have invested heavily in knowledge, experience, and physical capital in order to respond to the demands of flagship companies in GPNs. Flagship companies control the marketing process and the knowledge of the market; they dominate new product innovation, and most important of all, they structure the transactions through the GPNs so that they have substantial market power to play off Taiwan suppliers against each other. Taiwan ODMs sell to a small number of flagship companies. The top five personal computer brand marketers make over 50 percent of world computer sales, including desktop and notebook computers (Dean and Spencer 2007). There are more than 10 highly capable, efficient, competing Taiwan OEM/ODM notebook manufacturers. The flagship companies, as architects of the GPNs, have exerted substantial efforts to maintain this configuration of market power. This follows a basic principle of business school education: "Economic rent arises from differentiation and migrates to wherever in the value chain scarcity is found" (Kay 2006). These networks are structured in a way that makes it extremely difficult for Taiwanese firms to earn much economic rent.

None of these challenges indicates that the existing model of Taiwan integration into GPNs is flawed, harmful to Taiwan, or doomed. Quite the contrary. This model of production is responsible for Taiwan's emergence to an unprecedented level of prosperity, and it will continue to be an important pillar of Taiwan's prosperity for the foreseeable future. But every strategy or organizational solution has costs and benefits. Heretofore, the benefits have strongly outweighed the costs, as this strategy has been highly compatible with significant knowledge transfer, rising capabilities, and increasing income. However, we are now in a historical phase of global economic change in which the costs of Taiwan's narrow insertion into GPNs are beginning to rise, while the benefits are, arguably, stagnating. This does not mean that Taiwanese companies should abandon successful business models. However, it does mean that a few of these companies should seek other approaches to growth through innovation in a new global economy, and that the Taiwanese government should support these efforts. The particular paths this relative handful of future successful firms will follow cannot be predicted, but a different framework of analysis can help us see in which general direction those paths are likely to go.

Modularity and a typology of innovation

Taiwan's rapid ascent, and its emergence as a global hi-tech factory, was made possible by modularity. Modularity can be defined as a characteristic of the design of a product or process, in which specifications and tasks are interdependent within units (modules) and independent across them. Design and production can then be concentrated on a single module, enabling a uniform and predictable interface linking that module with the next. Modularity, combined with electronic data transmission, is what made the disaggregation and relocation of value chains into GPNs possible. It is not a coincidence that modularity has had the most dramatic impact in the personal computer industry. The standard Wintel architecture was intentionally and successfully leveraged into a fully modular format by Intel engineers, in their quest to make their own CPUs (Central Processing Units) the dominant standard (Gawer and Cusumano 2002). Once that was achieved, modular design rapidly eroded the economic rationale for vertical integration.

Market-led standardization (through technical standards and design rules) of the interfaces between separate stages of production made it possible to transform PCs and related products into fully decomposable building blocks. This created ample opportunities for vertical specialization ("fragmentation") of the PC value chain, giving rise to the OEM/ODM arrangements discussed earlier. Subsequently, modular production has extended well beyond the PC industry. One outstanding case has been Taiwan's breakthrough success in the development of the semiconductor industry, which was due to the decoupling of design and fabrication by TSMC that culminated in the creation of separate IC foundries and fabless IC design companies. As with earlier forms of modular production in the PC industry, decoupling IC design and fabrication was based on shared interface standards, and well-documented and automatically checkable "design rules."

Modularity also gives a specific form to the innovation process. Drawing on an earlier paper (Ernst and Naughton 2007), I use a well-known taxonomy of innovation that distinguishes "incremental," "modular," "architectural," and "radical" innovations (Henderson and Clark 1990). This taxonomy of innovation is shown graphically in Figure 7.3. "Incremental" innovations take both the dominant component design and architecture for granted, but improve on cost, time-to-market, and performance. With "modular" innovation, new component technology is plugged into a system architecture that is fundamentally unchanged. This type of innovation has been a defining characteristic of the personal computer industry; for instance, the multi-functional USB port on the personal computer facilitates and exemplifies modular innovation.

"Architectural" innovations change the way components are designed to work together, but use existing component technology that is available on the market to

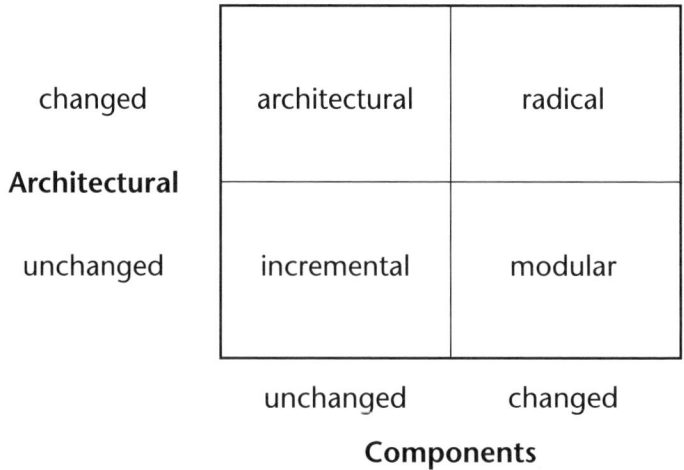

FIGURE 7.3 Typology of innovations.
Source: Adapted from Henderson and Clark (1990).

implement new designs. Architectural innovations thus introduce substantially new and distinct features to existing system architectures. They also build on a company's familiarity with market demands. Finally, "radical" innovations involve both the use of new component technology and changes in architectural design. They typically involve breakthroughs in both areas, such as the invention of the internet. These innovations receive the greatest attention, and high margins through premium pricing and strong market entry deterrents. However, radical innovations require an extremely broad base of capabilities, and involve huge risks. They are beyond the reach of most IT companies in China.

We can see that the focus of Taiwanese firms on incremental innovation, discussed above, is a logical consequence of their integration into GPNs dominated by flagship firms, in which they have been given responsibility for a production module. In this set-up, innovation and process improvement are naturally channeled into incremental improvement, particularly under circumstances of intense competition and cost pressures. Other types of innovation are more difficult for Taiwanese firms to achieve: radical innovations are of course rare and difficult everywhere. These firms also face barriers in their pursuit of modular innovation, since the definition of the module is generally, though not always, given by the flagship firm. Most important for our purposes, firms in Taiwan face obstacles in architectural innovations. Architectural innovations are those that are most likely to depend on contact with the end market. They emerge when someone has an incentive to meet a new market need, or to meet an existing market need in a fresh and unconventional way. In this respect, Taiwanese firms pay a penalty for their (otherwise very beneficial) integration into GPNs. They are slightly removed from the ultimate consumer in developed countries. Despite the excellent and efficient interchange of technical and market information between Silicon Valley and Taiwan (for example), firms in Taiwan do not have strong incentives to pursue architectural innovations. Architectural innovations are frequently "disruptive" in the sense in which Christensen (1997) uses the word, and existing Taiwanese firms have a strong interest in maintaining the existing configuration of GPNs.

We can see this by examining the concept of disruptive technologies more thoroughly. Christensen argues that established market leaders – he is mainly concerned with integrated device manufacturers, but the logic includes brand marketers who control GPNs – typically take the lead in the adoption of new component technology, while successful new entrants rely on architectural innovations. Technological complexity, and hence risk and cost, are lower for architectural innovations than for the development of new components, and architectural innovations lead more immediately to increased sales and profitability. Disruptive technologies bring to market very different products: they have features that initially only few new customers value. Products based on disruptive technologies are typically cheaper, simpler, smaller, and, frequently, more convenient to use. Incumbent firms, especially market leaders, generally fail to notice "lower-end" markets that may erode their market leadership. That is because they promise lower margins, their most profitable customers generally do not want products based on disruptive technologies, and the required break from routine requires a different organization from sustaining technologies. Developing disruptive technologies can sometimes be achieved with an organization of innovation with substantially lower overheads.

Disruptive, architectural innovations can make some firms very prosperous. However, the key requirement is that the firms have direct contact with a market that is large enough to make the innovative effort worthwhile. This is what Taiwanese firms have sacrificed for the substantial benefits of technology transfer and collaborative innovation with flagship firms in GPNs. While this has been a reasonable choice in the past – indeed perhaps it was the only choice for Taiwan at that stage of its development – as argued above, changes in world market conditions are increasing the costs and reducing the benefits of the existing configuration. However, those same changes are also creating new opportunities. On the basis of our discussion of types of innovation, we are in a position to explore those opportunities.

Three changes that are reshaping future opportunities

Three changes are reshaping Taiwan's economic environment. They are the rise of the China market, the disaggregation of research and development, and continuous technological changes that alter the incentives within modular systems.

Growing China market

It is obvious that the growing China market creates economic opportunity in many respects. I am here concerned with only one aspect, which is the opportunity to use proximity to that market to develop disruptive architectural innovations. Taiwanese firms are close to the China market in a way that they are not to the US market. Geographic and cultural proximity, combined with income differentials with the largest Mainland cities that have narrowed significantly, all bring the China market into clear focus for Taiwanese companies. Moreover, innovative activities with respect to the Chinese market are relatively open and unregulated. While the Chinese government intervenes in markets for core technologies, it leaves the field of play relatively open for market-oriented innovations. Moreover, the fact that the Chinese economy is relatively open means that key elements of high-tech components can be sourced at world prices. Ironically, it was mentioned above that the Chinese firm Lenovo outsources its notebook computer production to Taiwan ODMs. Similar practise is evident with respect to Chinese handset manufacturers, which have recourse to Taiwan OEMs sometimes for whole handsets, and sometimes for sub-assemblies. In any case, core components for handsets are easily bought from international companies (Liu 2005). This is the type of innovative activity in which we see many of the most interesting Chinese start-up firms concentrating. Conditions are ripe for a quick, opportunistic, low-cost approach to product innovation. Examples can be found in the handset industry and in the VCD industry. Another example is the Personal Handy-Phone System (PHS), or xiaolingtong. This fixed-line wireless system provides coverage in urban areas, and is much cheaper to use than a GSM system. For a very mobile society like the US, PHS would be very impractical, but in China this disruptive technology has thrived, even if temporarily. The PHS does not contain much real innovation (since it is basically adapted from Japan), and may not have much staying power. But it perfectly illustrates Christensen's point about underserved and underappreciated customers. This is the type of innovation that will be important in China, confounding pessimists like Nolan (2002), Rosen (2003) and Steinfeld (2004).

As the China market grows, this dynamic becomes more and more important. China has the size to serve as a lead market (Beise 2004) and the diversity of demand to generate economically significant lead users (Von Hippel 1998). *Some* Taiwanese firms will be well placed to take advantage of this opportunity. Most will not, but a significant minority may be in a position to exploit new product, market-based architectural innovations based on the China market. Such firms, by Christensen's logic, are not very likely to be the incumbent firms managing the subnetworks of the GPNs. Instead, they will be more entrepreneurial, maverick firms. One area where we might expect to see different patterns of activity in the future is in the area of low-cost computing. Already the market incumbents, Lenovo and Dell are stepping up their efforts to be reliable suppliers of computers in the US$300–400 price range (Nystedt 2007; Spencer 2007). It would not be surprising, however, to find, a decade from now, that this important new market had in fact been opened up by a maverick firm from China or Taiwan.

Taiwanese firms clearly recognize the opportunities. However, so far the most important response has been that of incumbent firms that seek to cooperate with the Chinese government over new technical standards. Cross-Straits cooperation on technical standards has been robust on video discs, and the creation of Sinocon (华聚产业共同标准推动基金会) in 2005 established a formal channel for cooperation with official Chinese bodies of 3G phone standards (TD-SCDMA), among other things (East Asia Economy 2007). Such efforts are good as far as they go. However, they tend to be driven too narrowly by a pecuniary motive (reducing royalty payments to existing IP holders), too dominated by government, and insufficiently entrepreneurial. Moreover, they have yet to return any obvious successes. If TD-SCDMA turns out to be a costly failure, the whole programme will be discredited. If, unexpectedly, TD-SCDMA thrives, the effort will retrospectively look very good. For Taiwanese firms seeking new opportunities for innovative development, standard-setting is a sideshow. Profitable opportunities will come from new products, with new attributes or fundamentally cheaper approaches. They will succeed in the marketplace long before they are mandated as standards by the Chinese government. The real opportunities are impossible to predict because they will only be seen by visionaries and captured by companies who have the incentives to be opportunistic.

Disaggregating research and development

Global production networks are being transformed by the introduction of research and development (R&D) into the logic of delocalization. The abundant supplies of low-cost skilled research personnel appearing in China and India are without doubt the fundamental drivers of this change. Increasingly, multinational firms are including China and India in their innovation strategies, creating global innovation networks (GINs) complementary to their GPNs (NSF 2004; Ernst 2006b).

Not surprisingly, Taiwan firms have also begun offshoring R&D to the China Mainland (Chen 2004; Liu and Chen 2006). Shin-Horng Chen (2004: 346) points out that Taiwan R&D in China is being driven by the needs and opportunities of existing China operations, rather than by traditional dichotomies between "high end" and "low end" processes. Instead, Chen sees Taiwan R&D evolving toward the needs to localize and qualify more suppliers, on the one hand, and toward market adaptation and exploitation, on the other. This type of adaptation has profound consequences for Taiwanese firms. First, it creates a more profound type of sharing with individuals and companies on the China Mainland, as cooperation extends into research fields. Further, it provides Taiwanese companies with much stronger capabilities to respond to and exploit market needs, as and when they are seen. Close interaction with suppliers and customers is one of the most important sources of innovative ideas – some would argue, the most important source. Adaptation of Taiwan R&D to the relative costs of R&D on either side of the Taiwan Strait will bring Taiwanese firms more opportunities for disruptive innovation keyed to the China market.

Re-aggregating modules

Modularity is not an inevitable and universal feature. Rather, modular production and innovation are the product of technological and economic relationships. While the trend in the direction of modularity has been dominant in both hardware and software in the past twenty years, there are exceptions and countervailing tendencies. For example, in the integrated circuit industry, the separation between chip design and chip fabrication may have reached a limit. As increasingly complex system-on-a-chip (SOC) designs are developed, closer interaction between design and manufacturing becomes necessary. We see this in Taiwan in the development of TSMC's business model in recent years, which has increasingly stressed closer cooperation with customers and a package of design solutions that are bundled with fabrication (Ernst 2006a). Similar trends are drawing IC design capabilities to China to be close to end-user demands. Patterns of rapid upgrading and increased complexity in that industry, clustered around Shanghai, were found by Obukhova (2006) in her survey, completed in 2005. Even when modularity implies that processes can be separated, business logic may demand that they be in constant interaction.

More generally, no matter how strong the technological forces that support modularity, businesses always seek strategies that link production more closely to market demands. As a result, modularity in technology does not necessarily imply that separate modules are managed by separate companies (even though that has been the trend in the PC industry in recent years). Of course, modularity may enhance the ability to respond to market needs by facilitating a decentralized approach to innovation of different aspects of highly complex systems like a PC. But responsiveness can also be achieved by coordinating responses to the market within a single organization. Thus, for a while it seemed that certain highly integrated Japanese corporations, like Sony, had hit the "sweet spot" of market responsiveness by institutionalizing a highly consultative process of product design and manufacturing through the company (Nonaka and Takeuchi 1995). But consider the alternative model of a company like Apple. Apple certainly is a brand marketer, and it outsources all of its production to ODMs in Taiwan and Singapore. But the real asset that Apple deploys, and which undergirds its brand equity, is its fierce focus on design for the end-user. Apple keeps its engineers on a tight leash, as it insists that every design solution be intuitive and simple to an ordinary user. This focus distinguished the iPod from hundreds of other cheaper MP3 players, but it was not enough to guarantee the iPod's spectacular success. Such success was achieved only when Apple was able to deploy its core design competence *simultaneously* to the hardware and the software (iTunes), while cleverly linking them together with a proprietary system. It was one of the great business coups of the new century, and it was achieved by a combination of a strong core competence along with a strategic re-assembly of the value chain. Apple was close enough to its target market that it could provide precisely the right bundle of characteristics that this market wanted.

This experience offers a kind of beacon to Taiwanese companies. It is not, of course, that any company will replicate Apple's particular strategy. Rather, the example shows that the Taiwanese firms that break out of their narrow insertion into GPNs will not do so by evolving down the existing value chain, becoming OBMs that compete with existing flagship firms. Instead, the break-out firms will be those that combine different stages – potentially different modules – of the value chain in unexpected ways that are driven by a keen appreciation of market needs. For a Taiwanese firm, that market is far more likely to be in China than it is to be in the US.

In terms of global business strategy, this thrust accords with the increasing emphasis on system integration, or the provision of integrated services to customers (Hobday *et al.* 2005). In part, as the share of value-added attributed to manufacturing declines around the world, and the share due to service increases, business strategies naturally follow the money and seek to bundle lucrative services with manufacturing. This leads to a strategic re-assembly of the value chain that positions the company to better serve its markets. While this kind of logic is especially clear in high-tech products, we see it in other areas as well. An example would be the Hong Kong clothing sourcing and logistics company Li & Fung, which has expanded steadily by providing customers with a gradually more complex package of design and delivery options made possible by electronic platforms.

With respect to their existing value chains, Taiwanese firms may find themselves stuck in asymmetrical positions with respect to flagship firms. At the root of the asymmetrical bargaining position of manufacturers and brand marketers, though, is the strong grasp on the US market that the brand marketers possess. Taiwanese firms are most likely to break out of that position by linking up to the China market, recognizing better ways to meet emerging market demands, and strategically recombining different stages of the value chain to meet those needs.

Conclusion

Past paradigms do not provide a very good guide to Taiwan's future industrial evolution. Evolution into own-brand manufacturers, along some path that leads from subcontracting to integration of manufacturing and marketing, has already proven to be a mirage. Concentration in specific manufacturing sectors, such that Taiwan remains the global hi-tech factory, will continue to be an important part of Taiwan's economic performance, but the cost and benefit ratio is shifting away from this pattern of production organization.

Fortunately, three changes currently taking place offer Taiwanese companies a good opportunity to rejuvenate their business models and create a new period of prosperity. By linking more closely to the China market, redistributing and building research capabilities that are close to that market, and strategically re-assembling new production networks, Taiwanese firms can create innovative products and companies with long potential life spans. The firms that succeed in this endeavor will be visionary, maverick, and highly entrepreneurial. Fortunately, Taiwan long ago demonstrated that it was well endowed with vision and entrepreneurship.

The policy implications of such a view are not unambiguous. Such processes cannot be planned by governments, and it is futile to try. The strongest support the Taiwanese government can give to such a process is to encourage a closer integration between Taiwan and the Mainland, and permit firms maximum flexibility in their choices about location of activities between Taiwan and the Mainland. Current policy impedes such entrepreneurship in a number of ways, including the "40 percent limit" on investment in the Mainland. Of course, these economic policy decisions cannot be made in a vacuum, and depend on cooperation from the government in China and agreement in Taiwanese society. However, for Taiwan the path to a mode of deeper globalization with more autonomy and more prosperity almost certainly leads through China. The alternative would be a quieter, and perhaps more comfortable, existence, but at the sacrifice of a great deal of dynamism.

Bibliography

Beise, M. (2004). "Lead Markets: Country-Specific Drivers of the Global Diffusion of Innovations," *Research Policy*, 33 (6–7): 997–1018.

Bernard, Mitchell and John Ravenhill (1995). "Beyond Product Cycles and Flying Geese: Regionalization, Hierarchy, and the Industrialization of East Asia," *World Politics*, 47 (January): 171–209.

Borrus, Michael (1997). "Left for Dead: Wintelism, Asian Production Networks and the Revival of U.S. Electronics." In Barry Naughton (ed.), *The China Circle: Economics and Technology in the PRC, Taiwan, and Hong Kong*, Washington, DC: The Brookings Institution Press, pp. 141–2.

Chen, Shin-Horng (2002). "Global Production Networks and Information Technology: The Case of Taiwan," *Industry and Innovation*, 9 (3) (December): 249–65.

Chen, Shin-Horng (2004). "Taiwanese IT Firms' Offshore R&D in China and the Connection with the Global Innovation Network," *Research Policy*, 33: 337–49.

Chen, Shin-Horng, Meng-Chun Liu and Ku-Ho Lin (2005). "Industrial Development Models and Economic Outputs: A Reflection on the 'High Tech, High Value-Added' Proposition," manuscript, Taipei: Chung-Hua Institution for Economic Research.

Chen, Tain-Jy, (2004). "The Challenges of the Knowledge-Based Economy." In Tain-Jy Chen and Joseph S. Lee (eds.), *The New Knowledge Economy of Taiwan*, Cheltenham: Edward Elgar.

Christensen, C. M. (1997). *The Innovator's Dilemma: When New Technologies Cause Great Firms to Fail*, Boston: Harvard Business School Press.

Collier, Paul and David Dollar (2002). *Globalisation, Growth and Poverty: Building an Inclusive World Economy*, Washington, DC: The World Bank.

Dean, Jason and Jane Spencer (2007). "Acer Seeks Happiness in Its 'Land of Sorrow,'" *Wall Street Journal*, April 5, pp. B1, B6.

East Asia Economy (2007). "东亚经济格局的变动及其对两岸经贸关系的影响 [Changes in the East Asian Economic Situations and their Influence on Economic and Trade Relations Across the Taiwan Strait]," *Yatai Jingji*, March 28. Available online at http://www.9max.com/research/html/2007-3-28/20073281044261.htm.

Ernst, Dieter (2006a). "Upgrading through Innovation in a Small Network Economy: Insights from Taiwan's IT industry," paper presented at international conference "High Tech Regions 2.0 – Sustainability and Reinvention," Stanford University, November 13 and 14, 2006.

Ernst, Dieter (2006b). "Innovation Offshoring: Asia's Emerging Role in Global Innovation Networks," Special Report, East-West Center and the U.S.-Asia-Pacific Council, East-West Center, Honolulu, July.

Ernst, Dieter and Linsu Kim (2002). "Global Production Networks, Knowledge Diffusion and Local Capability Formation," *Research Policy*, 31 (8/9): 1417–29.

Ernst, Dieter and Barry Naughton (2007). "China's Emerging Industrial Economy – Insights from the IT Industry," chapter 3 of Christ McNally (ed.), *China's Emergent Political Economy: Capitalism in the Dragon's Lair*. London: Routledge.

Gawer, Annabelle and Michael A. Cusumano (2002). *Platform Leadership: How Intel, Microsoft, and Cisco Drive Industry Innovation*. Boston: Harvard Business School Press.

Henderson, R. M. and K. Clark (1990). "Architectural Innovation: The Reconfiguration of Existing Systems and the Failure of Established Firms," *Administrative Science Quarterly*, 35 (March): 9–30.

Hobday, M. (1995). *Innovation in East Asia: The Challenge to Japan*, Aldershot: Edward Elgar.

Hobday, M., A. Davies, and A. Prencipe (2005). "Systems Integration: A Core Capability of the Modern Corporation," *Industrial and Corporate Change*, 14 (6): 1109–43.

Jiang, X. (2004). "2003–2004: Zhongguo Liyong Waizi de Fenxi yu Zhanwang [An Analysis and Outlook of China's Use of Foreign Direct Investments]." In G. Liu, L. Wang, and J. Li (eds.), *Zhongguo Jingji Qianjing Fenxi 2004 Nian Chunji Baogao [Blue Book of China's Economy Spring 2004]*, Beijing: Shehui Kexue Wenxian, pp. 202–27.

Kasahara, Shigehisa (2004). "The Flying Geese Paradigm: A Critical Study of Its Application to East Asian Regional Development," UNCTAD Discussion Paper No. 169 (April).

Kay, John (2006). "From Price Bubbles to Flat Sales: The Story of Champagne," *Financial Times*, 19 December.

Kojima, Kiyoshi (2000). "The 'Flying Geese' Model of Asian Economic Development: Origin, Theoretical Extensions, and Regional Policy Implications," *Journal of Asian Economics*, 11: 375–401.

Linden, G. (2004). "China Standard Time: A Study in Strategic Industrial Policy," *Business and Politics*, 6 (3): Article 4. Available online at http://www.bepress.com/bap/vol6/iss3/art4 (accessed February 9, 2007).

Liu, Meng-Chun and Shin-Horng Chen (2006). "Cross-Border R&D Networks and International R&D: A Quantitative Study of Taiwanese Firms," Chung-Hua Institution for Economic Research, April.

Liu, Xielin (2005). "China's Development Model: An Alternative Strategy for Technological Catch-Up," working paper, Institute of Innovation Research, Hitotsubashi University, March 22.

Lu, Q. (2000). *China's Leap into the Information Age: Innovation and Organization in the Computer Industry*, Oxford: Oxford University Press.

Market Intelligence Center (MIC) Taiwan (2006). "Taiwan IT Hardware Industry – Recap and Forecast," January 4. Available online at http://www.emsnow.com/newsarchives/archivedetails.cfm?ID=11648.

Ministry of Commerce Science and Technology Division (2006). "2005 Nian woguo gaoxin jishu chanpin jinchukou an qiye xingzhi fenlei tongji [High Technology Exports for 2005, Divided by Type of Enterprise]," January 26. Available online at kjs.mofcom.gov.cn/aarticle/bn/cbw/200601/20060101434158.html (accessed February 5, 2007).

Ministry of Commerce (2007). "出口企业性质 [Exports by Enterprise Type]," February 2, 2007. Available online at http://zhs.mofcom.gov.cn/aarticle/Nocategory/200702/20070204344012.html.

Mu, Q. and K. Lee (2005). "Knowledge Diffusion, Market Segmentation and Technological Catch-Up: The Case of the Telecommunication Industry in China," *Research Policy*, 34 (6): 759–83.

Naughton, B. (1997). *The China Circle: Economics and Technology in the PRC, Taiwan, and Hong Kong*. Washington, DC: The Brookings Institution Press.

Naughton, B. (2007). *The Chinese Economy: Transitions and Growth*, Cambridge, MA: MIT Press.

Nolan, P. (2002). "China and the Global Business Revolution," *Cambridge Journal of Economics*, 26 (1): 119–37.

Nonaka, Ikujiro and Hiro Takeuchi (1995). *The Knowledge-creating Company: How Japanese Companies Create the Dynamics of Innovation*. New York: Oxford University Press.

National Science Foundation (NSF) Division of Science Resources Statistics (2004). *U.S.-China R&D Linkages: Direct Investment and Industrial Alliances in the 1990s*. Arlington, VA: NSF, 04–306 (February 2004). Available online at www.nsf.gov/sbe/srs/infbrief/nsf04306/start.htm.

Nystedt, Dan (2007). "Dell Launches Low-Cost PC in China," IDG News Service in PC World, March 22, 2007. Available online at http://www.pcworld.com/article/id,130037/article.html (accessed March 28, 2007).

Obukhova, Elena (2006). "Liuxuesheng qiye tuidong Zhongguo jicheng dianlu shejiye kuaisu fazhan [Returnee Enterprises Stimulate the Rapid Development of China's IC Design Industry]," unpublished report (in Chinese). Available online at http://home.uchicago.edu/~elenao/semiconductors/obukhova_report.pdf.

Ozawa, T. (1995). "The 'Flying Geese' Paradigm of FDI, Economic Development and Shifts in Competitiveness," a background paper submitted to UNCTAD.

Qian, P. (2003). "Development of China's Industrial Clusters: Features and Problems," *China Development Review*, 5 (4): 44–51.

Rosen, D. (2003). "China Tech," *China Economic Quarterly*, Q4: 19–40.

Spencer, Jane (2007). "Why Lenovo Can't Tame US As Shipments Drop, Buyer of IBM's PC Division Shifts Marketing," *Wall Street Journal*, February 2, 2007, p. A14.

Steinfeld, E. (2004). "Chinese Enterprise Development and the Challenge of Global Integration." In S. Yusuf (ed.), *East Asian Networked Production*, Washington, DC: World Bank.

Suttmeier, P. and X. Yao (2004). "China's Post-WTO Technology Policy: Standards, Software, and the Changing Nature of Techno-Nationalism," NBR Special Report, No. 7. Available online at www.nbr.org/publications/specialreport/pdf/SR7.pdf (accessed February 5, 2007).

Taiwan Research Institute (China) (2007). "台商在大陆投资现状及发展趋势、现存问题有哪些？[Current Conditions and Trends of Taiwan Business Investment in the Mainland:

What are the current problems?]." Available online at http://www.chinataiwan.org/web/webportal/W5267023/Ushaotian/A398155.html.

Von Hippel, E. (1988). *The Sources of Innovation*, New York: Oxford University Press.

Xie, W. and S. White (2004). "Sequential Learning in a Chinese Spin-Off: The Case of Lenovo Group Limited," *R&D Management*, 34 (4): 407–22.

Yang, Yung-Kai (2006). "The Taiwanese Notebook Computer Production Network in China: Implications for Upgrading of the Chinese Electronics Industry," University of California, Irvine, Personal Computer Industry Center Working Paper (February). Available online at http://www.pcic.merage.uci.edu/papers/2006/TaiwaneseNotebook.pdf.

Note

1 According to a study by the Taiwan Board of Foreign Trade and branding consultancy Interbrand, the most valuable global brand equity out of Taiwan was TrendMicro, followed by ASUS and Acer. These are major companies, but not well-known brands in the US (TrendMicro is better known in Japan).

8

GLOBALIZATION, DYNAMIC COMPARATIVE ADVANTAGE, AND TAIWAN'S DRIVE FOR SUSTAINABLE DEVELOPMENT[1]

Peter C. Y. Chow

Introduction

Economic globalization is generally referred to as integration of national econo-mies into a globalized system through trade, foreign direct investment, capital and technology flows. The most noteworthy development since the 1980s has been the "functional integration" to internationalize economic activities across national boundaries (Dicken 1998: 5). This development does not only involve the quantitative process of opening trade regimes and liberalizing capital flows, but also the qualitative process of expanding all economic activities across national boundaries, including the movements of factors of production as well as segmentation of the production process. Among them, the increasing compartmentalization of manufactured produc-tion and the segmentation of components as well as parts across national boundaries, have led to the unprecedented economic integration in the world economy since the 1980s. The increasing trade-foreign investment nexus, international migra-tion, technology and capital flows were fostered by technological development and boosted by the economic liberalization undertaken in both developed and developing countries.[2] Hence, globalization and economic liberalization have proceeded hand in hand.

As a small open economy with foreign trade accounting for more than 100 per-cent of its total GDP,[3] Taiwan has no vital alternative but to cope with the trend of globalization. Since the mid-1980s, Taiwan has become one of the largest investors in East and Southeast Asia, and its economy has also become increasingly integrated through the trade and foreign investment nexus with many of its host countries in the region (Bende-Nabende 2003; Kreinin *et al.* 2000; Urata 2001). By examining trade competitiveness based on technology level (Lall 2000) and the trade speciali-zation index (Lall *et al.* 2005), this study investigates how globalization has affected Taiwan's dynamic comparative advantage over time, and how Taiwan can cope with globalization amid the rising regionalism so as to maintain its sustainable development. In this study, "sustainable" is defined as a persistent economic growth with the given resources endowments without eroding the current level of environmental quality.[4] For a trade-dependent economy such as Taiwan, sustainable development requires it to continually maintain its dynamic comparative advantages in the global economy by penetrating in the "niche markets" with its "niche products."

Since the 1980s, Taiwan has been pursuing its liberalization – a process propelled by both internal and external forces. These included currency appreciation after the Plaza Accord in 1985, which substantially undercut its comparative advantage in labor-intensive exports in the world market and a growing trade surplus, especially its trade surplus with the US, and the resultant swollen foreign exchange reserves, which mandated the lift of its control on capital outflows. Significant developments since the 1980s include the liberalization of capital outflow and outward foreign direct investment (FDI), the gradual lifting of restrictions on foreign portfolio investment in domestic capital markets, deregulation of the banking industry,[5] privatization of state banks,[6] and the phasing out of restrictions of trade and investment in Mainland China, both of which accelerated after Taiwan's accession to the World Trade Organization in January 2002.[7] After decades of export-led development primarily based on labor-intensive manufactures, Taiwan has reached the stage of "factor incongruity" (Ozawa 1992) and has been transformed from a labor-surplus to labor-scarce economy. Similar to what Japan did since the 1960s and accelerated after the Plaza Accord in 1985, Taiwan has to seek the "comparative advantage augmented type of outward FDI" for its sustainable development.

As a result, Taiwan has also shifted its status from being a net recipient to a net provider of capital flow in the world economy. Moreover, liberalization of outward FDI has enabled many of its multinational corporations (MNCs), notably the information technology and computer industry (ITC), to set up regional production networks overseas. Consequently, Taiwan has become one of the largest investing countries in Southeast Asia and China, and its economy has been fully integrated with those in the Asia-Pacific region without having formal bilateral and-or multilateral/regional trading agreements with those countries. The salient feature of Taiwan's globalization could be illustrated by its significant role in linking the global supply chain of ITC industry from Silicon Valley in California to many science and industrial clusters in East and Southeast Asian countries. The evolving structural transformation of its industrial production and changing composition of its exports toward more technology-intensive products have qualified it to become one of the newly industrialized countries (NIC). In fact, Taiwan would have been admitted to OECD had it not been disrupted by political factors.

The ongoing drive of globalization was complemented with Taiwan's dynamic comparative advantage and paralleled the global trend of the trade–investment nexus, especially in the Asia-Pacific region. This chapter is organized in the following order: First, I investigate the sequential order of liberalization that has occurred in order to cope with globalization. Second, I analyze the theoretical underpinnings of dynamic comparative advantage in the global context. Third, I discuss the division of labor based on the trade specialization index and level of production technology. Fourth, I address how Taiwan could break through the "spaghetti regionalism" of the proliferations of bilateral and regional trading arrangements, and policies to cope with the rise of China so as to maintain its sustainable development. The final section concludes the chapter.

Sequential order of liberalization to cope with globalization

As a late industrialized country, Taiwan along with Korea has arguably followed a similar development trajectory as that of post-war Japan. Yet, Taiwan's drive for globalization has far exceeded that of Korea in both inward and outward FDI. In terms of annual inward FDI flows as a percentage of gross fixed capital formation, Taiwan has a ratio that is more than double that of Korea before Korea's 1997 financial crisis, and far exceeded that of Korea most of the time after 1997. In terms of inward FDI stock as a percentage of total GDP, Taiwan far exceeded that of Korea most of the time except for the global IT recession in 2000–1. Much more significant evidence is found in Taiwan's outward FDI; since 1985, outward FDI as percentage of gross fixed capital formation increased steadily from 0.7 percent in 1985 to 13.69 percent in 2007, and outward FDI stock as a percentage of GDP fluctuated from 21.4 percent in 1985 to 44.84 percent in 2008. Since the US is one of the largest recipients and providers of FDI in the world, and Japan is the leader of late industrialized countries, Figures 8.1–8.4 show the time series of their bidirectional FDIs for comparisons.

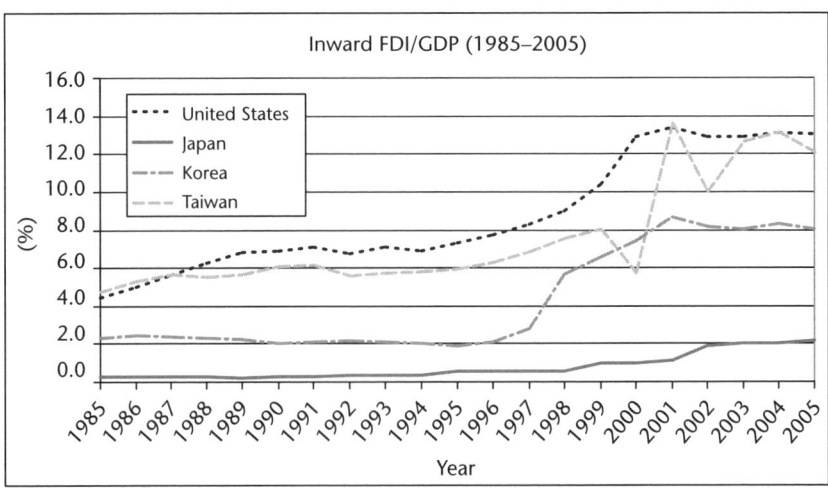

FIGURE 8.1   Inward FDI stock as percentage of total GDP in the US, Japan, Korea, and Taiwan.

Source: *World Investment Report 2004*, UNCTAD.

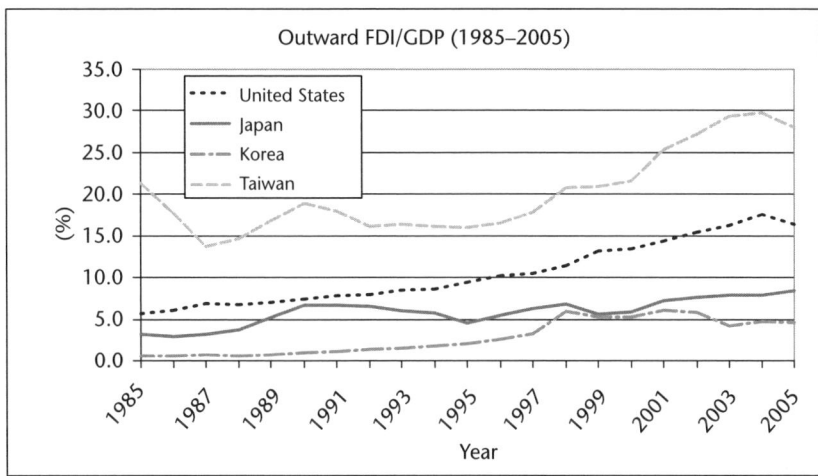

FIGURE 8.2 Outward FDI flow as percentage of GDP in the US, Japan, Korea, and Taiwan.

Source: *World Investment Report 2004*, UNCTAD.

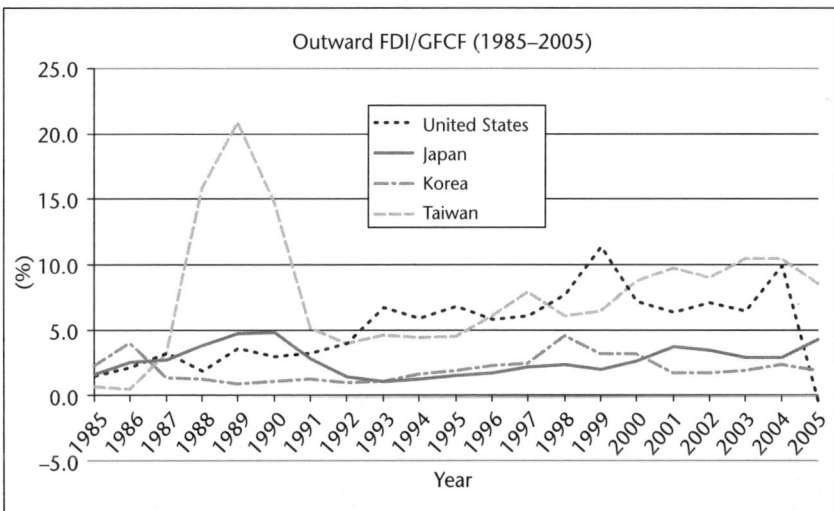

FIGURE 8.3 Outward FDI flow as percentage of gross fixed capital formation in the US, Japan, Korea, and Taiwan.

Source: *World Investment Report 2004*, UNCTAD.

In terms of geographic distribution, Taiwan received increasing inbound FDI from Japan along with a steady increase from Europe, but a declining trend from the US. Taiwan invested most of its outward FDI in Southeast Asia. After the 1997 Asian financial crises, the investment flows shifted to focus in China, accounting for more than 60 percent of total outward FDI after the late 1990s.[8]

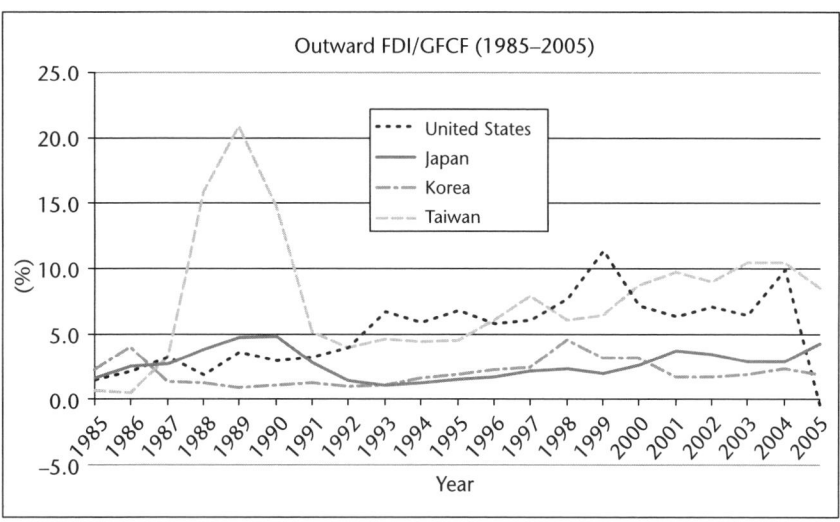

FIGURE 8.4 Outward FDI flow as percentage of gross fixed capital formation in the US, Japan, Korea, and Taiwan.

Source: *World Investment Report 2004*, UNCTAD.

Like most latecomers to industrialization, the development of the financial sector in Taiwan is far behind that of its real sector. Yet, Taiwan made modest progress with its financial liberalization since the mid-1980s. Deregulation of foreign portfolio investment in domestic capital markets followed a three-step sequential order of liberalization that began in the 1980s and accelerated in the 1990s.[9] As Taiwan's securities market has become more mature, a series of liberalizations of foreign

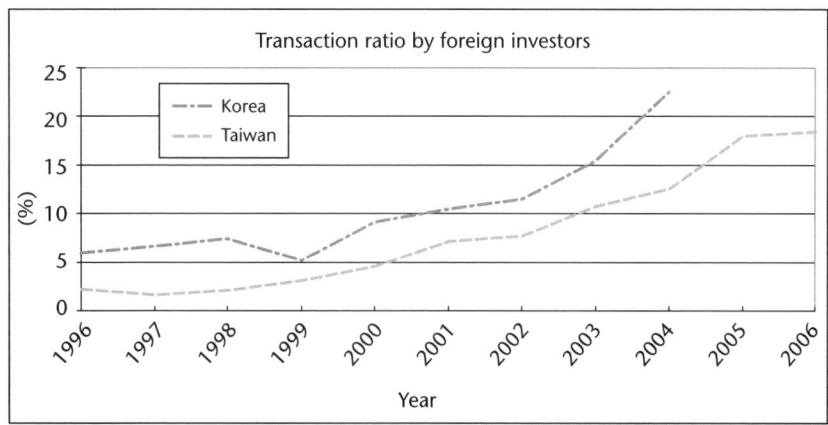

FIGURE 8.5 Percentage of foreigners' holdings of domestic securities in Taiwan, and Korea.

Source: Author's calculation from the database *Taiwan Economic Journal*.

portfolio investment including the abolition of the qualified foreign institutional investor (QFII) took place in October 2003.[10]

The percentage of foreign holdings of securities in the transactions of domestic securities increased from 2.1 percent in 1996 to 18.4 percent in 2006. By December 2005, the percentage of foreign holdings of domestic securities reached 30.17 percent, and the share of foreign stock in total capitalization of securities reached 31.8 percent during the same period. For comparison, Figure 8.5 illustrates the time series developments of the proportions of foreigners' holdings in stock market transactions in Korea and Taiwan. As we can see from this figure, foreign portfolio investment is much more significant in Korea than in Taiwan.

Theoretical underpinnings of globalization and dynamic comparative advantage

Literature on structural transformation in the NICs since the 1980s is voluminous. Ozawa (1992) argued that, similar to the development trajectory in post-war Japan, the NICs, notably Korea and Taiwan, would reach a "stage-compatible order of sequencing structural upgrading." After reaching that stage, the NICs would engage in a "comparative advantage augmenting type" of outward FDI to shift their development stage from the factor-driven to the investment-driven stage and even reach the innovation-driven stage. Henceforth, outward FDI would become a catalyst for the structural transformations in the NICs.

In his studies of East Asian development, Kojima (2000) analyzed the pro-trade-oriented FDI patterns in the technological leader and follower countries, and then extended Akamatsu's original "wild geese flying pattern" to outward FDI as the Kojima Model II. Narula and Dunning (2000) integrated the idea of an investment-development path with a trade-development path in the NICs, and presented a scenario similar to that of Japan's post-war development. Under this scenario, industrial upgrading and comparative advantage moved from the stage of developing the Hecksher-Ohlin industries (industries with standardized production technology), through the development of undifferentiated Smithian and differentiated Smithian industries, and finally reached the stage of developing innovative Schumpeterian industries (R&D-intensive industries). As a result, outward FDI in the NICs would shift from "resource-seeking, location advantage" to focus increasingly on "efficiency-seeking, market-seeking and asset-augmenting" types of activities in the process of structural transformation.

Incorporating trade levels and patterns into the investment development path in Korea and Taiwan, Dunning et al. (2001) argued that as countries proceeded along their development paths, both intra-industry trade and intra-industry FDI would rise as per capita income increased, with the growth of intra-industry FDI lagging behind that of intra-industry trade. Hence, both Korea and Taiwan have encountered a paralleled bidirectional investment with inward FDI concentrated more in technology-intensive industries and outward FDI concentrated more in labor-intensive industries and the lower end of high-tech sectors. The investment development path would not only cope with the trend of globalization, but also enhance the dynamic comparative advantage of home (investing) countries in the world market.

The conceptual framework and theoretical description of Ozawa's "trade-augmented FDI strategy" was based on Balassa's (1979) Revealed Comparative Advantage (RCA) index. Yet, using a general RCA index for all trade commodities as measurement of trade competitiveness has the drawback of neglecting the fragmented manufacturing process, which has become more significant since the drive of globalization. In fact, an RCA index of general commodities that fails to classify the product characteristics would address neither the technology level nor the degree of sophistication of export commodities. An alternative approach adopted in this study is to analyze the RCA index of trade commodities in accordance with the technology level (Lall 2000) and a sophistication index (Lall *et al.*, 2005) in order to further investigate the dynamic comparative advantage and changing division of labor between Taiwan and its major trading partners in the world. The next section will illustrate that Taiwan has generated its dynamic comparative advantage through upgrading its technological leverage and enhancing its vertical specialization through intra-industry trade to cope with the rising East Asian regionalism.

The changing technological level and product sophistication of trading commodities amid the new division of labor

Adopting the "technological capability" approach, which is similar to the neo-technology theory of trade, Lall argued that "comparative advantage depends more on the national ability to master and use technologies than on factor endowments in the usual sense" (Lall 2000: 339). As a latecomer to industrialization, Taiwan's role in the regional division of labor depends on its capability of exploiting its dynamic comparative advantage by continually upgrading its technological capability and the sophistication of the commodity structures of its exports.

To examine national competitiveness in the new trading environment, this study classifies export commodities by both the technology level *a la* Lall (2000) and the degree of sophistication by Lall *et al.* (2005). Combining the common approach of distinguishing export commodities by "resource-based, labor-intensive, scale-intensive, differentiated and science-based manufactures" with the OECD approach of "technological activity within each category" of product groups, Lall (2000) reclassified the technological structure of exports into three levels of technology intensities with seven product groups. Based on 3-digit SITC codes (revision 2), all trading commodities other than primary products and resource-based manufactures were ranked by their levels of technological intensities. Recalculating export commodities based on the three levels of technology by Lall (2000),[11] Taiwan has made much more significant progress in the high levels of technology-intensive products (HT I and II) than either in the medium (MT I, II and III) or low levels (LT I and II). The percentage share of low-level technology products (LT I and II) in total exports

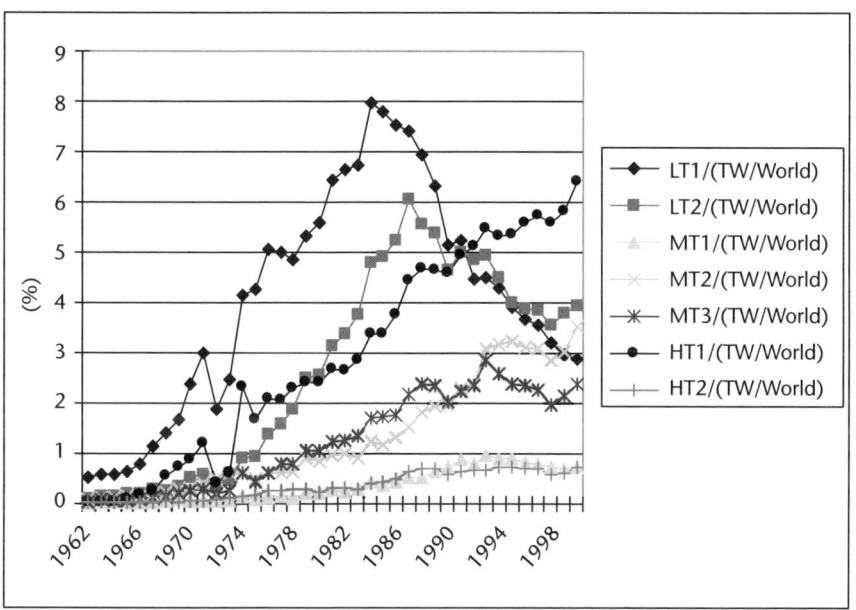

FIGURE 8.6 Distribution of export commodities by levels of technology, 1962–2000.
Source: Author calculation from the NBER–UN Trade Data.

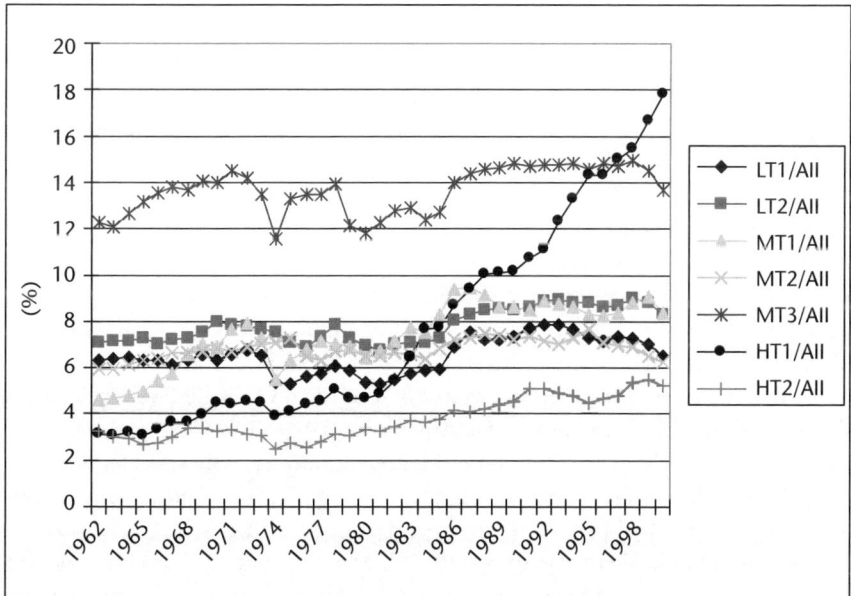

FIGURE 8.7 World market shares by levels of technology.
Source: Author calculation from the NBER–UN Trade Data.

decreased from 48.64 percent in 1985 to 20.66 percent in 2000, while medium-level technology products (MT I, II and III) increased modestly from 19.82 percent to 24.39 percent in the same period. The most fascinating development was in the high-level technology products (LT I and II), which increased from 16.49 percent to 47.41 percent, nearly tripling its percentage share in total exports as indicated in Figure 8.6.[12]

In terms of world market share (WMS), the low-level technology-intensive goods (LT I and II) decreased from 12.7 percent in 1985 to 6.84 percent in 2000, whereas that of high-level technology-intensive goods (HT I and II) increased from 3.82 percent to 7.17 percent in the same period. The most significant growth of WMS was in medium-level technology goods (MT I, II and III), which increased more than two times from 3.29 percent to 6.65 percent in the 1985–2000 periods as shown in Figure 8.7.

In a follow-up study, Lall *et al.* used the idea of an "export sophistication index" to measure product sophistication on the premise that "an export is more sophisticated the higher the average income of its exporters" (2005: 223). The sophistication index of exports normalizes each product to an index ranged between 0 and 100 on the basis of the weighted average of the exporter's income, and the maximum as well as the minimum unique sophistication scores of the dollar value for all products in the following way:

$$\text{SI (i)} = 100 \times [\text{US(i)} - \text{US(Min)}]/[\text{US(max)} - \text{US(min)}] \tag{1}$$

where SI (i) is the normalized sophistication index of product (i), US (i) is the unique sophistication score as the dollar value of product (i), which is a weighted average of exporters' income of product i. US (max) and US (min) are the maximum and minimum unique sophistication dollar values for all products. The sophistication index for 3-digit SITC codes were ranked into six levels in descending order with level 1 being the most sophisticated and level 6 the least.

For the 3-digit SITC, there are 181 products with 30 products each, except for the last group which has 31 products.[13] The composition of Taiwan's manufactured exports by the six levels of sophistication index is reported in Figure 8.8. As one can see, the most significant progress of shifting composition of manufactured exports was found at the medium level of sophistication. Combining levels 3 and 4, the shares in Taiwan's total manufactured exports were more than doubled from 30.37 percent in 1985 to 65.6 percent in 2000, whereas that of levels 5 and 6 (lower levels) combined decreased from 52.58 percent of total manufactured export to 15.94 percent in the same period. For the most sophisticated levels of product groups, i.e. levels 1 and 2 combined, their shares in total manufactured exports increased modestly from 10.46 percent to 14.74 percent in the same period.

Looking at the world market shares (WMS) of manufactured exports for Taiwan in the past decades, it is found that the most significant progress occurred in the product groups of levels 3 and 4. Their combined WMS increased from 4.12 percent in 1985 to 9.36 percent in 2000. It was also found that Taiwan has made modest progress

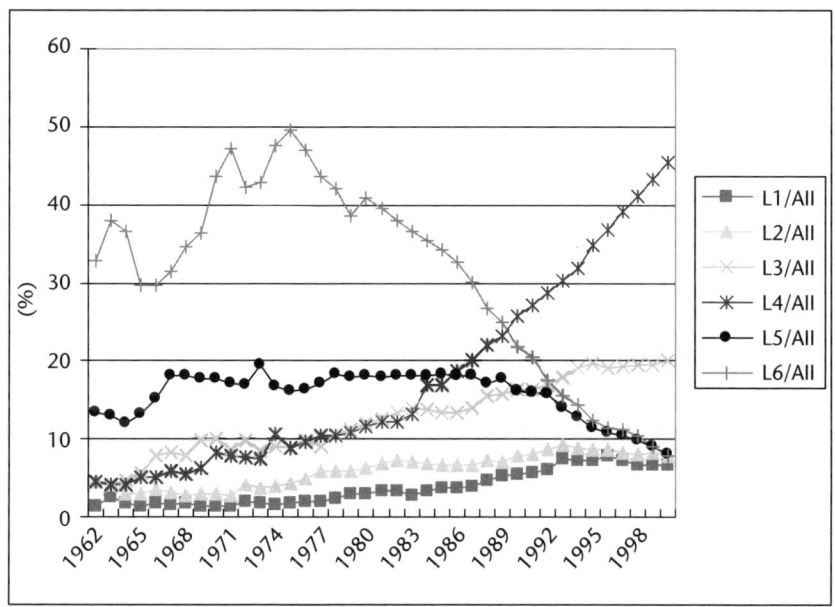

FIGURE 8.8 Distribution of manufactured exports by sophistication index.
Source: Author calculation from the NBER–UN Trade Data.

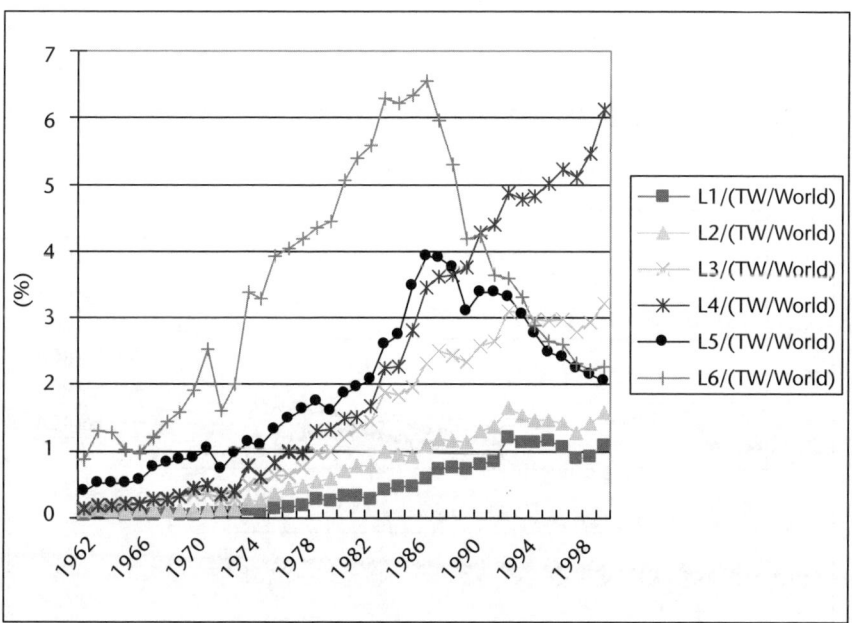

FIGURE 8.9 World market shares for manufactured exports by sophistication index.
Source: Author calculation from the NBER–UN Trade Data.

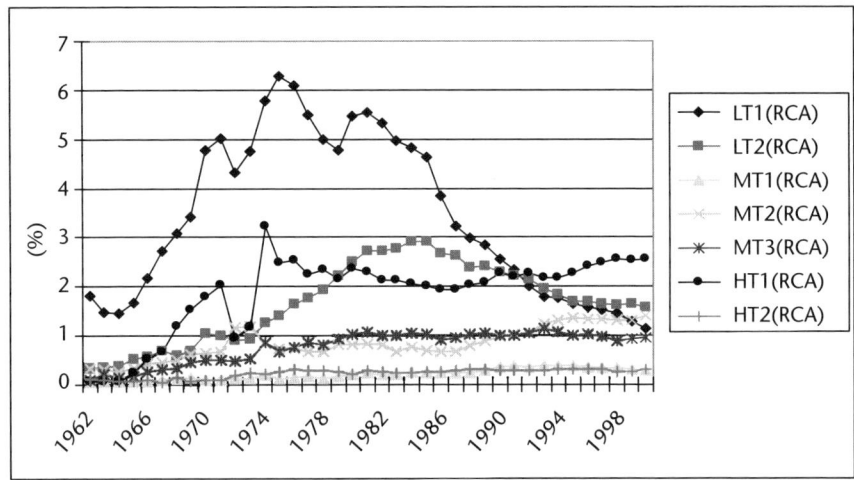

FIGURE 8.10 RCA index on levels of technology.
Source: Author calculation from the NBER-UN Trade Data.

in the highest two levels of sophisticated exports (levels 1 and 2). Their combined WMS increased from 1.41 percent to 2.67 percent in the same period whereas the combined WMS for product groups on levels 5 and 6 decreased from 8.97 percent to 4.31 percent as Figure 8.9 indicates.

Finally, Taiwan's dynamic comparative advantage in all levels of technology intensities is shown by their respective RCA indices as reported in Figure 8.10. An RCA index greater than 1 means the country has a comparative advantage, whereas an

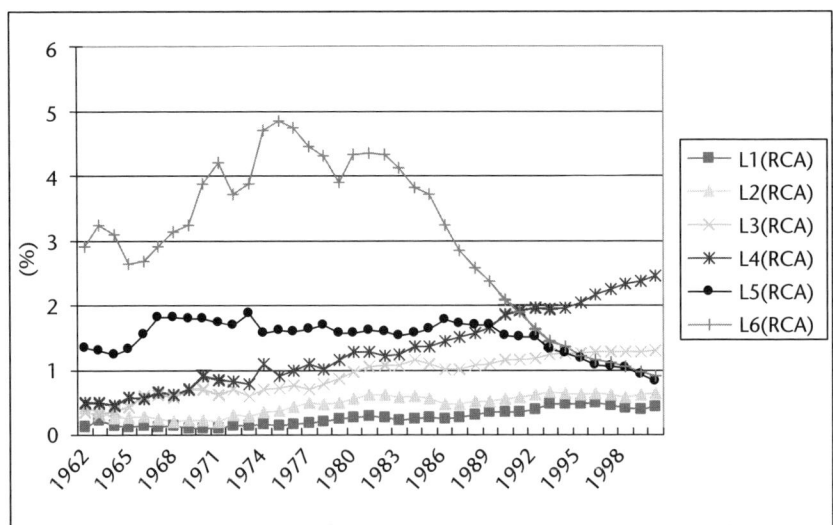

FIGURE 8.11 RCA index based on sophistication index.
Source: Author calculation from the NBER-UN Trade Data.

RCA index less than 1 means that the country has a comparative disadvantage on the export market.[14]

From Figure 8.10 one can see that Taiwan has gained comparative advantage in the world market with most of its export commodities. The salient product groups are high-tech level 1 (HT1), followed by low-tech level 2, and medium-tech level 2 (MT2), and there is room for further improvement in high-tech level 2 (HT2).

Looking at the RCA index from the six levels of sophistication index in Figure 8.11, one can see Taiwan's comparative advantage declined steadily in the lowest levels of sophistication (levels 5 and 6), yet increased significantly in those product groups on the medium and highest levels (levels 3, 4, 1, and 2). By 2000, Taiwan had the strongest comparative advantages in levels 3 and 4 with modest comparative advantage in levels 5 and 6. Since the classification of export sophistication is based on the weighted average income of exporting countries, the empirical evidence of changing comparative advantage from Figure 8.11 further reconfirmed Taiwan's current status as a high–middle income country between industrialized and developing countries in the world economy.

Coping with East Asian regionalism and a rising China

In spite of Taiwan's significant technological development and its role as one of the largest foreign investors in several countries in the region, the "bandwagon effect" of the China factor in Southeast Asian countries has prevented Taiwan from participating in any of the emerging regional trading blocs. The proliferation of free trade areas (FTA) in the past decade has been described as a "Spaghetti Bowl" of regional trade agreements (The World Bank 2004), under which Taiwan is an "outlier" in the emerging economic integration. Except for a few symbolic FTAs with some Latin American countries, Taiwan has not yet caught the tide of the emerging trading blocs. Whether or not Taiwan will be marginalized in the emerging Asian regionalism is a big concern.

Of course, one could argue that the marginal benefits of joining regional trade agreements will be reduced if negotiations of multilateral trade liberalization are completed in the near future. However, multilateral trade liberalization under the proposed APEC free trade area (APEC-FTA) is moving much more slowly than what had been anticipated (originally scheduled to liberalize trade among developed countries as late as 2010 and among developing countries in 2020) and the Doha Round has faced its deadlock. Moreover, even if the multilateral trade negotiations could be speeded up, the degree of trade liberalization within the APEC-FTA would not be comparable to those under variants of expanded ASEAN-FTA due to divergent levels of development among the APEC members. Therefore, the trade diversion effect of bilateral FTAs and plurilateral FTAs such as ASEAN plus China and ASEAN plus 3 (China, Korea, and Japan) could adversely affect Taiwan's trade and economic growth. The challenges of being an outlier in the East Asia economic integration is critical (Chen and Ku 2007).

The ongoing economic integration in East Asia has been mainly policy driven, rather than market driven. Therefore, the politically manipulated trading blocs in the Asia-Pacific region may not be consistent with market forces at all. Hence, there is still room for maneuvering for Taiwan to penetrate the proposed trading bloc through "tariff jumping" and other strategies to avoid being marginalized. The following five strategies focus on trade, investment and technology leverages without institutionalized trade pacts with other Asian countries. They are neither inclusive nor exclusive.

Market-driven versus policy-driven economic integration: Taiwan as a de facto partner of East Asian regionalism

Since the 1980s, Taiwan has become a de facto partner of economic integration in many Southeast Asian countries through its significant investments in those countries. The informal, non-institutionalized economic integration between Taiwan and Southeast Asia was carried out through the "functional approach" of market-driven forces.[15] The proposed regional trading agreement of ASEAN plus China and ASEAN plus three (China, Japan, and Korea) are primarily manipulated by China's "policy-driven" initiative to pursue its "good neighborhood policy" in the region. To what extent China's manipulations of policy-driven economic integration would distort and/or override market-driven forces of functional integration is not clear at the present.

In a market-driven process, regional trade arrangements follow rather than precede the economic integration. The trade-investment nexus since the 1980s has made Taiwan an integral player in East Asian economic integration and a significant actor in the global supply chain of ITC products. Hence, Taiwan does not need to wait for a formal FTA agreement with any country in Southeast Asia before further diversifying its destinations of foreign investments. Therefore, diversifying trade and investment destinations to Latin American and Southeast Asian countries would reduce Taiwan's asymmetric trade dependency on China and would complement the FTA negotiations with those Latin American and Southeast Asian countries.

Since the mid-1980s, Taiwanese enterprises have already established their production networks in many Southeast Asian countries as well as China. The expansion of the ASEAN-FTA to include China may challenge Taiwan's trade opportunities but not its functional approach of economic integration. Hence, the existing production and distribution networks built by Taiwanese MNCs in Southeast Asia and China will not be affected if those Taiwan-owned firms in Southeast Asia adjust their production and market orientation appropriately. The expansion of the preferential trading arrangements, such as ASEAN plus China, could discriminate against Taiwan's exports through tariff distortions, but not at all against Taiwan's FDI in these countries. Under such a scenario, Taiwan could still adopt its "tariff jumping" strategy through its outward FDI in these countries to build up its regional/global production, distribution and logistic networks so as to counter its isolation amid the East Asia regionalism.

Intra-industry trade and vertical specialization

Compartmentalization and disintegration of the production process in manufactured industries led to intra-industry trade, which used to characterize the trade pattern within industrialized countries only. After decades of globalization, intra-industry trade (IIT) has become more and more significant in the trade flows between OECD and developing Asian countries. Given the predominance of intra-industry trade flows in the region, technology leads and lags between countries, rather than the conventional trade theory of factor endowments, will dictate the new regional division of labor in East Asia.

Using the weighted average of the Grubel-Lloyd (1975) IIT index,[16] this study found that Taiwan's trade with the rest of the world has been steadily increasing through the ongoing expansion of intra-industry trade. On bilateral trade with the rest of the world, the overall IIT index of the three levels of technology-intensive products increased from 5 percent in 1962 to 54 percent in 2000, whereas that of the export commodities included in the six levels of "sophisticated products" increased from 10 percent to 56 percent in the same period. Among its major trading partners, Taiwan's trade with Japan had the highest IIT index with 53 percent based on technology levels and 54 percent based on degree of sophistication in 2000, followed by the US (29 percent by levels of technology and 30 percent by product sophistication), the EU (30 percent by both product groups) and China (19 percent by levels of technology and 21 percent by product sophistication). The trend of increasing intra-industry trade as shown in Figures 8.12 and 8.13 also demonstrate the degree of interdependency between Taiwan and its major trading partners.[17]

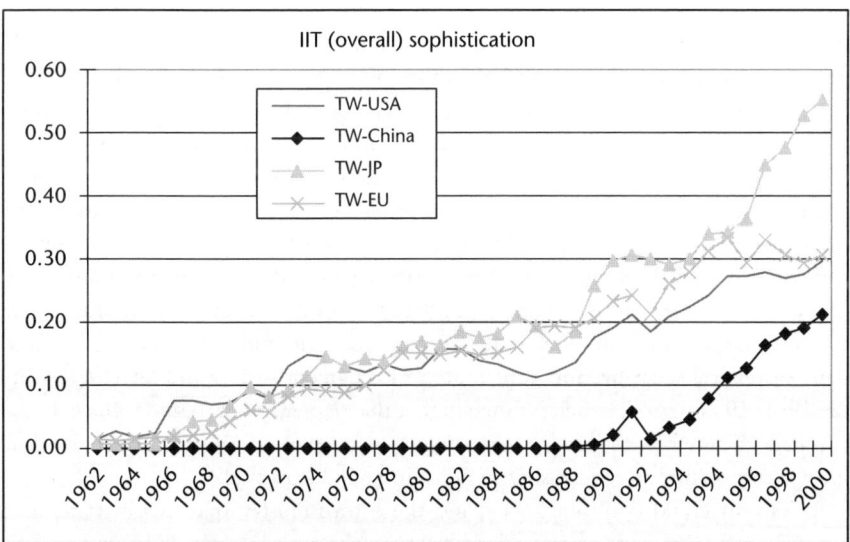

FIGURE 8.12 The overall IIT index between Taiwan and its major trading partners based on product sophistication.

Source: Author calculation from the NBER–UN Trade Data.

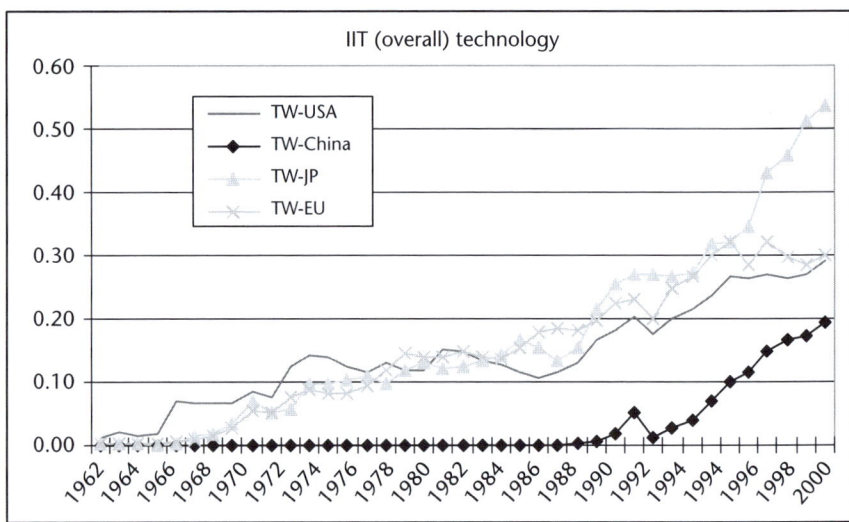

FIGURE 8.13   The overall IIT index between Taiwan and its major trading partners based on levels of technology.

Source: Author calculation from the NBER–UN Trade Data.

Fragmented production processes would lead to a vertical division of labor under which a country specializes in those segments of production chain or stages of the production in which it has the comparative advantage. In general, vertical division of labor among nations would increase the degree of interconnectedness and enhance mutual interdependency between trading nations. Hummels *et al.* (2001) defined vertical specialization as the proportion of imported intermediary goods in gross output times the amount of exports. Vertical share (VS) in a country is an export-weighted average of sector shares of VS.[18] Using the conventional "within" and "between" accounting, Hummels *et al.* decomposed changes in country-level VS shares into a) changes in sector VS intensity (the sector VS share of sector exports) and b) changes in the sector composition of overall exports (p. 89).[19] By using the input–output table for ten OECD countries plus those of Ireland, Korea, Taiwan, and Mexico – all together these 14 countries accounted for more than 60 percent of world trade – Hummels *et al.* found that Taiwan had made modest progress in the vertical specialization of its trade structure since the mid-1980s. The percentage share of vertical specialization contributed 51.8 percent to Taiwan's total exports in the 1961–1994 period, which is much higher than Korea, Mexico, and some OECD countries. Therefore, Taiwan could maintain its strategic position through vertical specialization amid the increasing trend of intra-industry trade.

If Taiwan could continue to expand the intra-industry trade with its trading partners, and increase its shares of vertical specialization in high-end intermediate products, then it would be able to upgrade its industrial structures by dominating the high end of intermediate products in the world trade. Consequentially, Taiwan would be able to mitigate the welfare loss of trade diversion, and become less vulnerable to the tendency of marginalization amid the East Asian spaghetti regionalism. Moreover, intra-industry trade with dominance in the high end of intermediate products could also hedge against the risk of Taiwan's asymmetrical trade dependency on China's market as addressed by Chow (2007).

In the past, Taiwan was known for its imitation and specialty in "original equipment manufacturing" (OEM). But for sustainable development, Taiwan has to move beyond its traditional OEM and gradually become an innovator. In fact, with its well-endowed human capital, Taiwan has the national innovative capacity to engage in the innovation-driven stage of development.

National innovative capacity and technology leverage: from imitation to innovation

In analyzing the development of a nation's competitive advantage, Porter (1990) classified the paths of development into four distinct stages: factor-driven, investment-driven, innovation-driven, and wealth-driven. Taiwan has transformed itself from factor-driven in the 1960s and 1970s to the investment-driven stage in the 1980s. In the past decades, Taiwan has moved to the innovation-driven stage by substantially increasing its R&D expenditures. R&D expenditures as percentage of GDP increased from 1.7 percent in 1991 to 2.62 percent in 2007.[20] Based on the number of patents granted, excluding new design, Taiwan was ranked as number four in the world, next only to the US, Japan, and Germany. However, based on patents per capita, Taiwan had an annual average score of 17.2 during the 1997–2001 period, which was next only to the US (28.6) and Japan (23.7), yet far above Korea (6.6) as shown in Figure 8.14.[21] Nevertheless, in terms of net export of technological services, Taiwan still is in deficit. In 1999, the ratio of exports to imports of technology trade in Taiwan was only 3 percent compared to 77 percent in Germany, 234 percent in Japan, and 275 percent in the US.

How can one reconcile the phenomenon of having high patents per capita with a deficit in technology trade? Chen and Liu (2001) argued that Taiwan's patents have a lower than average number of citations per patent. The science linkage index (SLI), which has generally served as a metric between patents and citations of journals (EI, SCI), indicates the interactions between patents and research output.

Between 1995 and 1999, the overall science linkage index in Taiwan was only 0.18, which is far below the world average of 1.97, whereas its counterpart in Israel was 3.27, in Canada it was 2.88, in the US 2.88, in Japan 0.51, and in Korea 0.42 (Chen and Liu 2001: Table 1). However, using the "Current Impact Index" (CII), which "measures the impact of patents taken out over the previous five years in terms of their current rate of citation," Hu and Mathews (2005) found that the quality of Taiwan's patents has been improving significantly since 1995, with a CII that increased from 1.01 in 1995 (cited from 1990 to 1994) to 1.25 in 2000 (cited from 1995 to 1999), which is far above the US (1.15) and Israel (1.01) in 2000. Therefore, Hu and Mathews concluded that Taiwan "had emerged as the world's leader in terms of patent quality."

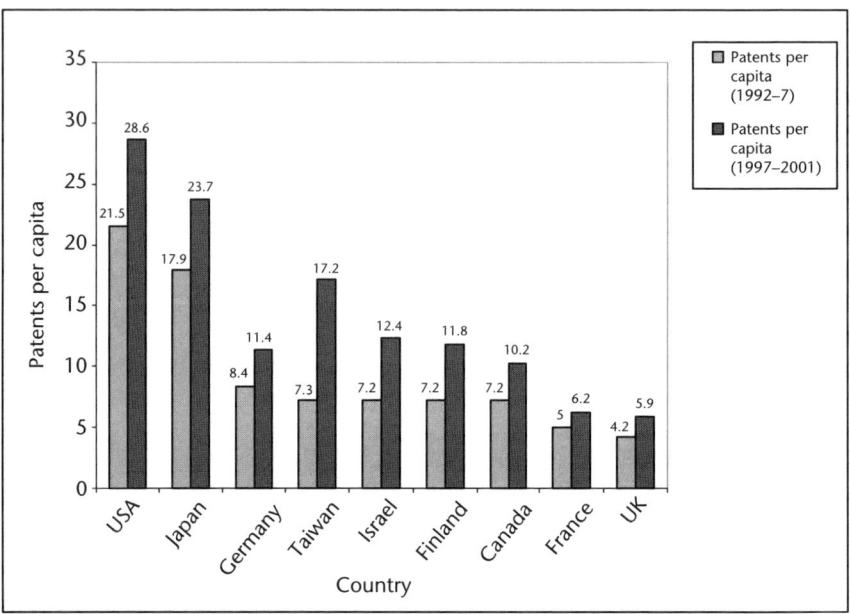

FIGURE 8.14 Top patents per capita in the US

Source: Author's calculation from U.S. Patent and Trademark Office. Available online at http://www.uspto.gov/web/offices/ac/ido/oeip/taf/cst_dsn.pdf.

The major difference between the quality of patents found by Chen and Liu (2001) and that found by Hu and Mathews (2005) is that the latter adopted a time lag between patents granted and the citation made. Perhaps due to its status of being a latecomer to industrialization, many of Taiwan's innovations are less "new" to the outside world. Therefore, it may take a while before Taiwan's new innovations are recognized and cited.

As Hu and Mathews (2005) pointed out, the innovative activities in the East Asian latecomer countries are more in "process innovation" or "new-to-the-country," rather than "product innovation" or "new-to-the-world." Hence, among the top patenting firms in Taiwan, most of them had specialized almost exclusively in the semiconductor industry, which focused more on manufacturing process rather than on activities that could receive royalties. The other reason is that most patents granted to Taiwan were in new product developments whose value-added was embodied in the product itself. Hence, many of Taiwan's patents were not able to receive the royalties. As a latecomer to industrialization, Taiwan's national innovative capacity had focused on "strategic specialization" by concentrating on selected industries such as semiconductor, computer, electronic and IT industries as Hu and Mathews argued.[22]

Hence, Taiwan's deficit in technology trade will be gradually improved in accordance with the accumulated and evolutionary process of innovation for the latecomer countries. It is interesting to find that, after the year 2002, Taiwan's largest semiconductor firm, TSMC, and some other active Taiwan companies were starting to gain valuable royalty income from so-called "late-arrivals" and particularly from China's companies.[23]

Innovation for latecomers is an evolutionary and cumulative process achieved through learning by doing. Through its long struggle for technological advancement, Taiwan is graduating from "imitation to innovation," as some scholars have argued (Hu and Jaffe 2001). As a latecomer to industrialization, Taiwan would need to penetrate world markets by continually identifying its "niche products" through patents, licensing and joint ventures with world-class high-tech firms, as well as mergers and acquisitions to catch up to the leaders in the OECD countries. Taiwan could also enhance the vertical division of labor between parent firms and overseas subsidiaries through its outward FDI and maintain its technology hierarchies at different stages of production in which it has the comparative advantage. Strategic components, parts and accessories, i.e. the "core functions" of the industries, would need to be kept at the headquarters of the parent companies in Taiwan, similarly to the "black box" of Japanese foreign direct investment strategy.

OEM to the development of indigenous "core industries"

Using the electronic industry as an example to illustrate the "positive feedback loop innovation system" (POLIS), Khan concluded, "Taiwan is beginning to build its structures of innovation that may prove to be self-sustaining" (2002: 302). For sustainable development in the long run, Taiwan has to upgrade its competitiveness by moving from OEM to develop its indigenous "core industries" in which it has "niche markets." Taiwan has to engage in innovation-driven activities, which are compatible with its development stage, through research and development to promote its indigenous technological capabilities and to increase the value of its exports. To maintain its technology lead in East Asia, Taiwan needs to integrate research output and patents with its indigenous "core industries" to achieve the "Schumpeterian model of innovation." In that regard, R&D resources need to be tied closely with the development of production capabilities so as to develop more recognizable, independent "core industries" in the world market.

Identifying the ideal candidates for Taiwan's "core industries" is beyond the scope of this study. Yet, one may try to identify them from Taiwan's patent performance in the US since the 1990s findings (Hu and Mathews 2005). Table 8.1 shows a list of the top eight innovative sectors that might have the potential to develop as Taiwan's indigenous "core industries" if the fruits of innovative capacities were transformed into production in the "niche industries."

As Taiwan shifts its status from imitator to innovator, the government will need to play an important role in industrial restructuring and the nurturing of its "core industries."[24] The government will need to set up a coherent and consistent research and development policy to shift from OEM to innovation, and to tie innovation to the development of indigenous production capabilities in innovation-intensive, Schumpeterian industries so as to reduce technology dependence on industrialized countries, notably Japan and the US. Moreover, as China is a formidable high-tech

TABLE 8.1 Top eight innovative sectors in Taiwan

	1996–2000 patent numbers	Global shares of patent (%)	CII in 2000
Semiconductors and electronics	3,375	11.35	1.61
Electric appliances and components	1,772	7.33	1.23
Industrial machinery	1,138	4.08	1.32
Misc. MFG	1,081	2.47	1.06
Computer peripheral	876	1.45	0.83
Misc. machinery	739	3.25	1.13
Telecommunication	682	1.43	0.70
Textile/apparel	660	1.46	1.57
Cumulative of top eight sectors	10,323 (66.6% of total patents)		
Total patents	15,502	2.98	1.25

Source: Derived from Hu and Mathews (2005) by the author.

rival, Taiwan would need to protect its research output as intangible assets with appropriate protection of intellectual property rights to maintain its technology lead in a competitive world economy. By doing so, Taiwanese high-tech firms could move to the high-value portion on the "Smile Curve."[25]

Policies on trading with and investing in China

The rise of China as a powerhouse of the global economy offers both challenges and opportunities for Taiwan's economic development. In spite of political tensions with Beijing resulting from China's claim on its sovereignty, Taiwan has been trading with and investing in China since the mid-1980s. Policies on trading with and investing in China have become one of the most controversial issues in the past three decades. Basically, Taiwan's policies are primarily motivated by economic incentives, whereas China's economic and trade policies toward Taiwan are highly motivated by political considerations of unification. Through the 1990s, Taiwan's economic interactions with China went through several steps of gradual liberalization on trade and investment flows, first indirectly through the third place, then directly after both China and Taiwan were admitted to the WTO.

Trading with and investing in a host country with a politically hostile regime is very complicated for the Taiwan government. On the one hand, domestic political pressure from Taiwanese businessmen would push for further liberalization. On the other hand, the government has to consider external effects of trading with and investing in a hostile regime and its resultant consequence on national security. Hence, previous governments have undertaken precautionary approaches to dealing with China; under the former presidency of Lee Teng-hui (1988–2000), after the initial period of liberalization, the government advocated a "go slow, be patient" policy to investment in China and a "Southward Strategy" to diversify Taiwan's outward foreign investment toward Southeast Asia.

Under the Democratic Progressive Party (DPP) Administration of 2000–8, economic and trade policies were twisted between "active opening and effective management" and "active management and effective opening" and resulted in significant growth in investment flows; the growth of trade flows increased from US$10.62 billion in 2000 to US$98.28 billion in 2008 and approved foreign direct investment in China increased from US$2.6 billion in 2000 to US$10.69 billion in 2008. Since 2000, China-bound FDI accounted for more than 60 percent of Taiwan's total outward FDIs and China-destined export accounted for 26.2 percent of Taiwan's total export (39 percent if combined with export to Hong Kong) in 2008. In 2004, China replaced the US as the largest export market for Taiwan. To some extent, one could argue that economic forces could not be halted by those precautionary policy measures at all.

New policy initiatives to engage with China

After President Ma Ying–jeou took office in May 2008, the Ma administration took strong initiatives to engage in rapprochement with China by signing a series of trade pacts and operating direct flights across the Taiwan Strait. The most controversial policy dispute between the Ma administration and its opponents arising from these initiatives has been the signing of the Economic Cooperation Framework Agreement (ECFA) with China. According to the official website of the government,[26] the ECFA is a precedent of a free trade agreement (FTA) under Article 24 of the WTO under which "substantially all" trade flows across the Strait would liberalize within a reasonable period of time, usually within ten years or so.

According to the official website, the ECFA includes liberalization of trade in commodities, including tariffs and non-tariff measures, trade in services, investment protection, intellectual property rights, and economic cooperation. Essentially, the ECFA includes three parts: a) normalization of cross-Strait trade flows under the WTO, b) preferential trade arrangements with a list of "early harvest" of 539 commodities of Taiwan's export to and 267 commodities of import from China, and c) coordination/cooperation of industries and division of labor.[27]

The Ma administration advocated that the ECFA would not erode Taiwan's sovereignty or political autonomy and would even lead Taiwan to sign multiple FTAs with other countries. Nevertheless, China's president Hu Jian-tao declared that any trade pact between China and Taiwan must be based on the "one China" premises, under which Taiwan is part of China. Hence, critics suspect that the ECFA is not on an equilateral basis under the WTO framework, but is merely another version of the CEPA (Closer Economic Partnership Agreement) signed between China and Hong Kong under the "one country, two systems" formula. Moreover, there is no indication that Beijing will not block Taiwan from signing FTAs with other countries in the aftermath of the ECFA. Therefore, while President Ma advocated that the ECFA is a panacea to pull Taiwan out of the tendency of being marginalized from

East Asian economic integration, many critics consider that the ECFA is simply a prelude to first economic and then political incorporation of Taiwan by China. They feel that the ECFA, which will institutionalize the closer economic ties between China and Taiwan, may lead Taiwan to join the "One China or Cross Strait Common Market," which would grant Beijing the leverages to limit Taiwan's ultimate political choices. An ECFA without leading Taiwan to multiple FTAs with other major trading partners such as the EU, the US, Japan, and ASEAN countries would let Taiwan become peripheralized in the "China-centric hub." [28] The ultimate effect of the ECFA on the future of Taiwan depends on whether or not Taiwan could be more globalized to become a "near hub" in East Asian economic integration or to become a subset of the "Greater China Economic Zone" (Chow 2011).

Toward a mature economy: a twin-engine for sustainable growth

Outward FDI and outsourcing from the home country would inevitably lead to deindustrialization, which is generally considered as the second stage of development where there is a shift from the industrial to the service sector when economies mature. [29] This development would lead to significant structural transformation in the home country by enhancing the output and labor employment in the service sector. Studies on the effect of outward FDI on domestic economies in the industrialized countries lead to the conclusion that the structure of labor employment in the home countries would shift in favor of skilled labor generally and especially in managerial, marketing, and logistics (Blomstrom and Lipsey 1997; Desai *et al.* 2005; Lipsey 1994; Lipsey *et al.* 2000). Hence, deindustrialization is the inevitable trend in most mature economies.

Whether Taiwan's economy is mature or not, and to what extent the degree of deindustrialization should be pursued, is debatable. Nevertheless, once Taiwanese outward FDI accelerates through "tariff-jumping" or other strategies to avoid being marginalized by the emerging trading blocs, domestic production and employment structure inevitably would shift to "service-oriented" sectors as well. Hence, outward FDI could serve as a catalyst of structural transformation in the home country (Markusen and Venables 1997), not only within the industrial sector in terms of technology-intensity of manufactures, but also between industrial and service sectors.

In the foreseeable future, a twin engine of growth would include the "core industries" in the high-tech sector, as argued above, as well as the service industry once the structural transformation is completed in the near future. Statistics showed that the percentage share of the service sector in total GDP increased steadily from 57.6 percent in 1990 to 73.3 percent in 2008, whereas that of the manufacturing sector decreased from 31.2 percent to 21.7 percent in the same period. By contrast, the percentage of labor employment in the tertiary sector in total employment increased from 46.3 percent in 1990 to 58 percent in 2008, whereas that of manufacturing only increased from 32 percent to 27.7 percent in the same period. [30] Therefore, it is anticipated that labor employment in the service sector will increase steadily in the near future.

Conclusion

Though not without drawbacks, Taiwan has been pursuing the drive of globalization along with liberalization and structural transformation. While modest progress of structural transformation has been made amid its pursuit of globalization, Taiwan may face the challenge of being marginalized in the emerging trade blocs in East Asia, which is contrary to the "open regionalism" as the WTO/GATT had advocated. To counteract this tendency, Taiwan could play its role as a de facto player in the region as one of the major investors through its appropriate outward FDI strategy.

Outward FDI would not only serve as a catalyst of structural transformation, but also generate intra-industry trade between home and host countries. Taiwan's vulnerability to East Asian regionalism is mitigated by the interdependency of growing intra-industry trade. In general, intra-industry trade would generate a vertical division of labor, which could contribute to stability of trade relations between two trading partners. Intra-industry trade enhances the degree of interdependency and reduces the risk of sudden shock of market disruptions from either side for non-economic factors.

The emerging trading blocs could discriminate against Taiwan's exports, but not its investment and technology flows. To maintain its international competitiveness, Taiwan would need to expand the vertical specialization of its trade structure, and to become a dominant supplier of the high-end, technologically sophisticated intermediate products in the global/regional supply chain.

If Taiwan could continue its technology lead with its trading partners in the region, it would be able to maintain the technology leverage against the challenges of being marginalized because technology dominance could, at least partially, overcome the adversary effect of being excluded from the preferential trading arrangement in the Asia-Pacific region. Therefore, Taiwan has to continue to upgrade its structure of exports from low-end to high-end products and keep those industries with the highly sophisticated and high level of technologies at home.

Nevertheless, economic interdependency resulting from intra-industry trade has been challenged by the development of localization of Taiwanese subsidiaries, notably in China. Outward FDI, which is a complement to trade initially, will become a substitute for exports once foreign subsidiaries integrate with local enterprises. Therefore, the trade flows induced by Taiwan's outward FDI will be undermined as more and more Taiwanese subsidiaries integrate themselves with indigenous enterprise and Taiwanese subsidiaries locally.

Fundamentally, developing indigenous "core industries" to generate strategic leverage on intra-industry trade is the key to avoid being marginalized. Taiwan has to realize that it is graduating from the imitation stage and needs to reach the innovation stage. Therefore, much of its research output and patents have to be integrated into innovative, R&D intensive, Schumpeterian industries.

The effect of the ECFA with China needs to be monitored periodically and needs to be subject to public scrutiny. Whether Taiwan could be more globalized to become a "near hub" in East Asian economic integration depends on whether it could sign multiple FTAs with major industrialized countries. The ECFA with China would critically determine the future development path of Taiwan, economically as well as politically.

In the longer term, outward FDI and the structure of trade will generate strong repercussions on domestic industrial structures and labor employment. Taiwan would eventually face the inevitable structural transformation to become more service oriented as its economy matures. Nevertheless, Taiwan should not follow the Hong Kong model by moving most of its manufacturing industries to China and focusing only on the service industry. A twin-engine of growth is what Taiwan needs to further its sustainable development.

Notes

1 The provision of Taiwan's trade data by the National Bureau for Economic Research is acknowledged. I would like to thank Ti-Jen Tsao for his computation assistance for this study. However, the usual caveats apply.

2 Collier and Dollar (2002) argued that, among other developments, the increasing international migration and capital movements are the most spectacular phenomenon in the third wave of globalization in the world economy since the 1980s. In general, the first wave of globalization occurred between 1870 and 1914, and the second wave occurred between 1945 and 1980.

3 The sum of exports and imports in total GDP exceeded 100 percent in 2000, then dropped to 95.39 percent in the 2001 recession, but recovered to 99.65 percent in 2002 and increased to 108.79 percent in 2003, 118.7 percent in 2004, 121.1 percent in 2005, 130.3 percent in 2006, 135.9 percent in 2007, and 140.4 percent in 2008.

4 It is noted that there are broader definitions of "sustainable development" than as it is defined in this study. In general, it includes three dimensions on economic prosperity, environmental quality and social equity. Social equity in Taiwan, though deteriorated a little bit since the 1990s, is still modestly tolerable with a ratio of the highest fifth's income to the lowest fifth's at 5.98 in 2007, which is much more equitable than the comparable ratios of 6.8 in Korea, 12.9 in Singapore, and 9.7 in Hong Kong in 2008. The issue of environmental quality, except for upholding no further deterioration from the current level is beyond the scope of this study.

5 The Asian financial crisis of 1997 and challenges of financial globalization have prompted the government to drive for further reform of its financial sector. The first financial reform started in 2002, which included eliminating fraudulent practises and reducing non-performing loans (NPLs). The share of non-performing loans in total loans outstanding decreased from 11.8 percent in 2002 to 2.2 percent at the end of 2005. The second reform process ran from 2003 to 2008 and focused on regulatory reform to make Taiwan a "regional financial services centre." The government intends, for example, to facilitate mergers and acquisitions of banks, and encourage higher shareholdings by non-residents to about 25 percent of overall market capitalization.

6 Since 1989, the government has been implementing a programme to privatize state-owned enterprises. By September 2005, 34 state-owned enterprises had been privatized; the stocks of 15 more enterprises, including in the areas of petroleum, shipbuilding, water supply, tobacco and liquor, banking, and chemical manufacturing, were listed for privatization.

7 Outbound direct investments destined to China by Taiwanese enterprises with paid-up capital of more than NT\$80 million are limited to not more than 40 percent of their net

assets. In certain manufacturing, agriculture, services, and basic infrastructure construction sectors, the government has a list of prohibited items that are reviewed annually. Inbound direct investment from China requires approval by the government, in accordance with relevant regulations.

8 Statistics on Outward and Mainland Investments, Investment Commission, Ministry of Economic Affairs. Understandably, the figures of outward FDI based on approval could be underestimated due to underreporting of outward FDI prior to the lift of regulation of outward foreign investment.

9 The first step was for the government to authorize local securities investment trust companies to raise funds from overseas to inject indirect investment in the domestic securities market. In the second step, the government granted qualified foreign institutional investor (QFII) status to allow direct investment in the domestic securities market. The third step was to authorize direct investment in securities by overseas and foreign nationals, and finally to abolish the QFII system in October 2003.

10 The regulation on securities investment by foreign institutional investors, under which securities investment per company was limited to US$3 billion, was abolished on September 30, 2003. Foreign institutional investors are subject to a quota of US$5 million investment, while individual investors are not subject to quota restrictions. On May 21, 2004, the government allowed foreign investors to engage in certain futures/options trading. Foreign investors may invest in non-listed companies with the permission of the Investment Commission of the Ministry of Economic Affairs (MOEA). Foreign investors are currently not allowed to invest in arbitrage and speculative trading in Taiwan.

11 The three levels of technology were further classified into seven sub-levels by low-tech (1) low-tech (2), medium-tech (1), medium-tech (2), medium-tech (3), high-tech (1) and high-tech (2). The data source in this study is the trade data of the National Bureau for Economic Research, which refined Taiwan's export and import data from the data source of the United Nations.

12 The shares of all levels of technology manufactures in total exports increased from 84.98 percent in 1985 to 92.46 percent in 2000. These data also show that the shares of primary commodities and resource-based manufactures declined substantially in the same period.

13 I am indebted to John Weiss and Jinkang Zhang for their generous support in providing me with the scores of the 3-digit and 4-digit product lists of export sophistication.

14 The RCA index was calculated in the following way: $RCA_{ij} = (X_{ij}/X_i) / (W_j/W)$ where X_{ij} is the jth product exported from Taiwan, X_i is total Taiwan exports to the world, W_j is the total import of the jth product in the world and W is total world imports.

15 FTAs can discriminate against non-members in trade, but not in investment flows. The functional approach of economic integration means to integrate the economies between the host and home countries through FDI without signing any formal bilateral and or multilateral free trade agreement.

16 The IIT for each trading partner is defined as the following:

$IIT_i = \{$summation $(X_i + M_i) -$ summation of absolute $X_i - M_i\}/$summation $(X_i + M_i)$.

Alternatively, it can be written as:

$IIT\ i = 1 -$ summation of absolute $\{X_i - M_i\}/$summation $(X_i + M_i)$

where X_i is the export of the ith product; M_i is the import of the ith product; and the weighted average IIT is calculated by the product of $IIT\ i$ times the ratio of X_i/X where X_i is the export of the ith product and X is total exports.

17 The IIT indices based on different levels of technology and degrees of product sophistication are too voluminous to report here, but they are available upon request.

18 Vertical share (VS) is defined as $VS\ k, i =$ (imported intermediate/gross output) (export). VS share of total export $= VS_k/X_k = \Sigma_i VS_{ki}/\Sigma_i X_{ki}$ where X denotes exports. It can also be expressed as $VS_k/X_k = \Sigma VS_{ki}/\Sigma X_{ki} = \Sigma((VS_{ki}/X_{ki}) * X_{ki})/X_{ki} = \Sigma[(X_{ki}/X_k)(VS_{ki}/X_{ki})]$.

19 The decomposition formula is given by ΔVsk, t/Xk, t = $\Sigma\Delta$Vsk, i, t/Xk, i, t * 0.5 * (ωk, i, t + ωk, i, t–1) + ($\Delta\omega$k, i, t)*0.5*((VSk, i t/Xk, i, t + Vsk, i, t–1/Xk, i, t–1)) where VS k, t and X k, t are total VS and exports for country k in period t, and Xk, i, t are country K, sector i.VS and exports in period t., and ωk, i, t are country k, sector's shares of total exports in period t. Each sector's contribution is divided into a contribution due to "changes in sector-level VS share (within), and a contribution due to the changes in the sector-level export share (between)". See Hummels *et al.* (2001: 90–1).

20 From Table 6–1, *Taiwan Statistical Data Book* 2009. CEPD.

21 From the US Patent and Trademark Office (USPTO). According to the website of USPTO, the number of patents granted in 2005 for Japan was 30,341 (2,415 in 2009), for Germany it was 9,011 (1,197 in 2009), and for Taiwan, 5,118 (1,114 in 2009). By dividing the number of patents by their respective populations, Taiwan ranked as the second highest country as measured by per capita patents in both 2005 and 2009. For the cumulated total of patents granted from 1977 to 2009, Japan has 36,268, Taiwan has 17,256, and Germany has 11,041. Taiwan still ranked as the second highest foreign recipient of patents in the US, which has a cumulated total of 228,238 in the same period. See http://www.uspto.gov/web/offices/ac/ido/oeip/taf/cst_dsn.pdf.

22 Hu and Mathews (2005: 1348) concluded that one of the three key factors is "targeting certain industrial sectors and specializing their innovative activities in these sectors." The other two are R& D manpower, and promoting and effecting public R&D expenditures.

23 The author is indebted to Mei-Chih Hu for contributing to the recent progress of Taiwan's patents in the US and its technology trade.

24 Dani Rodrik (1995) argued that "getting intervention right" was what made Korea's and Taiwan's success stories.

25 The smile curve was innovated by Stanley Shih, founder of Acer. Chu (2001) pointed out that much of the growth in the "value-added" of high-tech industries derived from scale economies of production rather than from an increase in the ratio of value-added in total sales.

26 Available online at http://www.ecfa.org.tw/.

27 See Chow (2011) for detailed analysis on the ECFA and its implications on the US economic and strategic interests in East Asia.

28 Based on the econometric model of measurement of hub-ness in economic integration, Baldwin (2004) concluded that, due to the dominance of Japan's and China's markets, there is a bilateralism of "hub-and-spoke" scenario in East Asia. Opponents argued that, without signing multiple FTAS with some major trading partners such as the US, Japan, EU and ASEAN countries, the ECFA will lead Taiwan to fall into the "Greater China Economic Zone" and become a spoke in the China-centric hub. See Chow (2011) for more detailed analysis on this subject matter.

29 The first stage of development was to shift from the agricultural sector to industrial sector. The percentage of labor employment in the agricultural (primary) sector in the total labor force will decline, while that in the industrial sector will increase as development takes place. In retrospect, it took 50 years for the US to drop its labor force in the agricultural sector to less than 50 percent of the total in the 1860–1910 period. It took 60 years in Japan to achieve the same status from 1870–1930.

30 From *Taiwan Statistical Data Book*, 2009. Taipei. CEPD. Table 2–9a, "Employment by Industry."

Bibliography

Balassa, Bela, 1979, "The Changing Pattern of Comparative Advantage in Manufactured Goods," *Review of Economics and Statistics*, 61, pp. 259–66.

Baldwin, Richard, 2004, "The Spoke Trap: The Hub and Spoke Bilateralism in East Asia," Korea Institute for International Economic Policy, CNEAC Research Series, 04–02.

Bende-Nabende, Anthony, 2003, "The Trade-investment Nexus: A Literature Review, with Reference to East Asia" in Anthony Bende-Nabende (ed.), *International Trade, Capital Flows and Economic Development in East Asia: The Challenge of the 21st Century*, Burlington, VA: Ashgate Publishing Co.

Blomstrom, Magnus and Robert E. Lipsey, 1997, "Foreign Direct Investment and Employment: Home Country Experiences in the United States and Sweden," *Economic Journal*, 107 (445), pp. 1787–97.

Blomstrom, Magnus, Denise Konan and Robert E. Lipsey, 2000, "FDI in the Restructuring of the Japanese Economy," NBER working paper, Series 7693.

Chen, Hsing Hrong and Man-Chun Liu, 2001, "The Relationship between Industry and Academia under the Knowledge-Based Economy" in Jeff Lin (ed.), *Knowledge-Based Economy and R&D*, Department of Economics, National Taiwan University (in Chinese).

Chen, Tain-jy and Ying-Hua Ku, 2007, "Taiwan and East Asian Economic Integration" in Peter C. Y. Chow (ed.), *Economic Integration, Democratization and National Security in East Asia*, Cheltenham, UK and Northampton, MA: Edward Elgar, pp. 172–90.

Chow, Peter C.Y., 2007, "East Asian Spaghetti Regionalism: Will Taiwan Be Marginalized?" working paper, City University of New York.

Chow, Peter C.Y., 2011, "The Emerging Trade Bloc across the Taiwan Strait: ECFA and Its Aftermath on Implications to the US Economic and Strategic Interests in East Asia" in Cal Clark (ed.), *The Changing Dynamics of the Relations Among China, Taiwan and the United States*, Newcastle upon Tyne: Cambridge Scholars Publishing.

Chu, Yun-Peng, 2001, "R & D in High-Tech and Knowledge-based Industries: How to Overcome the Bottleneck to Enhance the Value-Added in High-Tech Industries" in Jeff Lin (ed.), *Knowledge-Based Economy and R & D*, Department of Economics, National Taiwan University (in Chinese).

Council for Economic Planning and Development, 2009, "Taiwan Statistical Data Book 2009," Taipei, Council for Economic Planning and Development, Executive Yuan.

Desai, Mihir A., C. Fritz Foley and James R. Hines, Jr., 2005, "Foreign Direct Investment and Domestic Economic Activity," NBER working paper, No. 11717.

Dicken, Peter, 1998, *Global Shift*, New York: The Guilford Press.

Dunning, John H., Chang-Su Kim and Jyh-Der Lin, 2001, "Incorporating Trade into the Investment Development Path: A Case Study of Korea and Taiwan," *Oxford Development Studies*, Vol. 29, No. 2, pp. 145–54.

Grubel, H. and P. Lloyd, 1975, *Intra-industry Trade: The Theory and Measurement of International Trade in Differentiated Products*, London: Macmillian Press.

Hu, Albert G. Z. and Adam B. Jaffe, 2001, "Patent citations and International Knowledge Flow: The Cases of Korea and Taiwan," NBER working paper, No. 8528.

Hu, Mei-Chih and John A. Mathews, 2005, "National Innovative Capacity in East Asia," *Research Policy*, (34), pp. 1322–49.

Hummels, David, Jun Ishii and Kei-Mu Yi, 2001, "The Nature and Growth of Vertical Specialization in World Trade," *Journal of International Trade* (54), pp. 75–96.

Khan, Haider A., 2002, "Innovation and Growth: A Schumpeterian Model of Innovation Applied to Taiwan," *Oxford Development Studies*, Vol. 30, No. 3, pp. 289–306.

Kojima, Kiyoshi, 2000, "The 'Flying Geese' Model of Asian Economic Development: Origin, the Theoretical Extensions and Regional Policy Implications," *Journal of Asian Economics*, (11), pp. 375–401.

Kreinin, Mordechai, Michael G. Plummer and Shigeyuki Abe, 2000, "The Trade-Investment Nexus," in Mordechai Kreinin and Michael G. Plummer (eds), *Economic Integration and Asia: The Dynamics of Regionalism in Europe, North America and the Asia-Pacific*, Cheltenham, UK: Edward Elgar.

Lall, Sanjaya, 2000, "The Technological Structure and Performance of Developing Country Manufactured Exports, 1985–98," *Oxford Development Studies*, Vol. 28, No. 3, pp. 337–69.

Lall, Sanjaya, John Weiss and Jinkang Zhang, 2005, "The 'Sophistication' of Exports: A New Trade Theory," *World Development*, Vol. 34, No. 2, pp. 222–37.

Lipsey, Robert E., 1994, "Outward Direct Investment and the US Economy," NBER working paper, No. 4691.

Lipsey, Robert E., Eric Ramstetter and Magnus Blomstrom, 2000, "Outward FDI and Parent Exports and Employment: Japan, the United States, and Sweden," NBER working paper, Series 7623.

Markusen, James R. and Anthony J. Venables, 1997, "Foreign Direct Investment as a Catalyst for Industrial Development," NBER working paper, No. 6241.

Narula, Rajneesh and John H. Dunning, 2000, "Industrial Development, Globalization and Multinational Enterprises: New Realities for Developing Countries," *Oxford Development Studies*, Vol. 28, No. 2, pp. 141–67.

Ozawa, Terutomo, 1992, "Foreign Direct Investment and Economic Development," *Transnational Corporations*, Vol. 1, pp. 27–54.

Porter, Michael, 1990, *The Competitive Advantage of Nations*, New York: Free Press.

Rodrik, Dani, 1995, "Getting Intervention Right? How South Korea and Taiwan Grew Rich," *Economic Policy*, (20), April, pp. 78–91.

United Nations Conference on Trade and Development (UNCTAD), *World Investment Report*, 2004, New York: United Nations.

Urata, Shujiro, 2001, "Emergence of an FDI-Trade Nexus and Economic Growth in East Asia," in Joseph E. Stiglitz and Shahid Yusuf (eds), *Rethinking the East Asia Miracle*, New York: Oxford University Press.

World Bank, 2005, *Global Economic Prospects*, New York: Oxford University Press.

Index